To Rose
With my very best Wishes

D a that

Shout About Life

D. A. Shout

Published by

MELROSE
BOOKS

An Imprint of Melrose Press Limited
St Thomas Place, Ely
Cambridgeshire
CB7 4GG, UK
www.melrosebooks.com

FIRST EDITION

Copyright © D. A. Shout 2005

Cover designed by Bryan Carpenter

ISBN 1-905226-30-6

Printed and bound in Great Britain by:
Bath Press Limited, Lower Bristol Road,
Bath, BA2 3BL, UK

Chapter One

It's a Wednesday, the sun has just shown its face and a still young woman, after hours of hard labour, has just given birth to a 7lb baby boy. She was used to this toil and sweating as this was her seventh baby. So it was on the 3rd April 1929 that I was born, not that I knew anything about that. I do know that throughout my life I was never a Wednesday's child – as the rhyme goes "Wednesdays child is full of woe" I can honestly say that I was never a woeful child. Without coming on too strong, I think I should have been born on a Sunday, because Sunday's child describes me a lot better. "But the child that is born on the Sabbath day is merry, bright, happy and gay." All through my life I think I have tried to be just that.

I don't remember much – in fact I don't remember anything before I was five years old and going to school. School was the Methodist Day School on Quakers Lane in Richmond, North Yorkshire. This was an old stone-built building, consisting of four classrooms, later to be five. All four classrooms catered for about thirty-five to forty children. The new room, as it was called, had a stage in it and all assemblies and concerts were staged there.

At the age of five you went into Miss Toft's class. This was the room on the left of the building and it was in this class that the first of my memories come to life. It was one morning and the majority of the kids had gone out to play in the playground but I didn't. Instead, I saw lots of pencils on the other desks, so I thought I could have them as the other children had left them. So I went round all the desks and picked up a handful of pencils. After the whistle had gone and everyone came back into the classroom and looked for their pencils, but couldn't find them, Miss Toft noticed that I had a handful of them and asked me if they were mine. Thinking that as I had collected them they would rightfully be mine, I said "yes" they were mine.

1

Now Miss Toft was no fool, so she took hold of my hand and walked me to the top class where she knew I had an older sister. She then asked her if I had come to school with all these pencils. Not wanting to make me out a thief my sis Florrie said "Oh yes". I went home that night with about twenty pencils. That was not the end of the story though. Florrie told mother that I had nicked these pencils and I got a jolly good hiding on my bottom. I never did that again.

Our family consisted of my eldest sister Daisy (called after Mother), Nora, Florence, Lionel, Dennis, me, Fred and the baby of the lot, Francis, who always got called Nancy at home. Daisy and Nora were not living at home when I started school; they were out working in service I think. We all lived at Fryers Yard. It was a small house and how and where we all slept I do not know, but how happy we were. My mother was a very organised lady, as one had to be in those days, living in a two up and two down house.

We all had our daily chores to do before we went to school. One of the jobs I had to do was to take my dad's breakfast or lunch down to the paper mill, which was at the bottom of Reeth Road. This is no longer there as it closed in the thirties. It is now replaced by two lovely big houses on the site. They replaced the dry cleaning factory, which was built after the mill closed down. Of course the mill owner's house is still there and called Howe Villa; the other two are Mill House and Howe Bank House.

Another errand was to go to the grocers in Victoria Road called Geo Bensons for possibly a half pound of Echo margarine, or take a jug for half a pint of treacle, which was got straight from the barrel. Another brother would have to take a bogey down to the gas works and get a bag of cinders. The gas works making gas from coal was always interesting to watch. We used to love to see the men open the furnace door and shovel the coal in. At times we saw them remove clinkers from the furnaces and there would be red-hot cinders and sparks flying all over, we thought it was wonderful. My mother used to take us children down to the gas works if we had whooping cough (I think it was). We were told it helped us breathe more easily and was good for the chest.

Another one or two of us had to go to the bottom of the market place to 'Cherrys', the fresh fish and fruit and veg shop – and a classy shop it was too. I remember them winning the window dressing competition year after year. Their fish and game window was marvellous, with pheasants, partridge, hens and cockerels all hung up and fish displayed in nets and baskets on the floor of the window. In the other window they displayed a selection of fruit and vegetables, full of colour and freshness. In those days all the shops in the town used to take part in the competition and I can imagine the thought and competitiveness of all the owners. Back to what we had to go to Cherry's for was to get two pennyworth of bruised fruit. When we got home, mam would cut off the bruised bits and give us the rest. This was the only fruit we got and we thought it was good too.

Another errand was one of us would have to go to Robson Wood and Co in Finkle Street to the house behind the shop for some dripping if they had any. That was really nice on bread, which we had for supper. So you can see we all had our work to do before we went to school.

Times were hard and all the working classes did much the same. I didn't know at the time but my father was often out of work and went without a meal sometimes so us kids could eat. I remember our Daisy telling me in later years that mam and dad often shared an egg for a meal.

But we were happy kids and loved playing outdoors. In Fryers Yard we would play with a stick or a ball and throw it at a pear tree overlooking our house, and it was a great achievement if we knocked off a pear or two. We ate them very quickly and enjoyed every mouthful. Until one day the owner of the pear tree caught us picking up two pears – he was raving mad and said we should pay for the pears and went to see our mam, who gave him no change and sent him packing, telling him he was a tight old fool or words to that effect. But after that we were not allowed to throw any more sticks into the pear tree.

I was six, I think, when we moved to a new house at Whitcliffe Terrace. We were number five and had a nice size garden on three sides of the house. Our house was the end one of four on the left-hand side of the road, with numbers one to four on the other side of the road. Before I go on to living at Whitcliffe Terrace, just before we moved my brother Lionel died and although I don't remember a lot about it I do remember him lying dead upstairs, but I do not remember the funeral. In those days children didn't go to funerals. He had been ill for quite a while, I think it was his heart, and being so young myself I didn't really know him.

Anyway back to our new house. We thought it was a palace because it had three big bedrooms, a living room, kitchen and bathroom downstairs. I had not seen a bathroom before, and when it came to bath-time it was like going on a day trip to the seaside at Redcar in all that water. But best still, it was hot water not lukewarm. Before I get carried away about our new house let me finish telling you about life in Fryers Yard.

At weekends we would play in the yard until we got shifted for being too noisy or something similar. It was great fun when they started building the Zetland Cinema, which was of course next door to us as the saying goes. I remember one day going into a building which was next to be pulled down and finding large bags of cocoa and coconut which we shared and took home. My mother was delighted with it and told me that the building this cocoa came from was Nortons chocolate factory, which had recently closed down. This was about 1938. Sundays were always treated with reverence and we were not allowed to get dirty or go wandering off playing, because after our dinner, which was the best dinner of the week, mam would bungle us kids off to Sunday school. This was held in the Wesleyan chapel and the entrance we used was in Ryders Wynd. The service, if you could call it that, started at 2pm and lasted one hour. The entrance to the main chapel, where there was a large pulpit and a balcony round three sides, was from the Market Place. All the day school concerts were held in the church and were very well supported by the children's parents and friends.

After leaving Sunday school we would take our time and walk home. On arriving home we were very quiet, as we had been told to be, because mam and dad always went for a rest upstairs on Sunday afternoons. Woe and betold if we started arguing or got too noisy waking up mam and dad, we knew what to expect. When we got into the living room, mam had always laid out on the table four pieces of apple, sometimes orange, for us four children, i.e. Denis, me, Fred and Nancy. We all knew which was our piece of fruit as they were cut into different sizes. The oldest, Denis in this case, got the largest piece and me the second largest and so on to Nancy getting the smallest. I could never understand why Denis got a bigger piece than I did and so on. Sunday evening saw my father don his bowler hat and with mam, would go to church, leaving us kids in the charge of one of our older sisters.

Every year as Whitsuntide came along and Richmond held its Meet celebrations we would welcome my Uncle Will (Dad's brother) and Aunt Alice from Hartlepool to our house, along with the rest of the Hartlepool Cycling Club. Mam would give them all a cup of tea and a biscuit. In those days it was known as the N. Yorks and S. Durham Cyclist Meet and clubs from all over that area came to the Richmond Meet for the weekend by bike. We thought we were the tops because my uncle was an official of the meet and he would let us into the castle grounds without paying to see the concert. People used to stop and think "what are all those bicycles doing outside this little house?"

Uncle Will was my favourite uncle and I never got tired of seeing him. He kept coming to Richmond throughout his life, along with his friend Mr Maw. Two great fellows they were and sadly missed when they died. However the ties with Hartlepool continued as his son, my cousin Bill and his wife, kept coming and it was always a pleasure to see them. Bill was like his father in as much as he had that happy smiling face and temperament.

At school I had now gone into Mrs Ormanstun's class, who I must have liked because I can't remember anything outstanding that she or I did during my year and a bit with her.

I will now get back to moving to Number 5 Whitcliffe Terrace, the year I think was 1939 and the start of the Second World War. Now it was all hands on deck to set the garden and grow some vegetables for the table. I've already said that that it was like a palace, except that the toilet was still outside the back door – you had to pass the coalbunker to get to it. My God it was cold in there and nearly every winter we had burst pipes due to the frost. We soon learnt that as soon as the first frosts came we had to put an oil lamp in there near the pipes. We had tried candles but they didn't give off enough heat, hence the burst pipes and having to call out Bart Emerson, the plumber, to come and thaw us out and mend the pipe. You did not wake up in the middle of the night and go to the lav; you would have frozen to death. Instead there was always the po to go on.

At this time the Hampshire Steam Laundry had been set up in one of the old paper mill buildings and dad was working there. The manager of the laundry was a Mr Tom Berry who thought a lot of my father and trusted him implicitly regarding the running and maintenance of the steam boiler, which kept the whole works working. There were some real stories told about my father at the laundry, all good ones I hasten to add. One good one is that one day the ministry boiler inspectors came and told dad that he wasn't doing the job right, and if he did such a thing or something he could get more steam up in less time. They told this to Mr Berry, the manager, and he asked my dad what he thought. Dad replied that if they could do what they were asking him to do then prove it, because he told them that boiler couldn't work like that. But if they wanted to prove it dad would not go into work the next morning until mid-day so as to give them a real chance to prove themselves. Mr Berry then said to the ministry guys: "I bet you £10 each that you can't run this boiler the way you say it should be run, but I warn you now old George there knows what he is talking about, are you taking my bet?". "Yes," said the boys from the ministry. "Right George," said Mr Berry, "you have the morning off but don't go away". "Thank you," said dad, "I won't". Well morning came and the laundry started work at 8am, Dad used to start at 7am to get enough steam up by 8. The ministry guys were there at 6.30am and started getting steam up. At 8 they only had a quarter of what was required, so no one could start work. Mr Berry was now getting a bit miffed as the saying goes and told the boys he would give them another half hour to get steam up, and then if they hadn't they owed him £20 plus £20 for old George who would show them how it was done. Of course by now you can guess the answer. At 8.45am Mr Berry sent his car to pick up dad from home and bring him to the boiler house, where the two boys, now shirtless and sweating cobs, were getting nowhere. I can just imagine a great big cheer when my father walked in and told the two of them to get out of the boiler house. Dad had steam up in half an hour and everyone was happy again. None more so than my dad when Mr Berry gave him the £20, which was about a month's wages, that he had won.

Talking about my father reminds me of one day when I was playing about in the garden and he walked in with what I thought then was a tree trunk to saw into logs for the fire. At this time I was only a child but even years later – possibly fifteen or twenty years later – I saw him do the same. He was as strong as an ox even at seventy years old.

Back at school the new room was now ready and we held our first assembly there. The room was painted blue and cream if I remember correctly. It was new and modern and had a stage at one end and a stock room at one side. I was in this class and my teacher was Miss Bainbridge, later to become Mrs Reed. She was all right but could be a bit short tempered, and when you did wrong she used the ruler on the back of your hands, not flat ways but edge ways. This was the worst form of punishment I have ever heard of before and after. Anyway, some parent must have reported her and she was reprimanded most severely, she never used that ruler again. The headmaster, Mr Smith, had a short thick stick about fourteen inches long, one and a half inches in diameter and painted green, and he was not afraid to use it. More about him later.

The time now is about 1940 and I was having lots of fun. My friends at school and long after were Teddy Jenkins, who lived across the road from me on the corner of Reeth Road and Whitcliffe Place, and Bertie Catt who lived across the road in the second house up the hill of Whitcliffe Place. Bert was brought up by his grandma, a lovely lady we all called Granny Mudd. She was a lovely old lady who lived with her son Tom. Tom was the St John Ambulance Supt and gave me – or tried to – my sex education. He was asked to do this by my mother, who must have thought I needed it. I won't go into the lessons.

Ted, Bert and I were great friends and did everything together. Going to school one day we had another lad that lived up the street with us,

The author, aged 11

Bathing pool and falls. Reeth Road, approx 1930/40.
Now a car park.

Lenny Turner, and on our way to the school we had to pass what was called Joplings Field. This is now built on and called St Hilary Close. Anyway, this one day as we passed we saw that a circus was being put up in the field, I should say that the big tent for a circus was being erected. Also two elephants were walking about but chained to a stake in the ground. We went to investigate what was going on. Into the field we went and straight up to the great big elephants. One in particular looked enormous. We were just looking, or more correctly staring, at them when the big one raised its trunk from the ground and snatched Lenny Turner's cap off and ate it. For a moment we just stood dumbfounded, then turned and ran off to school, swearing we would get our own back on that circus. We did. After school we again went to the circus and low and behold the two big drums from the band were just outside the tent (big top). So Lenny put his best foot forward straight into one drum and then the other. All we heard was a man shouting, raving and waving his arms, but he had no chance of catching us. When Lenny told his mother how he had lost his cap she didn't believe him until we backed up his story. Mrs Turner wanted to go and ask for payment for his cap but we persuaded her not to go due to us kicking the drums.

On another occasion one winter, Teddy, Bert and myself along with about twenty other kids were sledging down Whitcliffe Place. The snow was just right – it was hard which made the sledges go that much faster. In fact it got so fast that Teddy couldn't stop at the bottom of the hill and went flying across Reeth Road straight under and out of the other side of a petrol tanker. This frightened all of us and some went home very shaken by what they had seen. I was paralysed to the ground because the tanker didn't know that anything had happened and we couldn't see Ted for quite a while. It was only when we saw movement in the hedge across the road that Bert and I ran to see what had happened to poor Ted. He was dazed from running into the hedge and couldn't believe what he had done. From then on we collected ashes from the houses round about and spread them over the snow to bring our sledges to a quicker halt.

We had what I call good winters in those days, although my legs got sore and chapped, wearing only short trousers. One didn't get into long trousers until you were at least twelve years old. We had good neighbours and everyone knew everyone else in the street and round and about. On our row next door to us were a Mr and Mrs Kinchin, then Mr and Mrs Swan and in the other end house were Mr and Mrs Stevenson. Across the road numbers one to four were Mr and Mrs B Stevenson, Mrs Robinson, Mrs Shell and at number one were Mr and Mrs Proud.

After the summer holidays, back to school we went and I had moved up a class into Mrs Skelton's. The classroom was across the corridor to the top class, which Mr Smith, our head teacher, took. The doors into these two top classrooms were dead opposite each other and the top half of the door was glass panes. Mr Smith had a happy knack of looking through his door straight into Mrs Skelton's class and if he saw you not paying attention or talking he used to sail into the classroom and shout "Jenkins and Shout into my room NOW". We then got four of the best and sent back to our places. The trouble was we soon forgot that until he came dashing back in again calling out the culprits he saw talking.

Our Denis had left school by now, him being two years older than me, but our Fred and Nancy were still there. At this time of our life it was time to take our eleven plus exam to see if you were good enough or had the money to be sent to the Grammar School for boys or the High School for girls. I was told later on that some, if not all, my sisters had got the marks but the headmaster was kind in those days and knowing our finances couldn't afford it if they passed he failed them. Denis, who had just left school, went to work at a grocer's shop in the Market Place called Stablers. Nothing much happened in Mrs Skelton's class, not that I can remember anyway, so I'll move on and go into the top class as it was called where we had Mr Smith as master.

I was now about thirteen and remember Mr Smith, "Smithy" as we called him; he was a tall thin man and always wore either a black or navy blue suit. When you got to know him he wasn't a bad sort at all, but my wife when she was at school was frightened to death of him. When you got into the top class you had one or two afternoon sessions in the garden. The boys in particular loved this lesson and prayed that it would be fine weather, because we couldn't go gardening when it was, or had been, raining. When I look back I think that was the start of my interest in the garden, which I will enlarge upon later. On one occasion the four of us – Ted, Bert, Lenny and me – after gardening for an hour or so, had to go back into class. This day we called into the toilets on our way back to have a pee. Well boys being boys we got carried away a bit and had a competition as to who could pee the highest up the wall, while having a great laugh as well. Unknown to us, Smithy had heard us fooling about and before we could say Jack Frost we had a slipper across our backside and legs and scuttled back to our classroom. We were banned from gardening for a month. What was embarrassing was the girls in our class wanted to know why we were kept in; none of us dare tell them.

Another lesson you did when you were in the top class was to spend Tuesday afternoons at Bend Hagg Farm. This was a mixed farm of crops and cattle and we enjoyed this trip out every week very much. Looking back this was a very good lesson for pupils living in the countryside. We saw Mr Raw, that's what the farmer was called, sowing seeds the traditional way, and then he showed us how they used to sow them in the olden days using an implement called the seed fiddle. If you have never seen a fiddle it is worth going to a farm machinery museum or an antique fair to see how clever they were. On this particular day it was hot and we were in the milking shed, as it was called, and Mr Raw, who stood alongside Mr Smith, was demonstrating how to milk a cow. I was stood at the back of the group not paying much attention when I noticed a hosepipe on the floor beside me, so I picked it up and pointed it at Smithy. Unknown to me, Teddy was stood next to the tap that the hosepipe was attached to and you can guess what happened next. The rotten so and so Ted had turned on the water and out it squirted. He only kept it turned on for about two seconds but that was long enough to give a quick jet and spray over the class. The kids thought it was hilarious but Mr Raw and Mr Smith didn't. We returned to school and were duly punished. We had no playtime for two whole days, whilst the rest of the class were only kept in one day for laughing.

As you will have guessed, the Second World War had now started and the builders were in the playground building air raid shelters. There were two running the full length of either side of the playground. One was for the younger classes and the other for the top three classes. They had red brick walls and a reinforced concrete roof about one foot thick. Inside there was a latted form running down each side to sit on. Once completed we had to have air raid drill and we in the top class had a great time in those shelters. Boys and girls together in a darkened room, well I ask you to use your imagination what went on. Needless to say we all came out smiling and waiting for the next drill. Also at this time (we thought the war was a great game) with a shortage of labourers on the farms, school children got twenty half days a year off school to go potato picking. We were given a card with twenty boxes printed on and when you went picking the school or farmer marked in one box the time and date you were there. We soon got to know who not to go to because they only paid five shilling a day. There were buses laid on to take you to farms as far away as Dishforth some twenty miles away. These were the best-paid ones as you got seven and sixpence a day and they were only half days really. Also you got a sack of spuds to take home with you. One of the best we went to was Lord Zetland's home farm, where we got ten shilling a day, a glass of fresh milk to go with our lunches and a bag of potatoes.

Talking of Lord Zetland has reminded me of one of our farming afternoons. Instead of going to Bend Hagg farm, we went to Lord Zetland's because he had just had installed one of the first grass drying plants in the country. I found this fascinating because if they couldn't get the hay in, they brought it to the drying shed. This consisted, if my memory serves me right, of three great big beds, which were heated from below and dried the grass. The beds would be about twenty yards square. Every time we went to his lordship's we got a cup of fresh milk. I remember this so vividly because the milk was very fresh and had a slightly pinkish colour to it, but I have never tasted milk like it, it was just super.

I was enjoying my stay in the top class now I think, because we didn't seem to have as many class lessons. What with the garden, the farm, potato picking and woodwork lessons which the boys did (the girls did cookery – they went to the old High School in Frenchgate for that). Our woodwork teacher was a Mr Jobling or Jopling, I'm not sure now, but he was a character too. The boys were allowed to walk to the woodwork class without a teacher being present and sometimes this took a little longer than was allowed because we never hurried and played games on our way there. Everything we made we made by hand using only hand toolsWe never had any electrical tools such as jigsaws, drills, etc, like they have today. I remember I decided to make a tray and Mr Jobling said: "Shout, you had better make it six inches longer and wider than your measurements on account of your poor way of doing dovetail joints." I chuckled to myself, as I knew he was right, and I did need those extra inches in the end. My tray started out to measure eighteen by sixteen inches but ended up being sixteen by twelve inches. We took woodwork class as an afternoon off and played about enjoying ourselves.

One day one of the boys brought in a live bullet and we decided to fire it. We put it in a vice, secured it, got a nail punch and with a hammer gave it a bang, right on the spot where the firing pin would have struck. There was one hell of a bang and the bullet just missed his foot. Well, that brought the class to a sharp halt; everybody wanted to know what had happened. Mr Jobling went from white to red to blue with anger or rage or fright because I think he thought one of us had been shot. When I look back on that incident I don't ever remember any repercussions. I think it was a matter of keep your mouth shut and say nothing.

People often found live bullets if they were out for a walk over the moors, as the soldiers from the barracks across the road used to do their training there. I never thought at the time that I would be one of those soldiers doing my training on those same moors one day in the not too distant future.

It was now getting near the time for me to leave school but there are still one or two things that I did, or we did, we being Teddy, Bert and I, that I should mention. For instance, some days if Miss Bainbridge was off sick or something, Mr Smith would send two of us to look after her class, usually it was Bertie and myself. This was a mistake as in that class was Bert's younger brother who got a little stroppy when told to behave or just "shut up" by Bert. But it did pass away a morning or afternoon very enjoyably.

Another thing that happened in the new room was in the morning assembly of the top two classes. We would be singing "All things bright and beautiful" or something like that. It was always a snappy hymn tune when all of a sudden Teddy Jenkins would blurt out some other song and then fall over in a deep faint. The whole class thought this was hilarious until they realised poor Ted was in a heap on the floor. The teachers soon brought him round and after a short while I had to take him home. By then Ted was feeling okay and we enjoyed our walk home through West Fields. I didn't hurry back to school.

In those days all the kids used to play with tops and whips, boolers and shirlers, and in the season, conkers. It was always a great shame when you got beat after having a twenty two-er or some number like that. We always added a number or two on for good measure, so if mine had knocked out four other conkers, I would say mine was a sixer or sevener just to be a bit cleverer. I'm sure everyone used to lie about how many conkers theirs had destroyed but it was still great fun.

In those days I don't remember friends or anyone having a bike, so it was wonderful when our Denis came by a bike. I don't know how or where he got it from but it was a bit of one-upmanship that I learnt to ride this bicycle. All my friends wanted a go on it and so it was that we all had scabby knees and knuckles when going to school, through falling off the bike.

The war wasn't going very well at this time and the country was now in the grip of rationing of food, tobacco, clothes and furniture, and we at home had to grow vegetables in the garden. Dad was a good gardener when I think and look back at the garden. Everything seemed to grow well and it was nice to eat new potatoes straight from the garden. Also we had a lot of salads. I remember in the summer we had home grown lettuce, radishes, beetroot and spring onions. All year round dad was planting and harvesting stuff such as cabbage, sprouts, cauliflowers, carrots and turnips. We had a little garden about twelve feet by four foot under the front window and this was the only patch that dad grew a few flowers in during the war.

The war is going on and as a child it appears there's not much happening in England (although London and the cities were getting bombed), except that now we have a complete blackout system. This meant that once dusk fell and we switched on the lights inside and drew the curtains no light must be seen from the outside. On patrol these nights were air raid wardens and if they saw a bit of light showing from your window or door, not only would they shout "put out that light" but they would have you up at court the following week, where you would be fined and told to get blackout material for your curtains. This happened to us once and I shan't forget the look on my dad's face when he had to go to court and was fined ten shillings.

Nearly everyone smoked in those days, I think it was the "in thing" to do. You could smoke your cigs outside okay but you were not allowed to strike a match. So what happened was they made little gas jets set in a circular case and wall-mounted. We had these gaslights in the market place. With the set back in the circle, they could not be seen from above and these were what the chaps used to light up. One of these jets I remember was on the wall of Horners the mens outfitters, trading at the time as Hodgsons. For all the precautions that were taken, the courts were always very busy every Tuesday.

My friends and me didn't have any of those worries though; we just kept on playing and misbehaving I suppose. In Richmond we had a natural bathing pool, which was formed and made when the paper mill was working. The mill made blotting paper mainly and used a lot of water; consequently the river was dammed and diverted by building a wall along a stretch of the river from the dam, so forming a long pool. Once the water got to the top of the wall it flowed over onto a sloped bed making a waterfall. When the river was low you could walk across the top of the weir to Billy Banks Wood. There was a footpath over the dam which of course they needed to raise or lower the water flow. As I said, with the dam it made a superb bathing pool. The council put up changing cubicles for men and women; also there were two sprung diving boards.

To get to the bathing pool you had to go along the Reeth Road past the cemetery to the milestone and cross the road into the field. There always seemed to be an ice cream hut there, or the "Eldorado stop me and buy one" ice cream bicycle and sidecar. The sidecar had two drums of ice cream on it, with chrome coned ice cream lids. On fine sunny days the place was filled with people having picnics or just enjoying watching people playing, swimming and diving. From the Reeth Road entrance you went into this field which fell down hill and then uphill and then down again to the water's edge, this making a hill where everybody sat and watched in comfort. This wasn't the only way to the pool though; you could go off Reeth Road down Mill Bank way, which brought you to three big ponds. These were created, so I am told, to do with the water supply to the mill. From the pond nearest the mill ran a flow of water, which was called the mill race; this ran alongside the house called Mill Cottage and under the road making it a bridge. Some days later in my life but still at school I think, Mr Berry would have us kids throw empty tins in the race and with his 22 rifle he would shoot and sink them. The cottage is still there today but the ponds went many years ago. As a child we were allowed to go to these ponds and in the summer time we would take a jam jar with a piece of string round the top which made a carrying handle and catch tadpoles by the hundred. The frog spawn I thought was just like bullet sago or tapioca. Needless to say, the tadpoles didn't live very long in the jam jar and down the loo they went.

My mother was always doing something; I can't remember a day when I saw her just sitting on the sofa or chair having a rest. Monday was always washday and I suppose all the other days were too. Tuesday the ironing would be done. Baking took up a large proportion of her time, as she baked all the bread we ate as well as rock cakes. Eating those rock buns was something else. I didn't like them very much but ate them just the same. I relate now what a wonderful woman my mam was. She would get us up in the morning, I cannot remember what time it would be, but up we got and dressed. Mam always saw that we got washed properly and that our fingernails were reasonably clean. We must have got washed in the kitchen sink because that was the only sink/washbasin in the house. The sink was next to the door into the bathroom. The bathroom was just that, it had a bath in it and that was all, no toilet or washbasin. Years later when Denis was older he must have got sick of having to get washed in the sink so he fitted, or he got fitted, a washbasin in the bathroom. I thought then that we were posh because no one else had one in their house.

While we were getting dressed and washed in the kitchen mam would be doing our breakfast. I don't ever remember having a big fry-up, bacon, egg, sausage, black pudding or anything resembling that, but we never went hungry. In the kitchen we had a large wooden table and about four chairs, a gas cooker behind the back door and that was about that. Hung on the back door was what my dad called the "cat of nine tails" which he said he would use on our backsides if we were naughty. It was a piece of leather about two feet long and split into nine strips up to halfway. Although he called it the cat of nine tails, I only counted seven.

Christmas was always eagerly awaited and from about November we would be told to behave ourselves or Father Christmas wouldn't be calling. We never forgot that and we tried very hard to be helpful and good to each other. Christmas day always came to us very early, when we would gallop down the stairs to see what Santa had left us. We were never disappointed; we would get a small toy, an apple and orange, a bag of monkey nuts and some chocolate money. We all played with our toys until it was dinner time. Christmas dinner consisted of, if we lucky, a chicken or if not a chicken a rabbit, and plenty of vegetables and Yorkshire puddings, followed by Christmas pudding and rum sauce. I think my mam and dad must have saved up for months to buy a small bottle of rum. It was a feast we thought, and after dinner we were allowed to have a pick off the mistletoe, which my mother used to make each year, using two or three hoops, usually off apple barrels, which we got from the fruit shop. They were crossed over each other and one round the middle the other way and tied. Then they were covered with coloured tissue paper cut to make it look frilly. After that all the tinsel decorations and little bags of sweets such as dolly mixtures and wine gums were hung on it, and this was our after dinner pick off the mistletoe. Usually we had a pick off the mistletoe every day until all the sweets had gone. To this day I still like a mistletoe in our living room as well as a Christmas tree, only now we decorate the tree and mistletoe for ourselves, our family and most of all now the grandchildren, especially when they were younger.

One New Year's Eve, as kids, we were sent to bed at our usual time and as custom would have it mother woke us at eleven thirty or thereabouts and in our night attire we came down stairs to see my dad let in the New Year. Mam would put dad out of the house about two minutes to twelve o clock and then after Big Ben had struck twelve, my father would knock on the door and mam would welcome him in. He would give her a silver coin, a piece of coal and some evergreen. Today, a lot of families celebrating New Year still keep that bit of tradition going. I know we do, as do all our family, and long may it continue.

Earlier I mentioned the mill ponds and forgot to tell you what we did on them. In the summer we would gather driftwood from the banks of the river and with a bit of cord or rope we would make rafts and sail on the ponds using a long pole to move us. Many a time the string would come undone and the raft would disintegrate and into the water we would go. That meant a good hiding when we got home but I always thought it was worth it. Anyway it never put us off doing the same again. In the wintertime it was a different ball game, as the ponds froze over and the ice was quite thick. Lots of people – men, ladies and children – would flock down to skate on them. As children and later as adults, we would create one big slide down one side of the largest pool, which was the middle one. It was sheer black ice about forty or fifty yards long. You didn't a need long run to have a full-length slide. It did have a sad touch to it, as sometimes one or two people would end up breaking bones or being badly bruised with not being able to stop at the end of the slide and crashing into the bank side.

If you carried along walking along the side of the ponds on the footpath, with the river flowing on the other side, you came to the weir and dam at the bathing pool that I mentioned earlier. I never remember the bathing pool getting frozen thick enough to walk on. I suppose the river being one of the fastest flowing in the country would not allow it to freeze. The river has always had casualties, some fatal, even up to this day. Further up stream the river got very deep and the bigger boys would play there. I remember them tying a thick rope on a branch overhanging the river and they would swing on the rope into the middle of the river and let go. It was good fun to them and they created a big splash when falling into the river. Needless to say I never tried this, as I couldn't swim. In fact I didn't learn to swim until two or three of my mates went to evening classes to learn. We were all married men then and the pool we went to learn in was at the Sandes Soldiers Home at Camp Centre – more about that later.

When I was twelve years old I had to get a part-time job; this I did. My older brother Denis was already working at Clarksons the Chemist in the Market Place. One day when I went to meet him I saw in Peacocks the Butcher's shop window "boy wanted for three mornings before school and all day Saturday". This was to deliver meat to people's houses on Tuesdays, Thursdays and Fridays before school, so I had to start at about eight or earlier. On Saturdays I was working delivering orders all morning to as far as the Isolation Hospital on what is now called Green Howard's Road. That is now offices for the district council. I had a great big basket to put the orders in. It was the size of those big baskets one used to see farmer's wives with when they were going to market to sell their fresh eggs. Anyway, I found the basket nearly as heavy as the orders of meat I put in them. Joe Peacock would give me some orders that he thought I could carry and off I would trundle. I worked very hard to get all the orders delivered thinking that then I could go home, but alas that was not the case. I would have a sandwich for my dinner and then sweep the floor using sawdust and water, and having no more orders to get out would wait for my wages, which was five shillings per week. I didn't have to wait too long if Mr Peacock was in the shop by himself, he would always say "how much did I say we pay you lad?" I just smiled and said "five shillings Mr Peacock". He then went into the draw cash till and handed me two half crowns. "Thank you," I said, "can I go now?" "Yes, yes, yes," he would reply and I would be off like a shot before Mrs Peacock came back from her dinner break. She always stood looking out of the window with her arms folded and staring into space. I could stand there sometimes until half past four before she would say "you can go now". I never used to say "thank you" to her, the miserable old soul she was. In Peacock's shop was the best chopping block I've ever seen before or since. It was a tree stump about thirty inches high and the actual block you would have thought was polished wood. That block got more looking after by Joe than his wife did, I'm sure. The shop was next door to the chemists, which was called Timothy White and Taylor's, now called Boots.

Out of those five shillings, which I had to hand over to my mam, I got sixpence returned as pocket money. On a Saturday afternoon I was rich and if I had got off early, I would go to the matinee at the cinema and then half of it was gone. It was well worth it though seeing "Roy Rogers"and "Zoro rides again" and other films like that. Sometimes if there were two or three of us and we were a trifle noisy we would get thrown out by the manager but would get back in by climbing through the men's toilet window. Mr Anderson who was the manager soon got wise to that little trick and would fasten down the window.

Every year we looked forward to the Sunday school outing, which was a bus trip to Redcar. Mother would make sandwiches and rock buns and pack them into a carrier bag, along with a towel, which was to dry our feet after paddling in the sea. Along we would go to the church where the bus went from. Mother must have saved a shilling or two for this trip because she always bought us something, even if it was only a stick of rock with the letters running all the way through it. We thought it was great and had a marvellous day every year. The only other time we went on a holiday was to Whitby and we went for a week. I don't know how old I was then or how we could afford it. I think my mother must have met a landlady when she was on holiday in Richmond and a friendship developed. I do know that dad enjoyed the pub in Whitby as it was very near where we stayed.

In those days mams and dads didn't play with the children like we do today. I think they must have had a lot more to do. There were none of the modern day appliances, which we take for granted, such as washing machines, vacuum cleaners, fridges and freezers, not to mention pressure cookers and microwave ovens. The most important thing that mams and dads did for us in those days was all the love and caring that they heaped on us. In other words they were always there for us, whether in happy or sad times. We in our turn try to do the same.

By now I must be in the last year at school and the desks had been removed in our class and replaced with trestle tables about six-foot long, with two of us to each table. The lessons seemed to be a bit more interesting but not that much. I couldn't wait to leave. The bit I enjoyed the most was the mental arithmetic at the end of the day. Smithy would start twenty minutes before we were due to leave and give us some mental arithmetic. The quickest one to get their arm up and he would see you and ask for the answer – and if it was right you could go home. It was a doddle for me, as I was good at mental arithmetic and got out early every day. When my mother asked me how come I was so early and I told her she said "well done, keep it up and you won't go far wrong". Of course she was absolutely right. That is the end of my memories at school that I can remember but if I do remember some tale or other that I think is worth mentioning, I will write about it.

Chapter Two

It is Easter in 1943, Thursday April 3rd to be precise, and it is my birthday and I am leaving school tomorrow. I say to myself thank god! I don't know how anyone can say the best years of their life was at school, because looking back they were not. Friday has arrived and I'm sure the sun must have been shining, as everyone was happy as they said their good-byes and saluted the school as we came out of the gate.

That was the end of one era and the start of another. I remember talking or listening to someone who said that once you have left school your life really begins, and that you will learn much more than you ever did at school. What true words.

Well I went home on that Friday afternoon feeling on top of the world. My mother was waiting for me it seemed, and said: "You can come down to earth now son, I'm taking you to get a job at the Co-op." Well! I was shattered. I thought I would have a few days to have a bit of fun with my mates but it was not to be. Off we went, mam and I, to see the manager of the Co-op, a Mr Robinson. I think mother had seen him before now as he said, "so this is Dougie, is it?" As far as I can remember he didn't ask me any questions or talk to me much at all. It was mam who did all the talking. The one thing I do remember is him saying "well I'll see you on Monday laddie at 8.30 prompt". So that was that, I was a working man. Mr Robinson called me laddie for many years; hence if you were under thirty you were a laddie.

I didn't have a very good weekend, work was beckoning me shortly, and on Sunday night sleep did not come easily. I awoke to a new dawn and got dressed; mam had made me breakfast as she always had, so up to now nothing had changed. It was after breakfast when I put on my coat and said to mam "right then I'm off, ta ra, see you at dinner time". My mam gave me a hug and told me to be a good lad and kissed me on the forehead. I was out and on my way to work and the start of a new life.

Everything seemed strange; I got to work just before half past eight and waited outside along with the other staff. One of the girls spoke to me and said in a nice manner "are you starting work today?" I nervously said "yes". She replied "don't worry you'll be alright". Working in the shop were four girls that I remember, the names being Margaret, Sadie, Enid and Sylvia who always got called Pearl. All four were really nice people. As for the male contingent, there were only four of us I think, Mr Robinson, Mr Thornbury or Thornbrough, Mr Dunn and little old me. Oh I forgot there was Charlie Hodgson our lorry driver as well.

The shop was one of the largest in the town at that time, as Hintons and Fine Fare didn't come till much later. Let me try and describe the layout inside the actual shop. It was a big square with a counter on the left-hand side, which was known as the grocery counter. Facing you as you came through the door was another counter but the customers didn't use it as a counter as there was always a display of about six-foot high in front of it. We put all the orders for delivery on that counter, and when they were boxed or parcelled and priced up they were put to the right hand side of the counter to be price checked and a check made out. These were not checks, as you know of normally, they were in books and the pages were duplicated with carbon paper and perforated about two inches long and one inch wide. There were about twenty checks to a page. Once the check was made out it was wrapped in the order form and twisted round the string of the box or parcel. On the check were the customers Co-op number and the cost of the groceries, i.e. 37188 £1-6-7 that read one pound, six shillings and seven pence. The customer got the check when she paid the deliveryman, Charlie.

On the right hand side as you came into the shop was the provision counter with the Berkel bacon machine at one end of it. Behind all the counters were fixtures divided into boxes where the different products were placed. The grocery counter fixture was seven or eight feet high, and on the top of this were placed packets of tea and such like. Bear in mind we had a large variety of teas in those days packed in packets of four and eight ounces; there were no tea bags then. The lower fixtures, which were much bigger, we packed sugar in, bags ranging from half a pound to four pound in weight. Remember the war was on and so was rationing. Half a pound or possibly quarter of a pound per person per week.

Under the counter we kept washing soap, one-pound bars of Newsleaf (Green), Congress (Yellowish) and White Windsor. We used to halve these by cutting them with a piece of string or wire. Also on the grocery fixture were three sets of four drawers, not very big but big enough to keep such as carb soda, tartaric acid and the various spices such as mace, ginger and nutmeg, all of which were sold loose. No pre-packs in my days then. Also under the counter were soap powders and under the order counter were Persil, Oxydel and Rinso in the property brands, Paddy and another which I can't remember the name of. Soap flakes 'Silvan' were the brand leaders and the Co-op's own brand was called 'Chrysello'soap flakes. All the Chrysello products were very good, such as baby soap and powder.

Behind the provision counter we stood the fats, such as a one hundred weight tub (1cwt) of Danish butter and lard twenty eight-pound blocks. Later cooking fat and margarine and of course eggs in fifteen dozen stacks of different grades. The bacon was cut as and when required, very little if any was pre-cut and displayed. It was always "that on the machine okay Mrs Blogs?"

In the back shop we had another counter where all the different products were weighed up into the amounts required. Sugar came in 2 cwt sacks, dates in boxes weighing 60lbs (they were the worst things to weigh and cut up that I ever had the misfortune to do). Soap flakes were another product that came loose and weighing them caused you to sneeze constantly, awful it was. Those being some of the lines we packed ourselves. On the floor on a stand was the barrel of vinegar, which was also sold in pints or quarts or whatever quantity you required.

In the corner of the back shop was the boss's office. I say office but really it wasn't the size of our toilet, which was the only one for the whole of the shop staff. Not only that, it was disgusting, never having been whitewashed or cleaned, that is until I became manager many years later.

The shop had two big windows, which were dressed in the good old way of window dressing, bags of colour but no theme or speciality. In between was the door. Next to the provision window was the loading room, this had a six-foot wide metal roller blind door and one had to be a Charles Atlas to push it up to open it. All our deliveries came into that room. Just behind the door were two trap doors leading down to the cellar, with a ramp slide for sending things down instead of dropping them. We used to put a sack full of empty sacks to stop things breaking.

In the corner of the loading room was the cash office. This cash office measured 7 foot by 2 foot 6 inches and was the home, if you could call it that, of a marvellous lady called Peggy Walker. She was a stalwart of that shop. No one, but no one, took more abuse and ranting and raving than Peggy. Let me explain; we didn't have cash tills in the shop, all money went to Peg via a set of catapulted cups on wires from the counters. There were two cups on the grocery counter, one at each end, one by the order counter, and at the end of the provision counter. Besides these Peggy had a window frame into the shop next door, which was the drapery shop, and she also took all the money from those staff by hand through the window. Now the ladies toilet was upstairs in the shop next door and if Peg wanted to spend a penny she had to lock her door and go through the grocery shop, into the street and into next door. Of course this took a little time, especially if Peg stopped to speak to someone on the way there or back. The way we got Peggy rattled was we used to bang on the wires – this made an awful noise up in her box and down she would come, feathers flying, saying "I've only got one pair of hands".

The cups were made of wood, cylindrical in shape, with a bayonet cap fitting to hold them into the other half, which was attached to the wire. A catapult was on the end and when you had placed all the checks and money into the cup you pulled this handle like a lavatory chain and it was catapulted up to Peggy's office. She in turn would take down the cup, look at the check and money and return the check and change, if any, down to the counter on the same line. If you were in Peg's box for any reason, and you weren't paying attention and listening, if one of those cups was sent up it gave your head a real knock The trouble was, not only did you get a bad head but the cup would return to the sender and then be returned again when the assistant saw it had not been up to Peg's. More hassle then from the customer for being kept waiting. Life wasn't easy in those days for poor Peg.

That was briefly the layout of the shop, but I must tell you my experiences upstairs in the warehouse, where I was employed as warehouse boy. The warehouse was the same as the shop below in size and I forgot to mention when I was telling you about the fixtures and fittings in the shop that at one end of the grocery counter there was a lift. This lift was two boxes each tied on a rope, and when one box was down in the shop the other was up in the warehouse. Now if the customer wanted half a stone of potatoes or one stone of flour, the counter assistant would put their head in the open space of the lift and shout up "Dougie, a stone of potatoes please". I would then weigh up a stone of spuds and send them down on the lift.

In the warehouse we had six large zinc or aluminium bins and in them we had balancer meal, layers mash and layers pellets, all for hens. In the other three we had two for flour and one for wholemeal. Each bin held two sacks of flour or wholemeal, but only one sack of poultry food. We always had about forty sacks of flour stacked on the floor and twenty sacks of potatoes. The flour was in twelve stones and the potatoes in eight-stone sacks. We had very large fixtures down one wall, which we stacked bags of flour in various weights, ready for when the shop shouted up for 3lb of flour so we didn't have to start from scratch and weigh it up. On another wall we had the potato bin. This, Charlie Hodgson and I filled up each morning before he went out delivering. The potato bin was six-foot high and five-foot square, at the front of the bin from about half way up the boards were loose, which meant we could fill the bin by removing the boards, putting in the potatoes then replacing the boards as we were filling it up. It was a lot easier than having to throw the potatoes in at the top of the bin. Charlie got carried away when we were filling the bin, he would get hold of the top of the sack by making two lugs and I had to get hold of the bottom, and when Charlie said "right" or "one, two, three" he lifted with my help and threw the bag into the bin, sometimes with me nearly behind it. But I had to hold on to the sack and let the spuds drop out. If I didn't and the whole bag of spuds went into the bin I was called all the names under the sun, such as "you useless so and so" and "if I had a dog half as daft as you I would have shot it years ago". A very colourful man with words was Charlie. I must say that it was he who taught me nearly everything, and to that man's credit, in all the years we worked together from being warehouse boy to manager, we never had one wrong word between us. Plus every day he would be in the same good mood and I repeat, every day. He told me when I was in the shop later on when we were talking that you should never bring your troubles to work and he practised what he preached. I tried and think I did that throughout all my working days.

Above the loading room was a room off the warehouse the same size and this also had two flap doors on the floor, which allowed the lift to come through with either a sack on it or the box. We had to swing it towards us to drop it on the floor and unload it. Very little was kept in this room as it was purely for unloading stuff that came up on the lift. In between the warehouse and the loading room were the stairs both from the ground floor and up to the attic. Once up to the attic, on your left was what we called the paper room, and in here we kept all the paper bags we ever used. There were parcels of sugar bags in sizes half-pound, one-pound, one and a half pound, two-pound, three-pound and four-pound and these were blue in colour. Then there were fruit bags in half-pound and one-pound sizes, confectionery bags in two sizes eight inches by eight inches, flour bags in three-pound, six-pound, and fourteen-pound – these were white in colour and quite strong. Also potato bags in three and a half-pound, seven-pound and fourteen-pound size and they were a dark brown colour. Grease proof paper by the reams, large sheets and butter paper, pre-cut to quarter, half and pound size, also plain greaseproof which was plain cut in the same sizes. Then there was cheese paper – the best way I can describe that is that it was like lining paper which you used when wall papering. This paper we had to cut into sizes ourselves.

There were two colours of dried fruit bags, blue and a colour I would call port. We had currants, sultanas, raisins and dates all to weigh up. The shop staff did that though, not little me in the warehouse. I had enough to do, like one and a half tons of potatoes and round about a ton of flour as the two main products to weigh up. The paper room was to the left at the top of the stairs and was a good size room, about twenty-foot by twelve-foot, and all the attic rooms were underdrawn with floorboards stained and varnished. It looked quite nice and spacious; you could walk about quite normally without banging your head.

The grocery shop had the use of the whole length of the attic, being the only entry to it. It went from Rosemary Lane round the corner into Finkle Street. I always wondered when I was a child what was in the dome situated right on the corner of the building above the drapery shop. It had two small windows in it and you could see into Newbiggin and Rosemary Lane from them. It certainly wasn't a lavish room, plain red brick walls, which were whitewashed and nothing else. Nothing was ever kept in there all the time I was at the Co-op. The attic turned left from the dome and about twenty yards on was the Committee Room. This room was done out like a boardroom, with a large substantial polished table and eight polished carver chairs situated round it. This room was used every week as the local committee met here. One week they met on a Friday at 4.30pm and the following week on the Saturday. At the Saturday meetings a representative from the main board from Darlington would attend and keep the local members up to date regarding the society. Without going into the history of the Darlington Co-operative Society (DC.S), the local committee were elected and were quite powerful. In the old days they hired and fired all the staff and the grocery manager had to report to them each week. I have in my possession two minute books from this committee and believe me they are powerful reading, the first one being from the year 1897.

I have given you the layout of the shop and diversed a little bit but now let me tell you about some of the day-to-day workings of the warehouse. I would turn up for work at eight- twenty five, being five minutes earlier than the starting time of eight-thirty, and be in the warehouse spot on time. My first job was to work with Charlie, carrying the orders from the shop to him. He stood in the middle of the back of the lorry and as I gave him an order, he would place it in the right place and in order of delivery. When all the orders from the shop were on the wagon I would have to get all the orders from upstairs that I would have put up, i.e. the stones of potatoes, flour and other products like hen foods, Charlie would then place the warehouse products with the customer's order. While we were loading these orders the provision hand would be making up the bacon orders. Let me explain about all these orders, and how it worked.

The first thing that the staff who were putting up orders did was to get all the orders for one delivery and make a list out for the stuff required from the warehouse. The list read like this:

Mrs Jones
Gayles
1 stone potatoes
1 stone flour
2 stone layers meal.

Briggs
Ravensworth
2 stone flour
½ stone bran
½ block salt

And so it went on until all the orders had gone through. Also listed was the bacon because you couldn't pack bacon the day before so the following morning the provision hand's first job was to get the bacon list and wrap and bag it up with the name on it. Sometimes the poor provision hand, who had been busy serving customers, would keep Charlie waiting, and Charlie being Charlie he would jibe to the poor soul "are you going to pay me overtime for keeping me waiting, I could have been at Skeeby by now". Also there was the vinegar list, which having vinegar in the barrel, meant we always had to keep some empty bottles.

The wagon now fully loaded; all Charlie had to do was get a money float from Peg and away he would go and we would only see him again when all had been delivered, that would be about four-thirty. After cashing in he would come and help me sort out tomorrow's journey. If I hadn't finished he would help me, Charlie was good at stringing up bags of flour or potatoes, anything really. It was he who taught me the best way to string up a bag of whatever. This was to fold the top of the bag in the normal way and using both hands, lay the string across the top and let your hands run down each side, holding the string tight and flip the whole thing over and tie using a slip knot and locking it. Then wrap the string around the first two fingers of your left hand and snap it. This took some time to master, but when you kept getting sore fingers you learnt quickly to get it right. It was always a party piece to show people how you could snap string just like that.

Anyway, getting back to the day's work after the delivery wagon had gone. Let me say first about the wagon. It was a 'Dennis' with a box cab and right hand gate gears, a 30 cwt short wheel base wagon. I will diverse a little for the moment and tell you stories about this wagon, Charlie and I.

The cab was made of wood and when I say it was a box cab it was just that. Straight back, front and sides, with plate glass sliding windows on the doors. I have to this day a scar on my left hand when the cab collapsed coming down Barrack Hill with 30 cwt of potatoes on. I remember saying to Charlie "I'm sure I'm holding back this load of potatoes" which were in sacks, his reply being "don't be so bloody daft". It wasn't daft when we hit a pothole in the road, the whole cab collapsed and the glass from the side window caught my hand and cut it. The steering wheel wasn't on an angle like they are today but straight up from the floor and there we were sitting bolt upright, Charlie with his hands on the wheel and both of us holding back 30cwt of potatoes with our backs. We must have looked a right pair of you know whats, riding back to the shop with everybody staring at us.

Another time we were doing a little job for ourselves with the wagon, which really we weren't allowed to use after working hours, which very nearly had a catastrophic ending. Charlie had seen a plantation being cut and knew that there would be quite a bit of timber lying about. So he said "we will take the wagon, fill it up with logs, sheet it down so no-one can see what we have on the wagon, and we will share the load". "Fine," I said, as it would be a great help at our house.

Dad always did the fire when mam was baking or cooking in the oven on the Yorkist fire range, which all the council houses were fitted with. Poor dad often got the wrath of mam if he had put too many logs on and the oven got too hot. The arguments that followed were always a treat to listen to and if some of the baking got a bit burnt, it was always dad's fault. He used to say, "I can't do right for doing wrong". Anyway, away Charlie and I went this Wednesday afternoon, this being the shop half day closing, to this plantation in the Washton Road. It didn't take us long and we soon had the wagon in the middle of the site that had been cut down. We loaded up the wagon, covered the back with the proper sheet for the job and made our way back to the road. The people that felled the trees were good, in fact very good, because they had sawn the trunks of the trees off right near to the ground, so when our lorry ran over one which was on a slope, the wagon went on two wheels, Charlie shouted "get over there" meaning for me to just about stand on the running board and he came close to me as the wagon went on two wheels, and he came out in a sweat that would have flooded the river Swale. I have never ever seen anyone come out in such a sweat so quickly and so heavily. We both nearly did the proverbial in our trousers. We soon got over it though and made our way back to town. We unloaded the wagon at Charlie's house first and then our house and then garaged it. That was just one of many things that we got up to in those hectic days.

Carrying on from before where I diversified about the wagon episode, now that Charlie had got loaded and on his way, I would get my list off one of the girls in the shop, who by this time had written out all the lists from the orders that had to be made up that day for the next day delivery, and take it upstairs into the warehouse. This was always the first job to do, so that tomorrow's delivery was ready. I would put the list on the table and proceed to write out all the bags what each customer wanted. Once that was done I had to complete the job by filling the bags with the product I had marked on them. It would be dinnertime before I got the list completed so at half past twelve, the shop would shut and we would all go to dinner, returning at one-forty, refreshed and ready to go. Back upstairs I would go, taking two or three at a time (those were the days), and get on with my work. Besides putting up stock ready bagged for the shop, there were great big forty to sixty-pound Cheddar cheeses to skin. These, though not all, were pigs to skin. The muslin that was the so-called skin was wrapped round them so tightly that it would peel of in about one inch squares. When they were very bad like that I had to wrap a wet sack around them and leave them for a couple of hours to soak. Looking back I don't think that did much good either. On another occasion the muslin would be covered in wax and then once you got a start it would roll of in one length. This was when I said "praise be" or "thank God" for that.

Another job that wasn't nice to do was cutting block salt into half or quarters, as people would ask for half a block of salt or even a quarter. We did this by a sawing action with string. Its funny how you remember some things, like the string we used for tying, every thing was 'No 5 Twine'. Useless information now though, isn't it. Talking about block salt reminds me that it was one of the products that Charlie and I had to go and collect from the railway goods yard. There were only two items that ever came by goods train, salt and flour. We would be notified or the manager would say that there were forty sacks of flour and forty blocks of salt to be collected by such and such a date. Hence Charlie and I had to make time to collect these goods in the morning before he went on his deliveries. It was very hard work for a boy of fourteen to sixteen to manhandle twelve-stone sacks of flour from a railway wagon to our wagon and then unload at the shop. I said to myself "thank goodness" when they stopped delivering by rail and brought it straight from the flour mills at Dunstan Gateshead, in great big lorries. It only had to be handled once then. That was the last of deliveries by rail we had.

Every Monday our own delivery wagon used to go to Darlington to our society's warehouse and get loaded with our weekly order which had been formulated by the previous Wednesday and sent by post. If we were lucky Charlie would get back with the load before lunchtime and we could make a start unloading it. It took all day Monday to unload and stack everything where it belonged. The bacon had to be taken upstairs into the warehouse ready to be boned. Once boned it was taken down to the cellar, where we hung it from the roof with 'S' hooks. Once again it was Charlie who taught me how to bone bacon, from hams, middles, spencers or just shoulders. I liked doing the middles as the ribs were no bother to get out, by just cutting round the end, and with a looped piece of string or wire, draw it along the bone and it came away as clean as anything. No meat at all was left on the bones, just like the boss liked it. He would get a bit pear-shaped if he saw a little bit of meat left on the bone "that's the profit you're leaving on there laddie". If we didn't get the bacon boned on the Monday it had to be done on Tuesday or when we had time. If that was the case it had to be taken to the cellar and hung, as it would have sweat, then we would have to bring it piece by piece to bone it back upstairs.

We got so busy in the warehouse that the boss decided it was too much for one person to do properly so he got another boy to help me out in the warehouse, and if I had a spare hour or so I had to come into the shop to pack goods in the fixtures. I got the jobs that they didn't like doing. Like packing in bags of soap under the counter, as you had to get on your hands and knees to do this, but I usually had company to do these jobs. One month after I had started work they started another school leaver but for the shop. This was a girl called Amy and we often worked together when I was in the shop. Amy stayed with me the whole time I worked for the Co-op and we have been friends up to this day. Anyway the lad they got for the warehouse was called George Thomas and George and I had some fun while he stayed with me. Mr Robinson, the boss, told George and I to go up to the paper room and sort it out, meaning put all the bags of one type together and generally clean the place. We soon did this, and started mucking about. In the paper room was a large cone-shaped fire extinguisher – red in colour and wall-mounted. Now I must point out that it was my job to check these extinguishers every month to see that the two bottles of chemicals inside were okay. I had shown George how to do this and put it back together, when he took it from me and pointed it at me as though it was a gun, shouting "bang, bang, you're dead". I forgot to tell him not to drop it on the floor as that would set it of. George did just that and I realised that we had only two or three seconds before it spurted out the foam. Just outside the room at the top of the stairs was a skylight, which opened upwards, and without hesitation I ran and opened this window, at the same time shouting to George to bring the extinguisher and hold it out of the window. Fortunately this he did without hesitating, just before it shot out all this white foam. It seemed to go on forever. At last it stopped and we were both relieved. We sat down for a minute or two before we filled the thing up again and put it back on the wall as good as new. We thought that was the end of it but it wasn't. At the back of our shop was a house, which the manager of Freeman Hardy and Willis lived in, being attached to the back of the shop in Finkle Street. Now the building came within ten feet of our warehouse, with the living room and above the bedroom, and when we came downstairs back into the warehouse we were surprised to see Mr and Mrs Danby looking somewhat puzzled by having their house wall covered in white foam. At first George and I were very frightened as to what was going to happen but after a little while we couldn't stop laughing, looking at Mr and Mrs Danby arguing what to do. Fortunately for us they hadn't come round to the shop to ask if we knew anything about it. Thank God, saved again.

Talking about the Danby's, they had a lovely daughter called Vera and I had a bit of a crush on her. Not forgetting it's wartime and all the windows had to be blacked out for precautions when there was an air raid. Well, we had a window looking straight into the Danby's bedroom but had to paint it black because we had no curtains to black it out. I used to open it and talk to Vera every day through that window, as she used the bedroom to do her homework from the High School. So it was only natural that I carved her initials out of the paint on the window. Of course it read VD and once when the general manager came to our branch, Mr Hall being his name, he saw this. He was not amused and asked who had carved it. Whether he believed it or not I was told to paint over it at once. I can't understand why some people get so agitated at seeing someone's initials displayed. Vera asked why I had painted over her initials when I told her what had happened she just laughed.

On another day George and I were fooling about, we were hitting each other and I picked up a parcel of paper bags and swung it on to George's head. I didn't see he was having a drink out of a bottle, and bang it broke his two front teeth. He called me all the names under the sun as he went to see Mr Robinson to ask if he could go to the dentist. George said he had slipped catching his face on the table as he fell. I don't think he believed him but I had to take him to the dentist, which unfortunately was just across the road. The dentist was Mr Groves and he built those two front teeth up so that you couldn't see that anything had happened. Now that there were two of us in the warehouse, if Charlie required a hand on his journey it was always me that went with him. In the summertime, well all the time really, I went with him when he had a load of potatoes to pick up. Being in the countryside we bought all our potatoes from local farmers. Charlie did all the negotiating on these occasions. You can see that there was always quite a lot going on in grocery shops in those days.

Every day was a busy day and you never knew what was going to happen that day. For example, George and I tipped a bag of hen meal into the bin and found a nest of mice had been in the sack. We put the lid down on the bin so that the mice couldn't get out and went and got the cat. I found the cat in Peggy's cash office sitting on a bundle of one-pound and five-pound notes. I must say at this time the cat had no idea what a mouse was I'm sure but we soon taught it. I took the cat upstairs and put it in the bin with the mice. It just looked at them, all four of them. George and I just kept watching the useless cat until it got the right idea. This is what we had been waiting for, for the penny to drop for the cat. We shut the lid I shouted to George "there's someone coming upstairs" – it was the boss. I hoped he wasn't coming to give us a hand to put up tomorrow's delivery list but he wasn't. All he was looking for was a clean sack, which he found quick enough and went back downstairs. It was a good job he was a little hard of hearing, because the cat in the bin was chasing the mice round and making a bit of a noise. So George and I were making as much noise as we could, weighing and stringing up bags of potatoes. After he had gone we took the cat out of the bin with a bit of a struggle because now he didn't want to leave his playmates. He didn't have long to wait, as we took a mouse out of the bin and put it on the floor so the cat could see it. The next hour was most interesting, watching the cat nip the mouse and then turn his head away, letting the mouse get away again, but the cat was looking. I think he had eyes in the back of his head. He played with all four mice and killed them in turn, and from then on we had very few mice come into our shop.

I must say whilst this little exercise was going on, who should come into the warehouse but Amy. I said "Amy come and have a look at this". Amy came round to where I was standing watching the cat play, and as soon as she saw the mouse being chased by the cat, she screamed and ran like hell back down the stairs. She told Alf the first hand what I was doing up in the warehouse, expecting to get me into trouble, but it backfired. Alf thought it was funny and told her she should have picked it up by the tail and brought it down and given it to Peggy. Amy said it wasn't funny and that she wasn't going into the warehouse anymore. Needless to say she soon got over it and life returned to normal.

The war was still going on but it didn't stop us doing much. One felt very sorry for London, Birmingham, Manchester and all the cities and large towns, as Hitler bombed them day and night. But we were getting the better of the war now and we were sending one thousand planes at a time over to Germany. We only bombed the places where they made the tools of war, such as the planes, tanks and ammunition, whereas Hitler was trying to demoralise the people of this country, by bombing the cities and large towns. As is recorded, he did not succeed. I would come home from work never knowing what we were having to eat for our dinner or tea but there was always food on the table and we enjoyed every mouthful.

In our house we had dinner at mid-day and tea after work, followed always by a good supper at night. Mam used to say "you cant go to bed or work on an empty stomach". Supper was always a nice meal as we used to have dripping and bread. The dripping we got from various sources, I know, but I can't remember them. Now and then we would have fish and chips. In those days one never thought of having fish and chips as a main meal; it was only a supper.

Having sat and thought for a while, I used to go to the Band of Hope and Junior Guild at the Methodist Church. I know we used to sing some rousing hymns at Band of Hope and Junior Guild but I don't remember what they were supposed to do for us. It must have been another extension of Sunday school. Now I do remember going to the Methodist Youth Club. This was started by a friend of mine's father, a man called Mr Wood, who as well as working on the camp, that's Catterick Camp, was a local preacher for the church. We had some great times at the club, one of which was we would form a drama group and put on a concert. Everybody was very friendly and we all soon became very good friends. Donald Wood, Jean Gates, Noel Richardson, Doreen Stevenson, Jean Gay, Keith and Peter Blades, Pat Mcombie, Evelyn Bainbridge, Dennis Forster, David Mansell, Joyce Thompson and Jack Harmsworth to name but a few. Little Mr Wood – we called him that because he was only five feet tall I think – kept a tight hold on our behaviour; he wouldn't stand for any hooliganism or any bad behaviour come to that. Part of our activities was the drama group and all the previously-mentioned members were in it, including myself. We decided to put on a play and then had to think as to whom was going to produce it. Mr Wood said he knew a Mrs Stant who was an excellent actor and producer and he would ask her to produce a play for us. Renee Stant came to the club and she put forward a number of plays which she thought we could do. We chose a two-act comedy called 'The Dumb Wife of Cheapside', and I would play the showman. The play was about a wife who didn't speak until she went to a fair and there saw someone who helped her to get her speech back. Then she couldn't stop talking. That was roughly what the play was about (I think, or on those lines) and Evelyn Bainbridge played the leading role as the Mistress Groat superbly. It was an Oscar-winning performance by her. Most of the time we enjoyed rehearsing this, but at one stage Renee Stant thought we weren't putting all our minds to the matter and told us all that she was packing it in. Mr Wood nearly had a fit and got us all together and gave us what for in no uncertain terms. As the concert was only two weeks away we said we would put a lot more effort into it. This we did and on the day of the concert we were nervous to say the least but Renee the true professional that she was saw us through and relaxed us. Even though I say it myself the play was well received and went through without a hitch. We played to a packed hall and all said they had enjoyed it enormously and suggested we do another one. In fact we did another two – 'The Bishops Candlesticks' and 'Old Moore's Almanak' which I played in – I took the part of Sir John Dullas Ditchwater. All our concerts were a great success, always playing to a full house.

This was in 1944 and we had the Germans on the run. My dad was still growing the vegetables and mam was still looking after all of us. Later on in the club we put on a pantomime called Jack and the Beanstalk, and I can remember seeing Donald Wood dressed up as a fairy, I think, and reciting this little verse which I shall never forget:

"I am the fairy of the wood
I go about doing good
For a bag of beans I sold a cow

I only have my mother now."

When it was spoken it was hilarious, just to see Don dressed up was hilarious. Mr Wood was a leader of the church and had to attend leaders' meetings and I must give credit to him, because he fought tooth and nail to allow the club to have dancing on the premises. The Methodist Conference, which was the ruling body of the Methodist Church, would not allow anyone to hold a dance on Methodist premises and of course our church leaders were governed by the rules. In the end we were granted permission to include a dance or two on our social evenings. This was all we needed, as who was going to keep count how many dances we had. Methodism in those days was really out of touch with what was going on in the real world. Richmond and all the nearby villages would have a dance every weekend. The troops – and there were I am told forty-five thousand on and around Catterick Camp at this time – enjoyed them to the full. They had only the town hall in Richmond and the village halls and the pubs to go to, and drinking as a Methodist was also taboo.

Richmond band, 1943

At the age of fourteen, fifteen and sixteen we didn't have a single girlfriend, but we went together and did things together in groups, and I must say we had some great times. We were fortunate in those days that there was plenty to do, as all the churches had youth clubs and we had competitions between us all. We would walk for miles, or go to the pictures. There were two cinemas in Richmond at that

time – the 'old' cinema and the 'New Zetland' cinema. Each had a
manager with a strong personality, who watched you as you paid the
three pence or sixpence depending on how flush you were. The old
cinema's manager was an upright man and wore a bowler hat and
never smiled, well I never saw him. The other manager was a little
dapper man, a lot younger than Mr French, and he was called Mr
Anderson. Now he looked liked a manager as he was always dressed
in evening suit with white shirt and black bow tie. He was a jolly man
but would stand no nonsense from us kids. The Zetland was favourite
with the courting couples as they introduced the double seats, which
were at the end of each row, except in the cheap seats.

Some nights three or four of us would meet, and not having much
to do and being broke, we would amuse ourselves by aggravating
people in their own homes, like knocking on the door and running
away. Or if there was a hedge, tie a line of cotton on the doorknocker
and hold it, hiding behind the hedge and keep knocking by pulling
the line of cotton. As soon as the door was closed we would do it
again. The person opening the door couldn't understand how anyone
could run away in such a short time. We did this trick on a house in
Gordon Crescent, I think it was, and when I saw who answered the
door, I nearly had a fit – it was Alf Dunne the under manager or first
hand at the shop where I worked. We did it three times and then ran
away but he must have recognised me because as soon as I got to
work the next morning he set on me like a tiger. "What do you think
you were doing last night frightening old people and causing wilful
damage?" "It was only a bit of fun and I'm sorry," I'm mumbled.
"Fun, fun you call that fun, I don't, I nearly called the police, I would
have done so if I hadn't seen it was you," he went on and on and in
the end the boss came to my rescue and told Alf to shut up, as he
was at work and had probably done the same thing himself when he
was my age. I had some horrible jobs to do that day. Mr Robinson
had stopped him shouting at me but he couldn't stop him giving
me all the rotten jobs to do. I was glad when that day was over and
went home and had a good tea. It didn't stop me getting changed and
going out after tea.

At home my dad was building a shed out the back with wood and
corrugated sheeting. It didn't take him long to do and it wasn't long
before all sorts of gear was in it. All the garden tools, the spade, fork,
the different hoes and all the other large tools. Dad also kept the logs
that he had sawn up in there where it was dry. It didn't look very
nice but it did the job it was made for and lasted longer than we
did at Whitcliffe Terrace. There wasn't a toilet in the house; it was
outside the back door. Well not quite outside the back door because

the coalbunker was first and then the toilet. The coalbunker held about six hundred weight and the coal was tipped in through a lid on the top. The toilet was brick-built, about four feet square, with a toilet pan in the middle and a little window. In the winter we had to burn a lamp in the lav to stop the water in the pipes freezing. I can count on one hand and have fingers to spare the times I went to the toilet in the middle of the night; it was always so cold, even in the summer.

Every Sunday morning, it appeared to be my dad's job to cut squares of newspaper, put a string through them in one corner and hang them in the toilet. It was only when we had company coming that we put a toilet roll in the loo. It looked better than sheets of newspaper. It was interesting though to try and match up some of the squares and to try and read them whilst sitting and straining.

Another project that often took place in our home was mat making. Clip or hooky, my mother and father were masters in this trade and made all the mats in our house. We had a big clip mat in front of the fire, which was about five-foot by three-foot. Mother would have a rag bag in which she put all the clothing that was finished with, and when the bag was full she would cut the cloth first into strips and then into pieces about four inches by one inch. These were the clips and mam would then separate the colours, so when she drew a pattern on the canvas it always had a border in one colour and the middle was a mixture of colours. Sometimes mother would make flowers in the middle if she had enough clips of one colour. The hooky mats were made of old lisle stockings cut again into strips about one inch wide and then left in strips, as these were prodded into the hessian making loops. You could dye the stockings if you wanted a variety of colours. The hessian that the mats were made on was usually an empty two hundred weight sugar sack. These sacks were the best as they were tightly woven, which kept the clips in better. The hessian was sewn onto some webbing that was tacked onto some lats, two long ones, which had the webbing tacked on, and two small ones that had holes punched into them in a line down the middle. You made a rectangle by slotting the small ones through a slit on each end of the long ones, and putting a peg into one hole that made the right size and kept the sacking taut. One then had to place it somewhere so you could do your prodding. What we did in our house was to put one end on one side of the table and the other end over the backs of two chairs. This meant you could either stand or sit to work to work in the clips. Any callers at the house always wanted to have a go and surprise, surprise, none of us stopped them.

Chapter Three

Our house was a happy house as the saying goes. There was always a lovely smell about the place as mother would be baking bread and pies and those dam rock buns, about three or four times a week. Out would come the baking bowl, it held at least half a stone of flour, and after adding all the ingredients mam would punch and pummel it or should I say knead it. Then cover it over with a clean tea towel and place in front of the fire to rise. Dad had to get the oven just right if he wasn't working, by shoving logs on the fire and pushing them under the oven. I sometimes think that dad wished he was at work instead of stoking up the fire because it was very seldom right. It would be either too hot or not hot enough.

Mondays were always washdays and out would come the poss tub, I never can remember where it was kept, but on Mondays it always showed its face. Dinner on a Monday was always a fry-up, all that was left from Sunday dinner. I can still remember Mam possing the clothes with a possing stick or whatever they called it. Women in those days were as fit as a fiddle and as strong as an ox, if you got a clip across the face you didn't want another one.

Tuesday was ironing day and what the rest of the days were I do not know. But I do know my mother never seemed to have a rest. By now my younger brother 'Frederick Bernard', Fred for short, had left school and gone to work at Clarksons the Chemist which was in the Market Place. That left 'Francis Ada', the baby of the family, who always went by the name of Nancy, the last at school.

The war came to an end on the seventh of May 1945, that's the war in Europe; the war in Japan ended on the second of September in the same year and naturally there was great jubilation. It wasn't long before a street party was organised for all of us in Whitcliffe Terrace, Reeth Road and Whitcliffe Place. This was one big party. I don't know who organised it but I do know everyone helped to make it a day to remember and so it was. Tables were set up in the street decorated with Union Jacks and white sheets, which were used for tablecloths. Do remember rationing was still on and it amazes me to this day where all the food came from – jelly, trifle, scones, cakes and sandwiches all laid out for the kiddies. They thought it was their birthday I'm sure. That party was in the afternoon but at night it was time for all the mams and dads to let their hair down and they did. Drinks flowed and people were dancing in the street. Everybody was so happy; I've never seen any gathering of people before or after having such a good time. One thing that stays in my mind about that party was Mrs Conway dancing on one of the tables, swishing her skirt about and showing a glimpse of her knickers. Everybody gathered round, clapped and urged her on till she was exhausted. I can't remember what time the party broke up but I do know it was the best street party in Richmond.

The war was over, we had all celebrated, and then reality came back to us and we realised we still had work to do and carry on living doing life's little chores. At work George had left by now and for a while I was on my own again, but not for long. I thought I would be getting another boy to work in the warehouse, but no it was a girl called Audrey. Well Audrey and I got on very well thank you. Besides doing our normal work we used to play games, if you can call it that. It all started with playing truth or dare, and it wasn't long before we were daring each other to do things that made your mouth dry. This was when my sex education started and as teenagers we learnt from each other. Often it got a bit risky with people coming upstairs for one thing and another but it all made it so much more fun and we laughed about it. It was hard work from morn till night to keep our hands off each other. I was expected to work more and more in the shop, which I did, helping Amy and the other girls with filling up fixtures or weighing up sugar or dried fruit. Alf Dunne, Pearl and I got so good at weighing up sugar we would time ourselves to see how long it took us to weigh up two cwt of sugar in a variety of weights, i.e. 1/2lb, 1lb, 2lb, 3lb and the odd 4lbs. Alf was a brilliant man on the scales and Pearl and I would do the filling and wrapping and stacking. Pearl and I were equally good at doing this and used to swap over when we got sick of doing the one thing. The best time we did was thirteen minutes to weigh 2cwt into 1lb and 2lb bags and take it into the shop fixtures. We never bettered that time, but we did send out a challenge to the boss for him to choose any two of the other staff to try and match our time. Although Mr Robinson was a good man on the scales, he was not quite as good as Alf I thought, and they got nowhere near our time. We were called "clever sh...s".

We delivered on Tuesdays to Gilling and Hartforth one week and Hudswell, Downhome, Marske and Hurst the other. On Thursday we went to Skeeby, Catterick Bridge and Brompton on Swale. Friday was one week to Whashton, Kirby Hill, Gayles, Dalton and West Layton. The other Friday we delivered to Melsonby, Forcett and East Layton. Saturday was the busiest day delivering around the town. This had to be done in three separate loads, that's how big the town journey was. Wednesday, being half day closing, was left to do a few town deliveries if there were any, and other jobs as work required, such as picking up stuff that had come by rail or getting potatoes from the farm. It was always the day when Charlie and I boned and hung all the weeks' bacon.

I was coming up to the age of conscription by now and having the time of my life at work and at the youth club or anything we did in the evenings. Denis was in the navy serving on corvettes and destroyers and enjoying himself. I must say when he came home on leave he looked superb in his bell-bottoms and all that. He had got into the habit of having a drink as well and it pleased my father no end when he took him out for a drink, especially into the Buck Inn, which was dad's local drinking haunt. Dad went to the Buck every night for a drink, going into town on the twenty past seven bus from Reeth Road and returning on the quarter to nine bus. I never saw my father drunk in all my life, except for one occasion. It was when we were very young, that's Fred, our Nancy and me. On one New Years Eve, mam had let us stay up to see in the New Year. Well this year dad had one drink to many and had gone to sleep it off on the sofa. Now us being wide awake and full of fun and thinking dad would be feeling the same, we got hold of his legs and pulled him off the sofa. That was it, dad went crazy and mum quickly rushed us upstairs to bed saying "all being well I'll get you up again nearer the time" after she had talked to dad. It started off as a bit of fun and we didn't think it would end like this. Mam being mam must have sorted it out and at about quarter to twelve she got us up again and dad never said a word; he was just marvellous and got his melodium out of its box and we had a sing-song before mam put him out at two minutes to twelve. It was love and kisses from then on and we went to bed in another year after dad had let the New Year in.

Everything was going on nicely thank you when one morning in April just after my birthday an official envelope came through the letterbox with the letters OHMS on it, addressed to yours truly. It requested that I attend for a medical examination somewhere in Middlesborough; I can't remember the exact place for entry into the army. It was all new to me to have to go to a large town on my own and find the place where I was to present myself. It was no problem; I got the bus to Darlington and then another bus to Middlesborough. Getting off the bus I asked a chap where this place was and he directed me. Fortunately it was just more or less round the corner. Having a bit of time to spare after finding the building, I took a look round the shops, which I found very interesting. After spending an hour or so I went back to the building and found myself along with about fifty other lads in a long hall, all waiting to be medically examined. There must have been half a dozen or more doctors working here as when one's name was called you had to go to the door where the voice was coming from and I saw at least six different entries.

"Mr Shout" was called and in I went to this little room with a screen at one end and a washbasin on one of the walls. The first words that greeted me were "have a pee in this bottle and leave it on the window sill" which in fact was a window hatch. I saw the hatch open; a hand came out, got the bottle and closed again. At the same time a nurse came from behind the screen after changing some paper sheets on an examination couch. I thought "bloody hell" it's like a ghost house in here, the only thing that didn't move was the doctor, who was writing at a desk. It wasn't much of an examination, after having to cough twice, I was told I was A1 and would be sent a letter confirming this and the date and place where I would start my conscription.

When I got home I told all what had happened and proudly boasted about being A1 in health. My friends all called and wanted to know what the score was, then we went out. Nothing much happened at work at this time, except that Charlie wasn't very happy to be losing me in a short time. It was sad because Charlie wasn't fit enough to join the forces and he had seen all the fellows out of the shop get called up at the beginning of the war and now after the war was over he was having to see me go.

The last week in May the postman delivered that brown envelope and mam and dad couldn't wait to see where and when I was going. I picked up the envelope, kissed it and deliberately opened it very slowly. "Hurry up son I have to go to work," said dad, so I adhered to his wish and proclaimed that I was to present myself to the barracks at Richmond on June 5th 1947 at 10am. And so started a new chapter in my life.

Well I packed my bags as the saying goes, and after kissing my mother and saying so long to my dad, off I went to do my bit. In my bags were my shaving brush and soap and my razor was in my pocket; that was all I had to take, along with a bit of money for NAAFI breaks – about £1 I think. It said in the letter to report to the barracks at Gallowgate and I thought, as would any other Richmond lad, that Gallowgate meant Gallowgate camp, which was built for the army complete with a square for marching. So up Westfields behind our house I went, as this was a direct route to Gallowgate. When I got there they put me in a lorry along with three other lads who had got there by taking a taxi from the station and took us along the road to the barracks at the top of Barrack Hill, as we know it, but the correct name of course was and still is Gallowgate.

Once there we were ushered onto another lorry with a covered back and chairs inside to sit on and off we went down to the station to pick up more recruits with a sergeant in charge. We had to stay in the wagon while the NCO went into the station. He came back after half an hour, leading another twelve lads. They wanted to know how we had got into the wagon, as they hadn't seen us on the station platform, so we told them. That lorry ran a shuttle service from the barracks to the station all afternoon, meeting the later trains and bringing back more lads. The lorry took us to the Gallowgate camp that I first went to and I thought "well it's been like a mystery tour up to now".

About five-o-clock when everybody was here, we started our GSC training by listening to an officer telling us what was expected of us in the next six weeks. He said we would be gradually wound up to peak fitness starting tomorrow. That guy told us a whole bunch of lies when he said we would gradually get to terms with fitness. If he thought that getting roused at five-thirty in the morning, or should I say the middle of the night, was gradual then he was the only one. I've never heard so many moans and groans in all my life. A corporal came in ten minutes later and pulled the blankets off anyone who had not put their feet on the ground and shouted "outside in half an hour, washed, shaved and ready to go to breakfast".

I went to the washhouse and it was just that, a row of aluminium troughs with a shelf at the back where you could stand a mirror to shave. The only thing was, nobody had told us we had to bring our own mirrors or looking glass, so for the time being we all shaved without one. I did get one though from the NAAFI the following day and told my room mates that the NAAFI sold them. They soon sold out and so we shaved with one another. The team spirit had already started. Shaving was terrible because if you were not in that damn washhouse early you washed and shaved in cold water and in 1947 it was a cold June. I substantiate this by telling you on our third night there, we woke up with snow on our barrack room floor, as the door had blown opening during the night.

There would be twenty of us in our barrack room, ten iron beds either side with a round stove in the middle of the room. We only got a little wood and coal to burn so I thanked God it was June and not January we were here. Anyway at six-thirty most of us were outside standing about when the corporal came along and told us to get felled in or should I say he shouted "fall in". After a count he found he was missing two or three. He told us to stand still while he went looking for those that were missing. He returned pushing three lads on the double and told them to get in line along with us, and then with a few words that I hadn't heard before gave them the biggest dressing down I've ever heard, and told us all those famous words "you're in the army now".

We were still wearing our own clothes when he marched us off to the cookhouse for our breakfast. This was to be our first parade each day, marching to the cookhouse with our mugs, knife, fork and spoon. We were given forty-five minutes to eat and then parade outside where we were dismissed. Today being our first full day we were kitted out, so straight from breakfast we marched back to our billet and were told to "fall out" and be outside again in ten minutes. It was a bit of a rush to put your things away and have time to go to the toilet, but one had to do it. We fell in and marched to the QMS (Quarter Master Stores) to get kitted out. It was a joke. We went into this room with one long counter down each side and behind the counter were fixtures filled with all the bits and pieces of our uniform and kit. Behind each section was a soldier who looked at you and told you your size. No tape measure or anything resembling one was used. It was the eye of the man behind the counter who determined your size. When I got to the counter he said in a nice crisp voice "size 4" and handed me a battle dress comprising of top and trousers. Moving down the line "cap size" was bawled at me

"6 $^7/_8$" I replied and straight away a beret was on the counter. "Next" came a voice and I had two sheets thrown at me. By now my arms were getting laden with clothes, etc, and beginning to get a bit heavy. "What size boots?" came next, "six and a half please," I said, "no half sizes, take a seven" and was given two pairs of boots weighing about two-ton. Next came our kit – a belt, large pack, small pack and a kit bag. The last things we got were a set of denims. Our corporal then told us to put as much gear as we could into our kit bag and carry the rest. Once again we got lined up and with kit bag over your shoulder and holding the other gear the best you could we were marched back to our barrack room. "Halt," came the command, "stand at ease, stand easy" said the corporal. "Now listen," he started saying, "you now go in, lay your kit on the bed then proceed to put it in your locker, tidy like, after get dressed in your battle dress. You do not have your shirts showing at the neck, your tunic to be buttoned up to the top. Boots and gaiters to be worn also. Right I'll give you thirty minutes then I'll be in along with your sergeant to inspect you." On the nose, thirty minutes later in came the corporal with a sergeant and shouted "stand by your beds". It was as if lightening had struck, from hearing all the talking to one another and mickey-taking, it became deathly silent. Isn't it strange how soon you learn who your superiors are – and woe betide you if you don't do as you're told.

We looked a real pretty lot, just like Captain Mainwaring in 'Dads Army'. The sergeant walked down one side and up the other without saying a word and looked at the corporal and he didn't say a word. Reaching the place where he set of from he said "stand easy" and we did, not knowing what was coming next. He looked a nice guy, not tall by any means but immaculately dressed and said: "Now lads you're starting a new life and you will be in the army for at least two years. It is our job to get you fit and train you in army life." He went on in a very nice way explaining what we would be doing, it would be hard, very hard at times, but if you listen to your instructor and do what he tells you, we'll get on fine. "Now go and get your dinners and get back here in one hour and we will get down to brass tacks straight away." That was the first and last civil speech I had all the time I was in the army. But he did turn out to be a nice person. It seemed to be all go all the time, hardly having time for a smoke, so I wondered what it would be like later. As the sergeant had said, it was hard and very hard at times and this was our first day. This was the first time we went for a meal and didn't march there.

The food was quite good really, the ones that moaned were the ones who never got a decent meal at home I thought, because if they'd had good meals they would have realised how good these were. After dinner our group would go into the Naafi for a cup of tea and a decent chair to sit on while we drank it and had a smoke. The hour we were allotted soon passed and back to our room again we went. Both NCOs were there when we got back and straight away showed us how they wanted the bed made every day, and how the blankets were to be folded and laid on the bed. Our lockers also had to be laid out in a certain manner. You just weren't allowed to throw every thing in there and close the door; because these were part of the barrack room inspection we had every other day. Then we were shown how to dress, you wouldn't think that a tunic had to be put on or should I say worn in a certain way. The berets were to be one inch above the eyebrows horizontally across the forehead and not on a slope. We were even shown how to polish our boots, how to get rid of the bobbles on the toecaps. This was done by putting plenty of polish on the toecap and with the handle of a toothbrush belting them down until it was smooth. It took more than once or twice to get it to really shine. I became an expert at this and it was to pay off later in my training.

You always get one or two who think they know better and didn't bother, then moaned a bucketful when they were reprimanded. The corporal said he didn't want to see anyone firing their boots as this would lead them to be put on a charge for defacing government property, and the punishment was about fourteen days CB (Confined to Barracks) and extra drills. Our duty that night was to get our boots to shine, so as one could see to shave with them, so we were told.

At about nine-thirty I'd had enough and my boots were better than everybody else's, so two or three of us went across to the Naafi for a change instead of resting on our beds. It was about ten-thirty when I got into bed and slept like a baby until that bloody bugle sounded at six a.m. That was my first real day in the army, and now another day has dawned and I wondered what was in store for all of us today.

On the third day, we paraded outside our hut and marched to the square. This was something new, going to the square for a bit of square bashing. I and the rest of the squad, which was what we were now called, now started to learn what being in the army was like. "Shut your gobs, no talking while marching," the corporal bawled us at. I smiled along with some others and the corporal again bawled at us: "You don't smile when you are on parade and marching is being on parade, so wipe that smile of your face." I thought "he isn't being very nice today, he must have got out of bed the wrong side".

Onto the square we came and the command was "halt", and halt we did. He then went on to tell us all the different commands there were and how they were used. We did them all in turn, from simply turning left or right, how high you should swing your arms. I was surprised at how many lads couldn't march. Some swung their arms with the same leg; others just seemed to walk. All these faults were soon rectified in the days ahead, as we spent more time each day on the square. The thirteen studs we had on our boot soles, I thought, wouldn't last long at this rate of exercise but they did.

The first part of the parade each day was an inspection of our dress and if our belts weren't blanco'd correctly, or the brasses not polished or a bit of Brasso had gone on to your belt or uniform, you were in trouble. That meant you had to clean the ablutions or latrines that day, and I can tell you this, the ablutions and latrines were cleaned each day, the NCO in charge saw to that. It meant you got no time to relax at night, no going to the Naafi or any other social activity until your job was completed, examined and passed okay.

One day we were paraded and marched straight to the army barber, who came to the camp one day a week. If your hair was a bit too long and you were pulled up about it on parade, you had extra duties to do, so you can see one couldn't do right for doing wrong. I always kept my hair cut reasonably short and never had any remarks from the NCO about it. After about a week we were marched from Gallowgate Camp along the road to 'The Barracks', the HQ of the Green Howards. This was the HQ of all our GSC training; there we got our rifles from the armoury. We were now completely kitted out.

It was lovely marching that half a mile to the barracks, it seemed as though in my mind we were in daylight again. This was because we were never allowed out of the camp for the whole time we were to stay there and that turned out to be three weeks.

We were real soldiers now that we had a gun, more about that later, but I must tell you a funny happening. My mate and I were walking to the Naafi one evening when we saw a young officer approaching, so I said to my mate "here we go for our first salute" because we hadn't seen any officers previously. He got to about twelve feet away and up our arms went like clockwork and I could hear myself saying "up two three down two three" when all of a sudden the young 'one pipper' officer shouted at me "soldier come here". I went and stood to attention right in front of him. "You have your gaiters on the wrong way, look, they should be like mine." I looked and said: "Sir my gaiters are on the same as yours." He looked down at his own and found they were on the same as mine. "Good God," said he, and briskly walked away with a face the colour of beetroot. The trouble was I couldn't find anything wrong with them, so I came to the conclusion he must have seen them from a different angle. Anyway it did not stop us from going for a drink at the Naafi.

We did an awful lot of square bashing while we were at Gallowgate and you could feel yourself getting fitter each day. Once a week we had PE with a specially trained instructor and worked out in the gym. I enjoyed that two hours in the gym, as I had never been in one before, never mind using all the equipment in there. Wednesday afternoon was sports day, and all the squad took part in various games. I enjoyed that too. After three weeks at Gallowgate we went to the main barracks down the road to finish our training. Before we were moved to the barracks, I remember one occasion when I noticed on the orders board that I was down to do a guard duty. This meant after our training, I had to change into my best battledress and belt and present myself along with four other lads to the guardhouse. There we were paraded and inspected with a small toothcomb, looking for any imperfections. I remember standing there still, perfectly still while the guard commander looked over me, then passed on to the next lad. I gave a silent sigh of relief as he found nothing wrong with my turnout. Then to my utter amazement I was picked as 'stick man'. This meant that I was the smartest man on parade and after asking the lads that were now on duty if they wanted anything I was free to go back to my billet. What did it for me was I was told my boots were polished like glass, so you see that all the effort you put in at the beginning pays of.

Whilst I'm on with guard duties I was put on one again, this was when I was in the barracks. It was posted on the board the night before, so you could prepare all your gear. It meant I could prepare for some visitors to come and see me at the crucial time. Right, I thought, after dinner I phoned the Co-op shop where I worked and spoke to Amy. I said I would love her till the end of her days if she would come and visit me at six p.m. and bring Pearl along also, because she being the elder could do all the talking. They say lighting never strikes twice in the same place; well it did for me, because I was chosen as 'stick man' again just as Amy and Pearl arrived. That visit got me off for the rest of the night and I thanked Amy and Pearl for being such good sports. In all my army time they were the only two times that I had guard duty and I didn't do one.

We were in a proper building now; one big two-storey stone-built block. Here all the company paraded each morning and it was the RSM (God in other words) who took it. His name was Richardson and I had heard of him being a Richmond man. He was tall, upright with a moustache. A formidable man who took control of the whole regiment. I do believe even the officers bowed in his presence when he took a parade on the sacred barrack square. Whether there were fifty or five hundred men standing to attention, he knew if you blinked an eye. His voice could be heard the other side of town when he gave a command. He was God. I was walking across the square one day, didn't see him anywhere, not that I was looking either, but I jumped three feet high when he bellowed "get of that square on the double". No-one had told me that you were not allowed to walk across the square; you learn something new everyday don't you?.

The first full day we were at the barracks we went on to the moor, which was also the racehorse trainer Harry Peacock's gallops. It was lovely to see these magnificent horses running round the moor. As soon as the horses came onto the moor, the army had to stop whatever they were doing. Sometimes I said: "Thank goodness for Harry Peacock's horses."

Let me diversify for a moment and tell you about our moor and Mr Peacock. The moor was owned by Lord Zetland who was principle owner to Harry Peacock's stables, although he had some very other notable owners as well. On average he turned out sixty plus winners every year. Also the other trainers in Richmond used the gallops on the moor to train their horses but they hadn't the number that Mr Peacock had. Doug Smith, one of the leading jockeys at this time, rode most of Peacock's horses and occasionally you would see him riding out on the moor some of the horses that would be fancied to win at the weekend. All the lads in the army used to love to watch the horses race round the moor. Some raced only five or six furlongs; the others would do a mile, mile and a half, and some up to two miles. The moor gallops, or should I say right around the moor, was two and a half miles, and I was later, along with the rest of our squad, forced to run round the whole moor, with bayonet fixed and shouting and bawling like we would have to do if we did a bayonet charge in a real war.

Once we had this to do, and off we set shouting and bellowing obscenities to each other, anything to make a noise and frighten the enemy. That was the thinking behind it anyway. After going about fifty yards one gets out of puff and eventually nothing came out of our mouths but we still had to go the whole distance. We got back to where we started and our lovely NCO said: "I didn't hear you after a hundred yards so off you go again and shout, squeal or cry but a noise you will make or we will stay here all day until you can run at least a mile shouting." We started objecting and saying we were knackered but he reminded us in no uncertain terms that we were being subordinate and would be charged if he heard another word. There were about twenty of us in our squad and we thought of a good idea to satisfy our NCO with his shouting. What we did was six of us at a time would shout, etc, for one hundred yards and then another six would take over and so on. It worked a treat, there was shouting all the way round. This time not all the lads made it right round the moor and were left to do cookhouse fatigue for a day. We could hardly walk back to camp but we did with a lot of effort helping each other.

Our marching and counter marching was getting good, so good in fact I know our sergeant had a big private bet that we would win the competition for the best squad at the passing out parade. This competition took in all the training exercises, marching, bayonet warfare, route marching and barrack room tidiness and cleanliness among them. It was really good to hear all our boots hit the ground at the same time and the same goes when we did our rifle drill, all you heard was one big slap on the butt of the rifle not a run of slaps like a machine gun.

We changed our corporal when we came here to the barracks. The one we had to start with I'm sure had been enlisted about a month before us and didn't seem to know much about bayonet drill. The new corporal was a regular, ugly looking so and so, and in the airborne regiment and a real soldier who had served on many battlefields including Arnhem. He took us on the moor and tested us, so he knew what we could or couldn't do, but before we went there he put us through our paces on the square. He was so laid back normally but changed once on the square (he might have been frightened by RSM Richardson) but I don't think so. He was a true soldier, who in war I would like to have beside me.

We knew our square bashing impressed him by the way he would have us do the same drill over and over again, so as to prove it wasn't just luck the first time how good we were. The bayonet drill we did later on the moor was another thing though. We lined up with the dummy soldiers in front of us and gave the command "on guard". Well we were taught by our young corporal to stand upright and point the gun with bayonet attached in front of us. "Good Lord," he said, "who the hell taught you to stand like that?" You know the reply we gave. On hearing this he said "forget all that sh. . This is how to be on guard" – and showed us. He turned sideways with his left leg bent and the right leg nearly straight and pointed the gun straight in front of him hiding his chest. The only part of him you could see was his left arm, none of his chest as he bent forward. "This way," he went on, "the only bit of you that can get hurt is your upper arm, not your heart or chest which would have done if you had stayed like you were". Once you saw this you knew it made sense and to prove it he took of his tunic, rolled up his sleeve, and there to see were bayonet marks that were meant for his heart. We looked round to see the other squads doing what we had been taught first and I brought this to his notice and he told me that they wouldn't last a day in a bayonet charge. As for the competition he said "what do you want to do, live or die?" "You're right," I said, "but the sarg has a big bet on I think and if all the others are doing one thing and we are doing something else, what is the adjudicator going to do". "Forget him," he said, "just do what I tell you" and we did just that. He really was a true soldier who you would trust your life with.

On another occasion we had instruction on the rifle and we were on the firing range. Before we started firing we had a lecture from him on the do's and don'ts of what to do with the rifle. He explained the mechanics of it and then we all had to dismantle and put it back together again. What we had to do if we had a bullet stuck in the breach and so on. I never knew there were so many rules one had to learn. After the lecture we got down in the trenches ready to start firing but the corporal stood behind us watching very carefully. He gave the command to fire five times at the target and not to forget what we had been told. I got myself comfortable in the trench and fixed my gaze on the target, taking aim, I pushed the butt of the rifle and gently pulled the trigger. BANG, it went off and I nearly sh. . myself with the noise and at the same time the kick of the rifle. I did it again and again, hitting the target each time, I was just about to fire my fourth shot when I heard the corporal shout "turn that gun away from me". "I've got one stuck in the breach," I heard this lad reply. "Everybody lie flat" came back the words from the corporal and at the same time lunged himself at the lad with the stoppage in his gun, knocked him to the ground and at the same time, somehow, took the weapon from him. "Right," he said, "everybody out that's getting out of the trench" and we did as we were told. It ran through my mind "is he going to shoot him, so as to make an example of him for not doing what had been drummed into him about what to do if a bullet got stuck in the gun?" We were sweating because of what had happened but the corporal was now calm and said "gather round, place your rifles on the ground, but first unload all unused bullets". Well we did this. He went on about what had happened saying "this illiterate, half-witted, stupid sod here" – he lifted the culprit up one handed by the scruff of his neck – "tried to kill us". His lecturing went on and on until no one was in any doubt about what to do with any form of malfunction with any weapon. That poor lad was never allowed out for the rest of the time we were at Richmond as punishment. The sergeant came over to us and asked the corporal "why were we getting a lecture?" The good corporal replied that we were asking too many questions and that we would now continue our target practice. That was one hairy experience.

By now, we, as a squad were getting it together, not only on the square, but also on the moor. We were quite fit as well and this was going to be put to the test. I'd heard of route marches naturally and now I was going to experience running in one. One Thursday morning we were told to be on parade with FSMO – that's 'full service marching order'. This includes small pack, large pack, belt with ammunition pouches and rifle. After an inspection to see if all our dress and equipment were up to scratch, we went on this short distance of a twelve-mile route march. Fortunately the weather as I remember was just right, cool, dry and a slight wind. This was the first time that we had to march in all this gear and it soon became apparent that it wasn't going to be easy. The Green Howard Regiment who were training us was an infantry regiment and marched at four miles to the hour. Now this doesn't seem very fast walking but I say to anyone or everyone you try walking at four miles per hour and see how long you can keep up that pace. It's a good job they got you fit before sending you on one of these marches.

I remember after about four miles one lad had had enough and dropped out, and after a few more miles another and then another only one mile from the barracks. Those that did not complete the march had to do it again three days later until they did it. By the time we got back, and our kit off, all we felt like doing was lying on the bed. The sergeant had other ideas of course, and in he came into our room and shouted "come on lads outside in three minutes in PE kit". Well you can imagine the language that greeted those few words. On went the PE kit and outside we paraded looking like a forlorn bunch of turkeys.

The army knew what it was doing and to be truthful after an hour in the gym believe it or not we all felt so much better, and next day felt fitter still. It was a good job too, because after a week, and with only one week to go to the end of our GSC training, we had the big route march to do. That was twenty miles in six hours – that's allowing a ten-minute break for a smoke after every four miles. Now that march made us soldiers, real soldiers. It took the boyhood away and replaced it with manhood. After nineteen and a half miles you can imagine we were nearly dead on our feet, but there was a lovely surprise waiting for us. Half a mile from the barracks the full band of the 1st Battalion had come to march us through the gates. I have never seen such a transformation in men marching as I did that afternoon. We marched like men inspired through the barrack gate and were halted and dismissed on the revered square. I learnt later that any squad that was marched through those gates had to be right up to scratch, like 1st Battalion Green Howards, or they were sent back a mile by the RSM and told to march like soldiers.

We are in our last week now and the first job on Monday morning was to see the selection officer. It was nine-o clock when we were marched to the office block and dismissed but told to go inside and wait for our names to be called. I went in after being called "029 Shout", sat down in front of a captain who was a nice guy, and talked for about ten minutes. This was because I came from Richmond and he wanted to know all about the place, as he had only moved here last week. I gave him a tour guide speech of all the places of interest and answered all his questions. He was most grateful. That little speech I thought to myself was worthy of a professional guide.

We eventually got down to business and he asked me what regiment or corps I would like to be in. "Well," I said, "I was a grocer, so don't you think the ACC (Army Catering Corps) would be right?" "Good

God, no man, you don't want to go with that shower," he replied. He looked at some papers in front of him and said "I see you have got some certificates in first aid". "Yes," I replied. "Well your best plan is to join the RAMC (Royal Army Medical Corps) and that's how I joined the ranks of the RAMC, one of the best moves I made in the army, even if it was not my idea to start with.

It was now Thursday of the last week of our training and we had the afternoon off to get ready for the passing out parade the following morning. All the lads and I pulled our gear out of the lockers and proceeded to clean and polish it. Looking down the room and seeing all the equipment on the beds, and some lad's blanco'ing their belts, others polishing their brasses and some pressing their trousers, all a hive of activity. We worked like beavers because we were scared stiff in case the RSM stopped by you on the parade inspection and remarked that your brasses had some Brasso left on them, or anything like that, your feet would never touch the ground on the way to the guard house.

Friday morning had arrived, it was eight a.m. and we were parading on the square in our squads, dressed in our denims. This was the start of the competition to see which squad was the best. The judges were the CO, another officer and the RSM. First we were all marched on to the moor and then put through the whole menu of battle exercises that we had been taught. Shouting, bayonet charging and belly sniping to name just a few. Our corporal was superb, he just said "think that we are on our own as usual and we will win this". I glanced at another squad who were doing their bayonet drill and it went through my mind "I hope our corporal's right" because we were the only squad doing it this particular way that he had taught us.

I saw the major, who looked a bit battle scarred himself, writing on his clip board and wondered if he was thinking the same as our corporal. The way they stood "on guard" exposing their entire chest can't be right. The major and co came to us and watched us go through our exercises and when it came to the bayonet drill, I thought "here goes, shor bust" and it went like clockwork. I caught the eye of the corporal and he had a (I can only describe it as a 'crafty') smile on his face. I said to myself "well he thinks it was okay so it must have been".

After all the squads had finished we went back to the barracks, changed into our best battle dress, and with rifle, paraded in our squads once again, and were inspected by the RSM. All went well with our squad I am proud to proclaim. We then all joined up to form one company for the marching and at the end of the march past I felt ten foot tall marching to the band (which I still think is the best band in the army) playing the regimental march. I think it's called the 'Bonny Rose of England'. There were some funny words to this tune, the first line was often sung "Take me back to dear old Richmond town where they don't know sugar from salt" or "Take me back to dear old Richmond town where they don't know shfrom clay" was the rude version.

In Richmond around this time the council had organised a tattoo in the grounds of Culloden Tower and the band that got the most cheering was our own Green Howard's. I have often thought since that the army at Catterick Garrison should organise more of this sort of entertainment, being the largest garrison town in the country.

Getting back to the passing out parade, after all the marching was completed, the major along with his sidekicks gave us the results of the competition that took in all the six weeks of exercises. As far as our squad was concerned it was no contest. We had won hands down by twenty points and we gained most of these through our corporal having had real battle experiences with bayonets. The adjudicators came to each squad to explain the markings they had given us on the exercises and it came as no surprise when the major remarked that our squad was the only one that could have gone straight into battle and he personally congratulated the corporal for such good tuition.

It was midday and dinner was taken, then we had to get all our kit together and when completed the whole company was marched down the hill to the railway station to catch a train to Darlington and from there we all went our different ways. When we paraded to go to the station it was raining and that put a damper on it, but I must say at this point that was the last time I was to see rain for twelve weeks.

Chapter Four

I had got my posting on the previous Thursday and was to report to the RAMC HQ at Crookham near Aldershot. I met two other blokes who were going in the RAMC on Darlington station, so we travelled together and good company it proved to be. We arrived at Crookham late at night and were shown into a room with four beds made up in it.

The guard commander told us to kip here for the night and to report to the guardhouse at eight in the morning. None of us took any rocking to get to sleep that night, and I was pleased that I had an alarm clock in my kit bag because it woke me up on time, which I couldn't have done left to my own devices. I got washed and shaved and reported to the guardhouse along with the other two guys. We were given our bedding and shown to our barrack room and told breakfast was from seven to eight.

The barracks at Crookham were all wooden in H blocks and slept twelve people. The one I was allocated to was full of new lads the same as me but who had arrived earlier than I, and as such I was the last one to get a bed. My bed would have been one that I might have chosen if I had been there first, next to a window in the middle of the room. A sergeant came in and introduced himself, told us to go and get breakfast and come back here and he would give us all our details, etc. He showed us where the dining room was, so off we went.

This was an experience I'll never forget. When we went into the dining room it was like going into a five-star hotel compared to what we had left behind in Richmond. All the tables had cloths on them and some even had a little vase of flowers in the middle. The big plus was that it was a cafeteria, with a good choice of breakfast foods, from cereals to fruit juices, porridge followed by eggs, bacon, sausages, tomatoes and also fried bread. I had never seen so much lovely food laid out for me to choose from. After going along the display of food and helping yourself to what you wanted, one saw displayed what was on the menu for next week. After dinner at night you even got to see what was available for supper, this was usually cheese and bread; well you can't have everything can you?.At each meal time an officer would visit each table and ask for comments on the food, the menu, the service and if you had any complaints. All the time I was there I never heard of anyone complaining.

It was hot outside, in fact it got so hot it started heath fires and for the twelve weeks that I was there it never rained once, and a squad or two of lads went fire fighting each day. We enjoyed our breakfast so much I think we were a tad greedy and ate too much. We trundled our way back to our billet looking at the gardens outside each hut, which I'm sure had been landscaped, as they were beautiful. The whole camp was immaculate – clean, tidy and not a scrap of rubbish anywhere. I wondered who kept it like this and soon found out when we got back to our room.

Our sergeant was, I thought, a canny sort of fellow who talked to us and told us that each morning, five days a week, we would be on parade along with at least five hundred others, sometimes even one thousand on the barrack square. From there we would go to our classrooms for instruction in the art of nursing. The sergeant then took us and showed us around the camp. Starting with the guardhouse where there was always someone on guard, from there to the Naafi, to the stores next and he told us to change our sheets and pillow cases every week, then on to the cinema, where we would spend a lot of time he said. "You won't see Humphrey Bogart or John Wayne but you will be chilled to the spine at some of the films you'll see," he said. I didn't like the sound of that, it sounded a little sinister I thought. From there we were shown the other classrooms which were done out like hospital wards. We weren't marching from one place to another but walking; very civilised I thought.

After walking right round the camp, the sergeant said we could have the rest of the day off to familiarise ourselves with what he had said and shown us. On departing he added that at the end of the drive to the camp if we hadn't noticed was a pub, and if any of us wanted to buy him a drink he would be there at about eight p.m. He chuckled and left. By the way the pub was called 'The Wyven Arms' and the product it sold most of was to my astonishment cider.

A lot of us did go down to the Wyven Arms that night and found it a nice old pub. Naturally there were a lot of medics in there and the atmosphere was smashing. Up to the bar I went and ordered three pints of cider off the landlord, he being a jolly chap with a real happy face said: "I bet you are new here, are you?" "Yes," I replied, "got here the day before yesterday". Handing over the three pints of cider he said: "Can I give you a bit of advice? You can take it or leave it, for what its worth, but have you ever drunk cider from the cask before?" "No," I said, wondering what was coming next. "Well its up to you," he said, "but I advise you that this stuff is the real 'I am' and will knock you out very quickly until you get used to it". "Right," I said, "thank you very much, I'll tell my mates". I gave him the money – I can't remember how much it was – and took the three pints back to our table and told the lads what he had said.

"Don't drink too much of this stuff as it will lay you out." Well I could see by the look on their faces that they didn't believe him for one minute and downed another gulp from their glasses. Our table was placed in front of a lovely log fire, which was giving out some heat. To this day I don't know why he had a fire lit on an evening as warm as that and why we were daft enough to sit at it. As an afterthought nobody wanted to sit there, that's why it was vacant. We downed our cider and one of the other lads went to get them replaced, half way down the second glass I thought "what are we laughing at" every time one of us would speak we would burst into laughter. It then dawned on me that we were being absolutely silly and were drunk.

We drank that pint and the other lad went to get a round in, staggering to the bar and requested "three pints please". "I think you and your mates have had enough for tonight don't you think chaps," he said talking to a bunch of regulars who were laughing their heads off at us three. Normally one doesn't remember what goes on when you are drunk but I can vividly remember all the ridicule and laughter that went on that night. To make matters worse just as we were going, in walked the sergeant. He gave us a wink and broad smile saying "have a nice walk home lads".

I don't remember getting back to our billet or getting undressed and into bed but I do remember the next morning. That was the first and last time I would get drunk I swore to myself. It was the first time but I did break my promise many years later. In all truth those are the only two times that I have ever been drunk, more about that later.

The day began hot and sunny, so we were told to parade in shirtsleeve order. "Thank goodness for that," came the shouts from the boys in the room. Once again as at Richmond barracks, we formed up in our squad outside the barrack room and marched to the parade ground, which was enormous in size, and I shall not forget the number of troops on parade there. What did take me by surprise was the marching, being trained by an infantry regiment I stepped out quickly and nearly tripped the poor fellow in front of me up, because the pace of the RAMC was less than half that of the infantry. It was more like a Sunday afternoon stroll in the park, very enjoyable in this heat. We were on the square every morning for one hour and then went on to our classrooms or at this time, change and go fire fighting.

My favourite was the classroom where we were given talks, lectures and demonstrations. Today they started us off with first aid, which I knew more about than the NCO who was taking us I think, because seeing how good I was he asked me to help the others. I enjoyed this, although I got the mickey taken by the lads saying such things as "who's teacher's pet then?" and so on. Not all were as complimentary as that but it was all good fun.

Another day we were in the cinema and the sun was belting down again, the film was about lice and creepy crawlies. The NCO in charge told us all to sit and listen. "Today you are going to see some films about lice and if any of you feel a bit itchy do not start to scratch yourselves, if you do you will start everybody of scratching. I will not be responsible for everybody's actions, so if you want to live don't scratch." The film came on and for about thirty minutes everyone was okay, then the cinema began to get warm then hot, then unbearable and of course some little runt down at the front scratched his head. Of course this was visible to all who sat behind him.

First one and then another one and before long the whole audience was just about bringing blood to themselves, so the NCO called a halt to the film by shouting up to the projection box, and told us all to take ten. That meant go outside for ten minutes and have a smoke to calm us down a bit. Was I glad to get out of that 'sweat box' and light up a cigarette. The remark was heard "who the hell started scratching, I'll bloody kill him?" The sergeant came out and calmed us down, then added with a grin on his face which stretched from ear to ear and said in such a charming voice and manner that it was time to go back in and start from the beginning again. "Awe come off it sarg, we can't go through that again it's like a hot house in there." "I know," he said, "I'm in there too you know, now get back in there and sit still," he shouted. As soon as we got back in the cinema we started itching again but had to suffer it for two more hours watching lice being treated with AL63 powder drop off naked men stood on paper sheets. You could hear the blooming things I'm sure when they hit the paper on the floor. Really it was our imaginations though.

There was a mad rush to get to the showers after that experience. It was so lovely to stand and let the water, hot it was as well, run all over your body, soothing and healing where you had been scratching.

Stepping out of the shower left you nice and cool and we soon put clean clothes on. It was bliss, bliss and more bliss.

In the evenings after work and dinner we often just sat outside reading or talking and enjoying the cool of the night. At times it was quite eerie as we could see the smoke from the burning moors and knew that some of our lads would be there flogging on beating back the flames.

Of course when it was payday, we could afford to go down the drive to the pub, and have half a pint or at the most a pint of that potent cider. I shall never forget that first night when we thought we knew better than the landlord and got completely legless.

Every day we awoke with the sun shining and the temperature already in the upper sixties or even seventies. After a few weeks it got to you and you began to pray for rain, but God I think thought it was the farmers' turn to have a decent summer and be able to get the hay in, and then the corn without being troubled by bad weather. This hot weather lasted the whole twelve weeks we were at Crookham. It was raining the day we arrived and it rained the day we left.

Back to our training; it was good fun but hard work at the same time. One day it was late afternoon and we were practising bandaging and the NCO said to carry on with what we were doing and at five o clock finish as he had to go and see someone. I was to supervise the proceedings; all was going well when one of my mates suggested we bandage a lad up like a mummy. Well yes I thought, we could have a laugh and a bit of fun, so I chose a really quiet lad and told him that I was going to show everyone how to do a body bandage. How I thought up and told all this rubbish I'll never know, but with a little help from the others this lad was bound from head to toe with only his eyes, nose and mouth left open. Even his feet with his boots on were all bandaged; he looked like a real mummy.

The time didn't enter our heads until the sergeant came back to see if we had left the place clean and tidy. He took one look at the mummy and said: "Alright you've had your bit of fun, now unravel him." We did this and he told the lad he had the rest of the day off for being such a good sport. We had to be good sports now he said, so go and change and be back here in ten minutes ready to go fire fighting. "Oh hell," somebody said, "whose bright idea was that?"

We went on the moors and we were lucky, the fire brigade had just got there and we helped them till midnight. That was the hardest night's work I'd done since joining the army. We still had to be on parade the next morning looking fit, fresh and fertile as the saying goes.

We continued our training; the weather never let up, red-hot during

the day and still hot at night. It was difficult to get a good night's
sleep, everyone laying on top of their beds trying to keep as cool as
possible. After a lesson in the classroom all you wanted to do was to
light a cigarette and lay on the grass to recuperate.

We had been working late one afternoon and a mate and me were
just walking slowly back to our room without a care in the world when
we heard this bugle play. Before I could stop and listen to the quality
of the bugle, we were bawled at "stand still". We froze in our tracks,
what it did for me though, was to listen to the best bugle playing that
I have ever heard. It was six-o clock and the 'Last Post' was played
under the flag outside the guardroom. I learnt another lesson then as
well, and that was that wherever you go in the army, all RSMs are the
same, true British soldiers. This time the RSM came over to my mate
and me and stated in such a manner that you didn't forget, that when
the bugle sounds you stand still, perfectly still until finished. I could
have stood all night and listened to that bugle and found out after a
few enquiries that the lads that played the bugle were boy soldiers.
They studied part of their time at the Knellar Hall, which is the army
equivalent of the Royal School of Music I believe. Although I got a
telling off that day I shan't forget it for the rest of my life. At nearly
six every night after that I used to make my way down to the guard
house just to listen to the bugle playing by those boys.

The weeks passed, the sun got hotter and we learnt more and more
and the fires were still burning on the heath. Then before you could
say 'Jack Frost' our training was coming to an end, and all of us were
looking forward to our first leave.

One began to wonder what you were going to do as soon as you
got home, get together with your home mates, go to the youth club to
see what was going on there, all sorts were going through my mind.
But we were stunned to learn that we had a big parade to do first and
that meant getting all your kit in order again.

All companies were to be on parade this day as Princess Margaret
Rose was coming to inspect the depot. In one way I was looking
forward to this, as I had never been close up to any of the royalty
and in hindsight I never wish to be as close again if they all act the
same as she did.

On any inspection, whether it be you're own CO or a visiting
politician they just walked round maybe saying "how's your father"
or words like that and pass on. That was the usual way of inspecting
whether it be the guard or a parade. Well HRH didn't do just that,
she stopped and remarked to the officer who was followed by the
RSM about how difficult it must be to polish the buckles on the back
of the belt. Well the poor sod that she had stopped at hadn't polished

behind the buckles; this of course showed up the officer and angered the RSM that one of his men had down let the whole of the RAMC. I would have bet my last shilling that if she had picked on any one else on the whole of that parade ground, not one other soldier would have had a dirty belt. That's what you call 'sods law'. One in a thousand. That mistake by that lad cost all of us two nights CB (confined to barracks) and us on our last week at that.

When the princess was leaving the officer gave the command "three cheers for the Princess Margaret". I've heard a bigger cheer when the local pub chucked everybody out at ten p.m. I'm sure that most of the lads on parade gathered that we would all be punished. It's a wonder that we didn't get another week's CB for not cheering.

Now I have said that our kitchens and dining hall were good, well on this day they were superb, like they were every time some dignitary came to the camp. Instead of displaying cheese and pickles for our supper there were pastries and sausage rolls. The trouble here was when we all went expecting to see sausage rolls and a variety of pastries we got our usual cheese. When we complained the next day to the officer who came round at dinner asking if every thing was okay, he said "yes I'm sorry about that but the meats didn't arrive in time to make them I am sorry" and walked on. If looks could kill he would have been dead before he reached the door.

It ran through my mind later that evening what miserable souls we were, complaining about one meal, and really not a proper meal at that as it was only supper, when we had the best dining room and meals in the country. In fact it was the showpiece of the British service, that was why we got a constant run of people looking around.

That was that, and now came our final parade. We had completed our training and after the passing out parade all we had to do was to get our orders telling us where we were being posted to and get our travel warrants first to go home and then to Chester, which was where I had to report to, No 7 Company RAMC. All went well on parade that morning; it was the first day since coming to Crookham that it was not hot, but cloudy and cool. This made it ideal as we were dressed in our best BD (battle dress) and not in shirtsleeve order like we had been for the last twelve weeks.

It was now ten a.m., the parade over and I'm in a queue now to get a) my pay and b) all my posting papers and warrants, etc. And then to go to the Naafi for a quick cup of tea, pick up my kit and get transport down to Aldershot station.

Before I finish writing about being stationed at Crookham there is one incident I forgot to mention and that was half way through our training, that would be six weeks after we got there, we got a weekend off. Now it was too far to travel home and too dear as well, so I decided to go to my eldest sister's home, which was at Worthing. Vic, being Daisy's, husband, was managing a garage there and they had a flat, which went with the job.

So off I went and spent the weekend with them. Now I had a very strange night sleeping there, the bed was a super feather one, and I soon relaxed and was just about to drop off to sleep, when the whole of my body started trembling and shaking. I thought "what's going on I don't feel ill" and then it subsided and finally went of all together. I pondered what it could have been but feeling very tired soon fell asleep. This happened twice more during the night, waking me up, and I began to get a bit frightened. I couldn't understand what was happening to my body, eventually I must have been so exhausted I fell asleep and didn't wake till eight a.m. when Daisy brought me a cup of tea. We talked while we had our tea and I said: "Do you know I had the most queer sensation last night; it happened just before I went to sleep and twice it woke me up during the night. My whole body started to shake, what could it be?" Daisy just looked at me and said: "You fool, it's the electric trains, the track is just over the road and they are silent running and cause some vibration." "Thank God for that," I said, "I thought I was going mad.".

Let's get back to where I was – Aldershot station waiting for a train to London. I didn't have long to wait and made my way to Kings Cross Station from where I got the train to Darlington. From Darlington I didn't wait for the train to Richmond, I got the bus instead, saving me having to wait for two hours.

On arriving home I was greeted with hugs and kisses which lasted, I'm sure, for about an hour. Everyone was pleased to see me, as I was to see them. Now you can't do much in a week so I decided to do as little as I could get away with. That's what I thought but it didn't work like that. First one and then another friend came over to see me and spend some time together, walking, talking shopping and of course the club, we did all these things and more. Before you knew it, it was time to say good-bye again and get changed back into uniform.

I'd had a marvellous time and was getting back to reality. I had made the travel arrangements during the week and they were, I can't remember the times, but from Richmond I went to Darlington, then to Crewe and then on to Chester to 7 Co RAMC.

Chapter Five

I arrived at 1400 hours and went through the usual procedure of drawing my sheets, etc, from the stores and getting settled in again. I was at Chester just over a week, but I had some good fun whilst I was there. All the lads and lasses were a real happy bunch and it was here that for the first time I would be working with girl nurses and sisters on the wards.

The hospital was quite large and drew its patients from a large area but I don't think it was as big as Catterick Military Hospital as it was called then. I learnt a lot in that short time at Chester, it was real nursing from emptying bedpans to bed baths and the usual TPR (temperature, pulse and respiration) and treatments such as dressing wounds, etc.

I had a night duty one day and reported to the sister in charge who paired me off with another lad and a girl on a surgical ward. Night shift started at eight p.m. and finished at eight a.m. All the staff were lovely people and we met on our break at eleven p.m. in the sister's office for a cup of tea. It was just my luck that a patient died on me at midnight, or maybe a little later, so with the help of the girl nurse we laid him out. The sister came along to us and said to take the dead man to the morgue and to get the other lad who was on duty with us to help usI called for him and told him that we would need a trolley, as we had to take a corpse outside to the morgue. He brought a trolley and told us that he had never seen a dead body before. I said "neither have I until now" but the girl nurse had and she kept me right. It was an awful night outside, raining and windy and the girl said to us "do you know where the morgue is?" We shook our heads and replied that we didn't. She said "well it's over the other side of the hospital, and you have to go outside as you are not allowed to go through the wards with a dead person on a trolley". The other lad and I looked at each other and said in unison "who's to know in the middle of the night?" "Right," said the girl nurse, "I'm not for going out in that weather, let's go through the wards. I'll go in front and check that no other sister or nurses are looking and you two push the trolley."

We loaded Joe Bloggs on the trolley and covered him completely with a sheet and set off with the girl saying this way and that way. We got a little behind the girl and she waved to us to hurry up. We took the hint to get a move on and duly raced round a corner into a ward of sleeping men, well that's what we thought. We must have cornered to quickly and as we entered the ward so Joe Bloggs fell of the trolley. "Good Lord," I said, and both of us quickly picked him up and put him back on the trolley, I swear it only took us two seconds to put him back on the trolley but it wasn't quick enough. The whole ward came alive with lights going on and men shouting, asking what was happening. I shouted, "go back to sleep, nothing to worry about" and we shot out of that ward before the sister saw us.

If we had been caught it would have been curtains for all three of us but fortunately no one complained and we were very pleased, to say the least.

As I said I was only at Chester for ten days and in that time I found my way round the city. What a beautiful city Chester is with the river Dee running through it and the two-tier shopping, as well as the famous racecourse. Glancing at the notice board (I think they called it Part 11 orders) I found out that I had been posted to a CRS (Casualty Reception Station) at Donnington in Shropshire (Salop) for short the following week. I had never heard of Donnington so I looked it up in a road atlas, I found it easily very near Wellington, Stafford and Shrewsbury. It was only a village really but the ordnance factory there was one hell of a size. The workers travelled to Donnington from far and near to work in the ordnance factory, it must have employed thousands in those workshops. All the buildings were numbered with the numbers painted white and six feet high with some being more that that.

One knew where to go once inside the depot, just follow the numbers and you couldn't go wrong. My address was CRS, Southgate, Donnington, Salop. The South Gate was the main entrance and the CRS was on top of an embankment at that gate. The staff consisted of three MOs, a colonel, a captain and a lieutenant; the nursing staff were a sister, a sergeant and five ORs. We also had stationed with us two lads from the RASC (Royal Army Service Corps) as ambulance drivers, another sergeant attached to us in the RAMC but he was the health inspector or something like that, he worked entirely on his own. I can't remember where he got his orders from. We also had lads from the ACC (Army Catering Corps) as cooks.

I took to these guys from day one and we really did enjoy our stay in Donnington. Little did I know that I would serve the rest of my conscription at this posting but as it turned out I couldn't have had a better one. Looking back I considered myself as a civilian attached to the army as we had no army drill or anything resembling being in the army. I remember the sister's name which was Hope, Sister Hope. She had been in the army a long time, in fact I would say it was her career, as she was not a dolly bird but a very good nurse. You couldn't shock her. I remember one day three of us were in the treatment room looking at a list of jobs that the sister had pinned on the board that needed to be done that day. One of the jobs was 'high dusting' and one of the lads said she must mean getting f...... high and dancing round the ward with a duster. "What I mean," came a voice from right behind us, "is get your duster and dust on top of the lockers and cupboards." Well we nearly did the proverbial in our pants, as not one of us had heard her come into the room.

The CRS was situated in a lovely place, getting the sun all day long, so we often sat outside the reception watching the comings and goings on. Our CRS had four wards and eighty beds but only on one occasion did we fill these beds, and that was when a boatload of soldiers docked in Liverpool suffering from dysentery. They had come from the Middle East. Ambulances from all over the place, both civil and service, went to the docks, picked up four patients and took them to hospitals, CRS or anywhere there was room to treat them. In our case once we had filled three of the wards, we took over some barrack rooms in a camp next door, belonging to the RAOC (the Ordnance Corps). We put soldiers in these barracks that only had the symptoms, not the works. Nine out of ten of these lads never developed dysentery and were soon sent back to their own barracks. The disease was so bad in our CRS that we had home office pathologists working alongside us, plus we got nursing help from local hospitals.

I found treating these patients very interesting but hellish hard work, as the treatment prescribed were M and B 693 tablets, starting off by taking six every two hours I think. This reduced as they improved and finally got down to taking two every six hours. At the same time they were never off the bedpans and a sample had to be taken every four hours to start with and given to the HO pathologists who did a sterling job in a cupboard room. Talk about being in the ShWe certainly were for about eight weeks plus. The sufferers, bless them, really did have a hard time but were the most likeable lot I ever nursed. They were in the RURs (Royal Ulster Rifles) and you couldn't get a better set of lads anywhere. Once they were feeling better they would not let any of us RAMC lads buy our tea, coffee, kit-kats, etc, from the Naafi; it was always on them. They thought the sun shone from our backsides!

Just along the road from our CRS was a little café called 'The Cartwheel Café' and this is where we went for a change from our Naafi. In the Cartwheel they sold rum-flavoured coffee, which was my favourite, and believe it or not they sold 'rock buns'. "Goodness gracious me," I thought, "only my mother made rock buns and how did she get them down here?" It was ironic that they looked and tasted like my mothers and I still didn't like them.

Myself and one of our lads called Pete had been in the café one night and were walking back to our place when we heard some awful groaning. At first we couldn't see anyone but after a few strides we saw a real big fat man who must have weighed at least twenty stones lying against a wall. It was evident he was in pain but at first we thought he was drunk. He wasn't we found and I ran and got an ambulance and called one of our MOs who diagnosed him as having a severe attack of colic. It took four of us to lift him into the ambulance, and the MO said to take him to Wolverhampton General Hospital which was the nearest civil hospital being twelve miles away.

Pete and I often went out together and would talk about our civvy lives. He was in the steel foundry at Sheffield and he told me how the leader of his team would have to walk a plank above the furnace and skim the molten metal of all its impurities. Pete added that they were given beer to drink and often seemed drunk. But no one had ever fallen into the vat.

We had been out one night down to Wellington having had a drink and a dance and went to catch a bus back to Donnington. As we turned a corner we ran into one holy fight. The RURs were fighting with the Ordnance Corps and pulling them out of the bus. In fact some were pushing from the front to the back and the others were pulling them out of the door at the back of the bus. Now we knew most of the RURs as we had nursed a lot of them in our CRS and when Pete and I got started on they went berserk and nearly slaughtered them. I got a punch in the face and Pete got a thump in the chest and neck. Anyway the lads got us into the bus along with them and were sorry for us getting thumped. On our way back I said to Pete that more than likely half of the lads that had been fighting would end up in our treatment room to be patched up within the hour. My prediction was more than right because the fighting continued long after our bus left and as soon as we arrived back the wounded started to come in. The lads that were on duty couldn't cope so Pete and I donned our gowns and helped.

We were still helping long after midnight; some of the badly gashed lads had to be sent to hospital. The trouble was some one or maybe more had been using bicycle chains and knuckle-dusters, causing a real mess on the faces. "Never mind," I said, "the RURs will be in in the next day or two showering us with gifts for being so good to them."

As I have said, we had two cooks in our happy group; one was a scouser and the other came from Wigan. Two smashing lads, and when they heard that we had been up till two in the morning Scouser came along and asked us what we would like for dinner. He said as a special treat we could have what we liked as long as we went along with the majority. We chose one of his specialities, liver and bacon with Yorkshire pudding. He did us proud that day and the patients we had in dock also benefited that day because he made it the main meal for all. The other cook Wigan was a grand lad also; he had the most infectious laugh that I have ever heard. Once you got him going he couldn't help himself and he would be doubled up on the floor, killing himself with laughing. On more than one occasion if he came out with us and he got into that state people thought he was ill and would slang us for not giving him some help as we just used to leave him, they didn't know him like us. After putting the onlookers in the picture they of course started laughing and before you knew it the place was in pandemonium. Sadly though one night in a café, a rather classy place, Wigan got into that state and we were all laughing rather loudly and enjoying ourselves and we got slung out. It wouldn't have been so bad but we were only half way through our meal but had to pay for the whole meal. We daren't argue with them as they would call the military police and they would come and cart us away for the night and charge us the next day. I said to Wigan "that's the last time you are coming out with me" but of course it wasn't.

Our sergeant was a lot older man, small in stature, about five feet three inches, and talked as though he had a short tongue and would splutter something terrible. A nice fellow for all that but he did get the mickey taken out of him. The lad we had in the stores was called Gledhill, I can't remember his first name as we always just called him Gledhill. Now he was a peculiar chap also, because at one time he seemed to keep himself to himself and we saw very little of him, except for meal times and then he said he would finish his meal in the store as he had a lot on to do. Gledhill wouldn't let anyone behind the counter and this set us thinking "is he sick or something?" We tried talking to him but he always said he was okay thank you! And he would buzz off back to his store. This went on for about three weeks until one day I went into the store when he wasn't there and found out what the problem was, if you could call it a problem, he didn't. There in bed was a young girl fast asleep. I quietly left and pondered what to do, whether to say something to Sergeant Gilchrist or forget about it and keep it to myself until I saw him. I decided the latter and when he came back I took him to one side and told him what I had seen.

He didn't seem a bit worried and told me to mind my own business, so I said "look Gledhill get her out of here today or I'll tell on you. You will get us all into trouble if this gets out". "I don't care," he said. This conversation went on for some time, unknown to either of us Sister Hope had seen me going into the stores and was going to ask me to get some sheets but decided she would get them herself. On hearing our slightly raised voices she stood and listened and had heard the whole story. To cut the story short she took it out of my hands and told him exactly what I had told him saying that if he didn't get the girl out now she would call the MPs. He wouldn't and she did, and the MPs came and took him away. That was the last we saw of Gledhill but we did learn later that he had been medically discharged from the army.

I didn't know that the army had health and safety officers or people that did that duty, until one day one of them was posted to stay with us. He was called Tom Johnson, I think, and held the rank of sergeant. One day I was doing nothing, as it was one of my days off, and Tom asked me if I would like to go with him for the day, instead of just sitting about in reception. I said "I would like to see what you do" and also it would be a bit of company for the both of us.

The first call was to the Pioneer Corps Camp and Tom was met by the duty officer. I got a surprise when he introduced me as his assistant and the officer duly shook both our hands. Talk about being shocked, I was, when Tom started laying the law down to this poor officer. He said everything bar the words to pull your socks up and get this camp into some decent order; it was a disgrace to the service. The poor officer stuttered and squirmed and assured us this would be done. We left after Tom told the officer that he would return in two weeks and if there wasn't any improvement it would be reported.

After signing out at the guardroom and on our way to the next destination I said to Tom "Bloody Hell! You had me blushing and shaking in my shoes the way you spoke to that poor guy, are you sure you're allowed to talk to officers like that". "Not exactly," Tom replied, "but I can't bear two pippers to run a camp like that and the only way to get things done is to shout at them and let them know you are in command". "Mind you," he said, "I couldn't get away with it in most other regiments but the Pioneers are the labourers for the army and they don't know any better."

This reasoning was emphasised at our next camp, when the duty officer handed us over to the RSM to show us around. This man, a regular of years standing, knew where he stood and where Tom stood. He knew Kings Regulations off pat and I'm sure could quote you chapter and verse for any query. Tom knew this also, so he was treated with as much respect as the situation required. However the camp was in excellent order and Tom told the RSM this, and complimented him saying that his report would be in the same tone. This pleased the RSM and he bade us good-bye. We got back to Donnington at about three p.m., just in time for a cup of tea that Scouse had made. It had been a most interesting and informative day out, having learnt such a lot about another one's work, or should I say duty. After that day out I went with Tom whenever I could get time off.

The weather was still holding up fine and warm and we only had half a dozen patients in dock. So we would take our easy chairs from out of the reception office and sit outside watching the different vehicles coming and going to the ordnance depot. It was on one such day that I was out there just sitting and talking, watching the lorries that were pulling guns going into the depot, that I nearly had a heart attack. Riding in an open top pick up truck was my youth club leader Mr Wood, 'Little Willy Wood' as he always got called.

I jumped up of my seat and shouted "hey Mr Wood, Mr Wood its Dougie". He caught my voice just before going into the depot. He stopped the convoy of vehicles and shouted back "I'll see you in ten minutes." "Who the hell are you shouting at?" asked the lads I was sitting with. "He's my friend's father," I said, "he also runs the youth club I go to, along with his son Donald, he's coming back in ten minutes and believe me you'll like him, he's a true Christian." Well you can imagine the remarks I received after saying that. "Oh we're going to entertain a bible puncher now are we?" "Yes," I said, "so no swearing from you bunch of heathens."

Mr Wood, who was the chief gun examiner at the ordnance factory at Catterick, duly called and I must say he was made most welcome by the lads, not because I had told them to be nice but because they really took to him. He told them he only came down to Donnington today for the ride out and to have a few words with his counterpart here. Little Willy told us he would be picked up here as soon as the rest of his men in convoy had unloaded the guns. It was strange to see a military convoy stop outside our CRS and pick up a civilian. We said our goodbyes and off went Mr Wood back on the road to Richmond. Seeing Mr Wood not only made my day but the rest of the week and I couldn't wait to write and tell my mam and dad what had happened. In turn I'm sure my mother would have told all her friends along with Mrs Wood when they went to the women's Bright Hour in church that we had seen each other and how lovely it was that I had given Mr Wood his tea.

The Bright Hour was the only place that I can remember my mam went to, I can't ever remember her going to the pictures or anything like that. Mam and dad did take us for a walk now and again but not very often; she always seemed to be to busy washing, cooking and mending, etc. It was grand when I came home on leave and could spend some time with them both, talking about how my elder brother was getting on in the Royal Navy and what had been happening whilst I was away. But however much you enjoy yourself at home there comes the day when you have to say "ta ta" and get back to your posting.

I'll never forget those partings as I always got a lump in my throat and didn't relax until I was on the train on my way back. It was strange that every time I came home on leave another Richmond lad did, and we used to meet, although never planned to, on Darlington Station. We both caught the Newcastle to Bristol express and got off at Birmingham Snow Hill Station. I crossed over to New Street Station but I honestly never knew where Roy Lowe went, that being his name; he lived in Sunnycrest Avenue with his parents and sister. I don't know whether I got the stations the right way round, it may have been the reverse.

Wellington was the nearest town to Donnington, being four miles away, and one day we were handed an invitation to a grand social evening organised by the Methodist Church in their church hall. After a bit of leg-pulling and mickey-taking, two of us decided to show goodwill and go. It was Pete Green who came with me to the social and I can categorically say that we had the most wonderful night. We dined, danced talked and met some beautiful people. Most were a bit older, some even old enough to be our mothers, but still we had a smashing time and went back quite often after that even the other lads came along and enjoyed themselves too. Wonderful people, true Christians spreading warmth and happiness to young men away from home.

Every time any of us had been out for the night the cook on duty would always leave a tray with some supper. Our cooks were good guys and if we wanted when they prepared the meal for the night duty, they would prepare one for you as well. Sometimes the meal that they left for the night duty nurse was far superior to the one they served up to us at midday.

I'll never forget one night all six of us had told cook to leave a meal out but hadn't told each other. The night duty meal was cooked to eat at two in the morning, and at that time the cook came and awoke us all, and much to our surprise we all got up to eat.

Scouse who was the cook on duty had decided not to leave a plated meal, as all the staff wanted one, so he had got up earlier and cooked us all a poached salmon meal with all the trimmings. It was gorgeous and we had a real party amongst ourselves. Next morning we all slept in and I was supposed to be on duty when the MO came in and roused me. It was Capt. Reynolds. After quickly getting dressed, not even washed or shaved, I found Capt. Reynolds in the kitchen, Wigan having given him a cup of tea. I apologised and told him it wouldn't happen again but he just smiled and said: "A good lie-in now and again does you good you know." "Yes sir," I replied as we walked into a ward and began to see to the patients.

Of the three MOs, Capt. Reynolds was a conscript like the rest of us as was Lt. Jaswin but Colonel Allen was a regular soldier and was much older than the other two. You could tell the difference between all three by their bedside manner. Capt. Reynolds was the perfect GP, quietly spoken and a good listener, whereas the colonel was the military man through and through, very good in surgery but when he spoke he was giving a command. Now Lt. Jaswin was Irish through and through, lovely dialect to listen to but a bit quick tempered. For example he had been on leave and on returning to his room in the officers' mess at North Gate, he found that someone else was living in his room. So without trying to find out why he was living in his room, he got all his clothes and kit and threw them out of the window straight onto the parade ground. I was told the RSM saw this and went straight over to see what the lieutenant was doing. Lt. Jaswin told him in no uncertain words that nobody was going to sleep in his room. Evidently quite a slanging match took place and in the end our MO duly told the RSM to go to hell and get it sorted out. "In the meantime I'm going home to Ireland so let me know and I'll think about coming back," he said and stormed off again. We never saw or heard of him again and we were left with just two MOs.

I was stationed in Donni for the rest of my service, which was supposed to be a total of two years including the training, and strange as it may seem, bar on one occasion the six of us, including the cooks, all remained until our conscription ended.

The only one time that was different was when we had an additional five Taffies with us. Now I don't know what it was but they kept themselves to themselves so we did the same. Thank goodness they only stayed about a month, which was about as long as we could have stood it. When they were gone we said we should celebrate, so the cooks put on a good meal, and along with the six patients we had in, we all gathered in the ward, and having previously bought some drinks, we celebrated till midnight. We bedded the patients, saw that they were all okay, and we just sat for a while in the reception. Well, time passed, and I said "where's Pete?", as we hadn't missed him until now. "Has he gone outside for a breath of fresh air?" somebody said and we went out to see if they could find him. He wasn't outside so we decided to do a proper search. The time by now was turned two in the morning and we were just about to go looking for him when there was a horrifying shout from the bathroom. One of the patients had gone for a drink of water and was startled to see Pete asleep in the bath, after being sick all over himself.

We were relieved to have found him but at that time of night to have to start and clean Pete up by giving him a new bath was beyond a joke. The general census of opinion was that we should have woke him and left him to it but he would only have gone back to sleep again. The next morning he was on duty and as fresh as a daisy, he brought the rest of us a cup of tea in bed. We were shattered and he was fit, fresh and fertile as the saying goes.

There was one time we seemed to be using more distilled water than usual and the MO told us to order some more. The sister duly did this but our supplies came from Chester. We had sent a patient to Chester by ambulance and they brought it back with them.

I was working in the treatment room one day – I can't quite remember what I was doing – but handling some equipment I thought to myself I could make our own distilled water. I'm not sure now what the equipment was but it could have been something to do with blood transfusions. I rigged up a distillery on a table, which was up against a wall in the treatment room, and with two Bunsen burners and glass tubes I set this contraption to work. Work it did and I could produce doubly distilled water all day long if necessary. The MO saw this working and said "it looks all right but I wonder if it is as sterile as it should be". "We can soon find out," I said, "I'll send a sample to the lab, it should be okay though as it's being distilled twice without coming into contact with the air or anything, and as long as I sterilise the bottle it flows into I can't see why not." The MO sent two bottles to the lab and got a sarcastic reply asking why he was sending them sterile distilled water to analyse. I should have had a bet with him that it would be okay.

Talking about betting, I have always liked a bet, as did my mother. I used to take her bets to Dolly Shields the bookmaker in Victoria Road. Dolly was a lovely lady and she ran that bookies by herself for years. Sometimes her brother would help her but he wasn't nice at all.

If he could swindle you he would and I had one or two arguments with him and it was Dolly who always came and apologised for him. One year, I think it was 1947, when Dante, a horse trained by Matt Peacock at Middleham, won the Derby it nearly bankrupted her. She was paying out winnings from that race for nearly a year but in the end everyone got paid. With Dante being a local trained horse nearly everybody was betting on it, some at long odds by anti post betting. Mam never put her name on the bit of paper she wrote the bet on, it was always 202, that being her nom de plume.

In those days there weren't any betting shops, or betting slips for that matter. Except if you placed a bet ante-post you took a price, say twenty to one, and that price you got paid out if the horse won, as against SP (starting price) on the day of the race. You got a big betting slip showing you the bet that you had placed. Sometimes I would have a bet ante-post trying to beat the bookies with the price but I never had a winning ticket or the price I took was less than the starting price.

I learnt a lot about betting while I was at Donnington. For instance, one night, when we had the Welsh lads with us, one of them said that they were having a game of cards that night and if any one wanted to they would be most welcome to join the school. Some of us did, including me, and we sat down after the eight p.m. ward rounds to play pontoon. Now I had never played cards for money before, so I was, to say the least, a little bit shocked when the person playing the banker said there was to be no limit as to the amount you could stake.

The boys round the table must have played cards before because they were staking £1 on the first card dealt to them without looking at it. What I thought was a reasonable bet was two bob on a good card but I had soon amounted enough money to play them at their own game. I think they were trying to be clever and show off but it backfired, as both Pete and I came out winning a lot more than we started with. The boyos from the valleys weren't a happy lot by the time they called time. Pete and I treated our lads to their Naafi breaks the next morning.

The CRS had a little Naafi just for ourselves and the patients that were with us. Now that wasn't a lot of people even when all the beds were being used but I think it was every six months that we got a share of the profits from it. We could do what we liked with this money, so every time we got a cheque we used to do something different. Such as hiring a small bus, filling it with drinks, eats and sweets and go into Birmingham to a theatre and see a show and if time permitted see a film as well. We always had a great day out.

There was one time our MO, Capt. Reynolds, said we should try something else. Now the captain was a sports fanatic, so it was no surprise that when the next payment came he said "we'll go to see England play Scotland at Wembley". This was something else that I had never done, see an international football match. Joining one hundred thousand others, it was a great experience and a jolly good time was had by all. Another time we went to Villa Park at Birmingham to see another international game. We had to spend the money or we wouldn't get any more and now when I think about it, it must have been every three months that we got some, because we went all over the country and I was only there two years.

Chapter Six

We were having a quiet time, not many patients to nurse – maybe five or six and only one or two of them were really sick. But the floors still needed polishing so our sarg said to the MO that we could do with some help to polish the floors, etc. The MO being, as I've said before, a good chap said "okay we'll send some in suffering from pendulum and plumbiosis" – in other words they were swinging the lead – and those lads could do the floors. It always worked well did that, because they were skiving off doing a kit inspection or a parade and we got off doing the hard graft of polishing the floors. Once all the floors were done we gave them another two days to relax and recuperate, and they were most grateful to us, treating us to our Naafi breaks.

There was always something different happening, like one morning an army lorry pulled up and the driver asked "where do you want these boxes dropping?" Someone replied "what are they?" as we hadn't ordered anything. "They are from Chester and I think they are Canadian Red Cross Comforts, as we have been delivering these the last two days." The MO was present, having just completed his ward rounds, and having a cup of coffee replied "put them in that empty ward sergeant". So with the help of a couple of us, that's where we put the four large wooden crates. Canadian Red Cross Comforts – none of us, including the MO, had ever heard of them – so we couldn't get into them fast enough.

The MO came out of the kitchen armed with tools to open the crates and set about the job with wild excitement. The first one we opened contained the most gorgeous fluffy blankets along with other bedding. I have never seen before or since such lovely blankets. "Are we sharing these out between us?" asked one of the lads, "or are we using them on the wards?" "Well it would be a pity to use them on the wards," Pete replied, "because you'd only need one or two people to be sick or spill something on them and they would be forever in

72

the laundry and I think that would be criminal." The MO thought for a moment and said "yes that would be wouldn't it, so the best thing to do is we all have one each, and that will leave two, which we will use on the examination bed in the treatment room". "Before we open another box get rid of these on to your own beds and put mine in my car will you," he went on. We all then quickly took the blankets to our room, dumped them on our beds and raced back to open a new box, or should I say boxes.

When we opened the other boxes it was like opening Aladdin's Cave – there were large tins of pears, peaches, apricots, fruit salad and other fruits, along with tins of cream, custard and other sauces. The last box was to be the best, as this contained boxes of cigarettes and a few cigars I think, but also boxes of sweets and chocolates. The next question was, what to do with all these delicious goodies?.It didn't take long to decide.

The boxes came from the good folk of Canada but did not specifically say that they were for the patients or for us. So we decided that as we only had half a dozen patients in, the MO could, if he wished, discharge all of them today and we could have a share out. Altogether there were eleven of us – three MOs, the sergeant, five orderlies and two cooks. The sister had been posted back to Chester and was no longer with us, so we set about sharing out the lot.

There was a lot to share out but we did the right thing by putting aside what the CRS should have first. What we decided was to think we had a full house with about forty patients and worked out the amount that we would need to give them something special for their teas for about two weeks, and we would keep that in the kitchen. After this was put aside the MO said "make twelve piles and share out each product in turn". It was surprising just how much we all got. Then it was "take your pile of goodies back to your bed space and store it the best way you can".

After that exercise was done I began to wonder how many trips home it would take to clear that lot. Looking back it didn't take many; two heavy packs soon got rid of it from my bed space.

Back to normal after all that excitement; nursing at its best was the order of the day. Sitting on the patients beds and having a constant supply of tea or coffee and chatting away about anything from sport to life in the army, and what we were going to do when we got demobbed. For me that wasn't long, as I had about three months left to doIt was during this time that more boxes of Red Cross Comforts came. This time it was mainly bedding and equipment, which we put straight on the wards except for two chiropody kits. These were superb kits; everything one needed to attend to one's feet. I was given one for myself, as I had been the one that saw to all the feet problems, and had remarked one time or another that I might take up chiropody when demobbed. So it was that I got one and the other I used in our treatment room.

We never had a dull moment all the time I was at Donnington. What with chatting up the girl in our Naafi, to playing tricks on ourselves or better still the patients. One time we were sat in the kitchen with nothing to do as we had got all our three or four patients wrapped up nicely in bed and Scouse had made a cup of tea, when someone suggested we had a bit of fun with the patients in the ward. "Like what?" came the reply from the two of us? "I'll tell you what," I said, "this afternoon the MO removed a cyst off a soldiers hand and used the ethyl chloride spray to freeze it, lets have a bit of fun with that".

"Yeah we could," said Pete, "we'll wait until they are all asleep and then we'll spray it around their bed heads and light it, chant some mumbo jumbo and they'll think they are in hell with fire over their heads on the wall, not knowing if its going to come on them." The ethyl chloride was in a glass cylinder about nine inches long and when sprayed onto the floor and a match put to it made a little flame which you could trail all over the place.

So that's what we decided to do. We waited till about eleven o clock when all was still and quiet, then set off to the ward. Normally we kept a small light on all night so we could see that all was well but this night we had switched the light off so it was total darkness. Next, two of us crept under a bed each and as soon as Pete got the ether trailing of the wall, and all you could see was this bit of fire running up and down and round the bedhead of one of the patients, we under the beds started wailing "ooh aar" and making a dreadful noise. This soon awakened one or two of the patients and one ran straight into the corridor screaming, the other was paralysed and speechless for ten seconds until he realised that someone was playing tricks with them.

He then went to put on the lights but we were ready for this and as soon as he touched the switch one of our lads grabbed his arm. This did frighten him and all hell broke loose as Pete put on the lights and they found it was us playing a joke on them. Looking back to that night it wasn't funny really and we were ashamed of ourselves for treating the poor patients in that way because it could have turned sour and someone could have got hurt. But that night we did have a good laugh.

The next day the patients were treated like royals, as we didn't want anyone to report us to the MO, but they didn't and took it all in good part. One genuine frightening experience though happened to me when I was on night duty. Not having any seriously ill patients on the ward, whoever was on night duty could sleep next to the phone in the reception room. This meant that you were there only to answer the phone, and if necessary deal with the problem – it didn't mean you were not on duty in the morning as usual.

Well this night I was on duty and had gone to sleep, when the phone rang. "Hello CRS Donnington," I said picking up the phone half asleep. "I've been run over by a train," came the reply in quite a normal voice. "I beg your pardon," I said, "what did you say?" "I've been run over by a train," came back the reply. "Get lost," I said and put the phone down. I was mad at having been woken up at two in the morning and now was wide awake. The phone rang again. I picked up the receiver and shouted down the line "if you know what's good for you, you'll stop this arsing about, I'm mad now". "No, no, I have been run over, the train ran over my foot and I've crawled to the phone; there were only two of us got off the train and he ran to a car nearby that was waiting for him." "Well where are you now?" I said. "Oakengate Station but please hurry as my foot is beginning to hurt," he said. Well you can imagine the conversation that followed that remark.

However, I got the ambulance driver out of bed and sent him off to pick him up, and then I called the MO and told him I had a bloke coming in, in about fifteen minutes, after having a train run over his foot. "What did you say? I'll be right up." That was not the reaction that I thought I would get but the MO on duty was the long-serving colonel and he never took anything for granted. If you said something to him it had to be right – that was his army training coming out.

When the ambulance came back we took the lad into the treatment room and put him on the examining couch, making him as comfortable as possible, although he was not in much pain. The MO came, took one look at it and said to me "try and get the boot off Shout but be careful". It was hard to know where to start and in the end the MO came over and with my help he cut off the top of the boot allowing me to slide his foot out. The poor lad never made a sound when I did that and the MO looking at his foot all crushed and no toes left said: "I'll give you some morphine and we'll get you to hospital as quickly as possible as you are going to feel real pain shortly." The nearest hospital was the General at Wolverhampton, twelve miles away, and that was where we sent him. We phoned the hospital and they were waiting for him when our ambulance arrived there. I was left with the boot with five toes sticking out of the toe cap, so to get my own back on the lads for playing a trick on me earlier, I waited until they were all seated round the table for breakfast with their cereal bowls in front of them. Then I did the most dreadful thing to them. I walked in holding the boot behind me and carrying a pair of forceps and getting hold of one toe at a time, dropped it into their bowls. At first they didn't know what it was; then the penny dropped and off I went like sh....off a stick with that lot chasing me. I ran off but they caught me and dumped me in a cold bath of water. As I said, never a dull moment.

I got my demob orders and was told I was to go to our HQ at Chester and go through the procedure of handing in my kit and getting paid up to date, and all the relevant papers attaining to being released. The date was in two weeks time so I had plenty of time to gather all my kit together and see that it was in good condition.

I had been in the army for about two years and had never had a kit inspection since leaving Richmond. It must be sod's law because the day that I was to go to Chester we had a kit inspection by some general and as I had all my gear ready to go to the station and then to Chester I had nothing on my bed to inspect. He stopped at my bed and I smiled and told him that I was on my way to Chester to be demobbed. He looked hard into my face and putting his hand on my shoulder said "listen to the news in an hour's time", smiled, and passed on. After he had left I said to Capt. Reynolds "what the hell does he mean by that remark?" "I don't know," he said, "but if I were you I'd get away now". "Right I will," I said and put my gear into the ambulance as I had previously arranged to do and went down to the station. The ambulance driver gave me a hand to carry some of my gear on to the platform but there pandemonium had broken out.

The place was full of MPs turning all soldiers back to barracks, as all leave and movements had been cancelled. I didn't swear but the air around me turned blue. There was nothing to do but to do as I was told and return to our CRS. On returning to my old abode the lads cheered saying "I didn't know that you liked us that much" but were flabbergasted when I told them what had gone on. "The general knew though, didn't he" someone said and of course we all had to agree. Anyway I got my own bed back and sorted my kit out back into the locker and shelves again. Once again I was back to square one, though I did say "that from now till I go again I'm doing only light duties". You can guess what the reply was to that remark. "We thought that was all you did." Rotten lot they were. Nothing much happened in the three months extra that I had to do and when the time was up again I said my goodbyes again and off I went to Chester.

It was a quick get out at Chester, as I arrived at midday and they had all my papers ready for me (probably from three months ago). I handed in my kit, got my travel warrants and wages, and was at Chester Railway Station at four-o-clock. My train to Crewe left at four-fifteen and from Crewe to Darlington at six-o-clock. I got home and was showered with love and kisses from all the family.

Chapter Seven

It wasn't until I'd had a cuppa and something to eat that I remembered that I had forgot to bring my chiropody kit with me. "Never mind" I said to myself "I'm not going back for it." It was late at night and mam and dad had gone to bed leaving Denis, Fred, Nancy and I talking. Fred told me he had just received his call-up papers and was going to try to get in the Royal Navy like our Denis had been and I wished him all the best.

We had a lot to talk about, especially the tales our Denis told us about his experiences in the navy and what Fred would have to endure. Denis had been at the Dunkirk landings and his ship had been torpedoed. All he said was that it was a bit hairy landing the troops. It must have been three a.m. before we retired and was I shattered, I didn't need any rocking that night to get to sleep.

I awoke the following morning feeling relaxed and comfortable just knowing that I hadn't got anything to do that day. I had woken up so I got up. Dad, Denis and Fred had gone to work and Nancy was getting ready to go to school. Not watching what was going on in the kitchen – that was until mam brought me in a lovely fry-up of bacon, eggs, tomatoes and two slices of fried bread. I hadn't had a breakfast like that since I had left home to join the army. It was too good really because I felt bloated all morning. I told mam that she wasn't to cook me a big breakfast like that again, much as I had enjoyed it, but toast and marmalade was all I was used to and that was enough.

My best friend Donald Wood had chosen to be a Bevan Boy and go down the mines for his conscription and he wasn't home at the moment but within a week or two he too was demobbed. We met up very quickly and soon we were back home doing what we used to do. The youth club was our first priority as this was where all the girls were. But I had to put first things first and that was to go and see if my job was still okay, knowing full well it was as it was law that one's job would still be there when they returned from conscription. So one day I went to the Co-op and saw Mr Robinson the manager and told him I was now out of the army and ready to start work again. That was a lie but only I knew that!.

The first thing I noticed when I went into the shop was that the chaps that had been in the war years had returned and Amy and Pearl were the only girls left. Alf Dunne, who had been first hand when I left, was now only a counter jumper, the same as the rest of us. The man second in charge, the first hand as he was called, was a Mr Walter Johnson whom I was to have some battle royals with later on. He was not a very nice guy but was a close friend of the boss. This made life a bit difficult I was to find later on. Mr Robinson said that I could start work straight away, but I said I would start the following Monday. This left me another weekend to get tuned up for the ordeal.

Monday came and back to work I went. After a brief introduction to the rest of the staff I found myself working alongside Amy again, putting up orders and being a general dogsbody. The staff now consisted of Mr Robinson the boss, Walter Johnson the first hand, Fred Paling provision hand, Alf Dunne chief counter assistant and Pearl Mudd, Amy and me, with Charlie Hodgson still driving the wagon and Peggy Walker in the cash office. There may have been some others but at the present time of writing I can't think of any. Oh! I just remembered we still had two cats. There wasn't the same atmosphere about the place that there used to be, everyone was just getting on with their work and saying very little. Even at break times there was never a lot of conversation going on unless the shop got busy and some of us were called in to serve or pack groceries for a customer, then the comment would be "why can't he manage, we always do". They were talking about Walter – he never liked being on his own for very long.

As I remember he wasn't a nice looking person, as he always had an angry looking face, and used to dash about pushing people aside. This upset the girls more than me but I made up my mind if this continued I would tell him in no uncertain terms that he should pack it in. Evidently I wasn't the only person with these thoughts as Fred on the provision counter had had enough of his bullying tactics. Now Fred was a tall guy, having served in the Guards, I think it was the Coldstream Guards, and one day he had had enough of Walter coming and pushing him about, trying to get something from behind Fred's counter. Fred got hold of Walter by the scruff of his neck and frog-marched him to the end of the counter and said: "Look Walter, I've had enough of you pushing and shoving everyone about. See that line (and with his hand drew an imaginary line at the start of the provision counter), don't you ever put a foot across it again or I'll knock seven bells out of you," or words something like that. "You're not in the army now and I was a sergeant major in the Guards, not a poxy corporal or whatever you were so keep out of my space."

This little fracas bought the shop to a standstill until the boss came out of his office and asked what was going on. Fred told him what had gone on and restated what he would do to Walter if he ever set foot over that line again. It must have been a bit difficult for Mr Robinson having to tell his best friend to calm down. The rest of the staff were delighted that Fred had told Walter where to go but it backfired for us. Walter left Fred alone but he took it out on us – we couldn't do right for doing wrong. This rift went on for a few weeks and Walter wasn't getting any better; in fact it looked as if the rest of the staff had sent W Johnson to Coventry.

Then one day he had a go at me, because after pushing me against the counter where I was putting up orders I said "there's no need for this pushing about Walter, pack it in". Well he went berserk: "If I want to push you I'll bloody well push you." He wasn't good looking at the best of times but now he was as red as a beetroot and I'm sure I could see steam coming out of his ears. He came up to me, stood right in front of me in fact, and poked his finger on my chest and said "who do you think you are talking to?" and still prodding my chest with his finger went on "when I want you to tell me what to do I'll ask you". "If your finger touches me once more on any part of my body I'll go straight up Newbiggin to the police station and have you charged with GBH." I said that because I thought it sounded good.

Walter was by now in a proper sweat and said something like "go on then see if they will take you seriously". That did it. I was calm and as cool as a cucumber when I replied, "okay I'll go and see if you are right". I thought I had better tell Mr Robinson what I was going to do, so I went into his office and related to him what had happened and finished by saying that Walter won't only get locked up by the police but they will call in the mental nurses and doctors and have him committed to York Asylum because he had gone absolutely mental.

Mr Robinson was a chain smoker, lighting one cigarette from the one he had just finished. Well, after listening to me the ciggies were lining up on his desk, he couldn't smoke them quick enough. "Laddie, laddie, just a minute," he said, "now listen to me we don't want to go along that route really do we." "I don't know about this 'we' business, you may not want to but I do." "Just a minute, just a minute," I remember him saying, "what I mean is I'll tell Walter that he must apologise to you and the others and make him promise not to do this sort of thing again." Mr Robinson was like a barrister cross examining me that day and the more he went on I thought I couldn't hurt him, like it would have done had I taken it further. "Okay," I replied, "for your sake I won't go to the police this time but if he ever just brushes past me again I'll have his guts for garters."

The boss followed me out of his office and I could feel all eyes were on me – was I going out of the shop or just back to work? And of course it was just back to work. The boss took Walter back into the office and we could hear raised voices coming from there. Fred, Amy and Pearl asked what was going on so I told them that we all needed an apology from him or I was going to go to the police. Fred said that I should have gone straight to the police as we all knew that they were the best of friends. "I was going to Fred," I replied, "but it wouldn't have been fair on Mr Robinson, "he never talks to or treats any of us like he does."

The boss had Walter in the office for over an hour and when Walter came out he said "I've been instructed to offer my apologies to you all". He then walked straight by us on to the counter and started serving a customer. Fred shouted across the shop "well are you going to apologise to us or was that it?" "What do you want, blood?" came the reply back from Walter. Life was never the same from then on in the shop and I am sure Mr Robinson got him promoted very shortly after that. He got the position of manager at a branch in Darlington and we never saw him again except on the occasion of his holidays, when he would come and have a word with our boss regarding transport or something as he and his wife went with Mr Robinson and his wife on holiday together.

Fred went out travelling for the orders. I don't know who used to do the travelling but Fred enjoyed it and I was trained to take over the provision counter. Alf became first hand again and things began to get back to normal with us all enjoying our work again.

Rationing was still on I think. It makes no matter if it wasn't because what I'm about to relate to you happened when it was. We all had our favourite customers and I used to look after mine. For instance if they had company coming they would tell me and I would give them a little bit extra of what they wanted. It might be half a pound of butter or lard or a few extra rashers of bacon, anything to help out. In turn they used to give me two shillings or even half a crown to show their gratitude. I always looked after the staff first but what used to get my back up was Mr Robinson, who would have me take a piece of bacon to boil or two pounds of sugar and sometimes both to people who were not even our customers. One of these was a manager of a big store in town; in fact the biggest store at that time, though not grocery. I didn't think that this was right, so one day I took this joint of bacon to this man and said "you know Mr X this isn't right, you aren't even one of our customers are you". I can still see his eyes looking at me, wondering what I was getting at. In the end after a minute or two when he had summed up the situation he said "do you like sweets?" "I love 'em," I replied and without further ado he put his hand into his top pocket on his jacket and pulled out about three books of sweet coupons and gave them to me saying "will that suffice?" I looked back into his eyes with the same look that he had given me and said "look forward to doing business with you Mr X, thank you".

As time passed and I became the traveller I did a lot of swapping coupons for my customers, such as if Mrs A was short of cheese and Mrs B wanted more cheese but wasn't fussy about eggs or something, I used to oblige all I could by swapping. Everybody was happy as they all got what they wanted. The traveller had a bike to get round the villages on, and what happened on the long journeys was Charlie would take me and the bike to the furthest point and I would work my way back on the bike. Sometimes Charlie would give me a hand and come into the houses of the customers that he liked as well as me. One such house was in Gayles and the lady that lived there was called Mrs Hart. This lady was most charming and gentle, and this day that we had called she told us that it would have been her son's 21st birthday had he lived, and would we have a drink with her to celebrate his birthday. "Off course we will Mrs Hart," Charlie replied, as he never refused anything but blows. I must tell you now that Mrs Hart was a judge of home-made wines, and renowned throughout the area for putting down the best wines.

Mrs Hart produced a bottle of wheat wine, which she said she had put down when he was born and had vowed not to open it until his twenty-first birthday. It was lucky that we had called on that particular day to celebrate with her. "Now lads," she said, "just have a small glass as this will be very potent and I don't want to get you into any bother." Charlie and I looked at each other and I think we were both thinking the same that there's not much in this glass. It was the best glass of wine that I have ever tasted to this day, golden in colour and crystal clear it was, she called it polished. Now I didn't like to say that I could drink another one of those Mrs Hart but I felt like saying it. I did say though that that was one of the best wines she had made. Now Charlie being Charlie didn't just think it, he said it. "Mrs Hart," he said, "I must go along with what Dougie has just said and without being rude or cheeky another one would go down very well."

I thought good old Charlie keep the ball rolling, Mrs Hart didn't want us to have another one really, she knew what effect it would have on us, but relented and said "be it on your own heads if you can't stand after it". The good old lady wasn't far wrong, as after we had had one more we said that we would have to go. Charlie and I got into the wagon and off we went. We only got to the bottom of the village when I noticed Charlie looking all over the place. "I'll have to park this thing for a while," he said. We pulled over to a lane end and before I knew it we were both out for the count. All I remembered before I went right out was feeling daft and giggly then blotto. Mrs Hart, who was taking her dog for a walk, saw the wagon and came to investigate, awakened us. "I told you boys not to have another one didn't I, now I feel it's my fault that you are in this state." "No, no," said Charlie "we were just letting our sandwich settle and must have dozed off." "Thank you Mrs Hart," I said, "for rousing us, we had better get going on our travels now, thank you again, bye bye" and off we sped. That taught me a lesson, never drink when working.

This was never going to be kept because Christmas came along, and with Christmas came cake, cheese and a glass of something stronger than tea or coffee. So it was, I had been travelling the village of Melsonby and not to be unsociable when offered a glass of wine, whisky or even lemonade and a bit of cake and cheese to wish them all the best for the New Year, that when I got on my bike I felt on top of the world. I had finished for the day and put my orders that I had collected into what was an obsolete cash bag fastened on to the back of the saddle, and made my way home. On the way out of Melsonby there were some hens in a field, so I stopped and put my hands into my pockets and brought out a cart load of Christmas cake which I had discreetly put there because one couldn't go on eating cake and cheese in nearly every house, so I used to slip most of it into my pocket the first opportunity I had. Now was the time to get rid, so I fed the hens and they seemed to lap it up.

After emptying my pockets on my way I again went, not a care in the world. Going down the bank which led into Gilling West I didn't notice that I hadn't fastened the bag on the back of the bike securely and my orders were being blown out. I saw them floating out of the bag but somehow I didn't care. Fortunately a United Service Bus was following me down the hill and to prove that there are always some good people about, the bus driver who lived a few doors away from me, kept stopping the bus and picked up my orders. I saw what was happening and waited for the bus to get to me at the bottom of the hill. The bus driver was Ronnie Johnson and he gave me all the order forms that he had picked up and asked me if I was okay. "Fine Ron," I said, "and thanks very much, I'll see you later." I can still see Ron shaking his head as he got back into the bus and made his way off to Richmond. When I got home my mam said "had a good day then?" "Yes," I replied, sat down and fell asleep for a couple of hours.

On another day I was travelling round the villages of Whashton, Kirby Hill, Gayles, Dalton, Dunsa Banks and Ravensworth on my bike as usual, and had done all those villages which left me one call on my way home, and that was to a farm off the Whashton Road, through a plantation and then through two fields to reach the house. It was dark, late afternoon when I knocked on the door and the farmer's wife opened it, and seeing me and knowing that I had come for her order said "oh we're just having tea I'll post it in thank you" and then she closed the door on me. This farmer was only registered with us for two ration books for bacon and sugar only. If it had been daylight the air around me would have been blue, bright blue. I thought that the least they could have done was to have scribbled a few items down that they got every fortnight, I could have done it for them myself because their order never altered much. The things that go through one's mind in those circumstances! I vowed I would not go back there again. I didn't like going there in the dark anyway, because once I was on my way through the plantation, when all of a sudden the damn gamekeeper leapt out at me. I nearly did the proverbial in my trousers. "What the hell's the matter with you," I shouted, "you nearly frightened me to death." It was Mr Crisp, Lord Zetland's gamekeeper and a very good one I believed. He thought I was a poacher. I just thought "who the heck would be a grocer".

On this journey you never got back in time to go to the shop, so you cashed in and did what you had to do the next morning. The first thing I did that morning after getting all the orders sorted out into journey order, etc, was to see Mr Robinson and tell him what had happened at Aske Moor Farm. I asked him if he knew where this farm was but he hadn't a clue so I finished my story by saying that it wasn't worth going all that way when they only had two books for sugar and bacon out of a family of six, all this and on a bike was no joke. He listened, then said "do you know when I was travelling I had a horse?" "A horse," I said, "get me a horse then, because you don't peddle a bloody horse". Of course he didn't get me a horse but I never went back there again; they always posted in their order.

It was on that same journey another time I was nearly frightened to death because I was pushing my bike up the hill from Ravensworth when I heard a cough. I stopped and listened but didn't hear it again until I started walking again. Pitch black it was and the cycle lamp wasn't much good, it gave very little light, but I went on walking and again the coughing sounded. By now I was getting a little agitated as you can imagine. "Hello," I shouted, "who's there?" You look around not wanting to make a fool of oneself but no one answered. By now I am getting scared, then all of a sudden a blooming sheep came alongside me, it had been following me. You don't know how relieved I was but I could have kicked that sheep from here to eternity if I could have got near it. Never mind it's all in a day's work I'm told.

On this journey to Gayles I called on a lovely old couple and the husband used to smoke quite a lot and when I was smoking he always had some of mine. It got a bit out of hand, because by the time I left there after having had a cup of tea and biscuits with them, the old boy had helped himself to half my fags and that meant I ran short before the day was out. There were no shops in these villages, so I decided I'll cap the old boy, I'll start smoking a pipe. The next time I went there I was duly equipped with tobacco and pipe, and asking the good lady if she minded me having a pipe instead of a ciggie, she replied "oh no I prefer tobacco smoke, please do". She had no sooner got those words out of her mouth when the old boy said "yes, let's have a pipeful, I prefer a pipe to a cigarette". Now I was worse of than before, because I had a pouch full of pipe tobacco and a packet of cigarettes. One can't win em all, as the saying goes, but it would be nice to win an odd one now and again.

Being the traveller was what I would call a good and bad job. It was good because you were working outside in the fresh air, you were your own boss and you got to know so many nice people that became friends. The bad side was of course you had to go out in all weathers, frost, rain and fog, the worst being the rain, but in hot weather you were pestered with flies and other insects. I remember on numerous occasions I would be cycling alongside a cornfield wearing an open neck shirt, usually white or cream, and all of a sudden I would be covered from head to foot in those black harvest bugs – you were uncomfortable for the rest of the day.

When I was not out travelling I worked behind the provision counter. There was always plenty to do, helping out whoever was working behind that counter, such as weighing up different weights of fats, butter, lard and margarine into quarter pounds, half pounds and a few pounds. The butter came in barrels weighing 1cwt and the procedure was, using the cheese wire, we sliced through the top of the butter about a four-inch deep layer. I had better explain what the cheese wire looked like. It was a piece of wire about twenty four inches long and fastened at each end was a round cylinder-shaped piece of wood about five inches long. You will have gathered that it was originally made for slicing a piece of the colonial cheeses, cheddar being the main cheese, and these weighed anything from forty to sixty pounds each. At one time we had a chap called Bill Rennick working as the provision hand and one day he was carrying into the shop half a box of eggs, which was fifteen dozen made up of six trays each holding two and a half dozen. Just at that precise time I had picked up one of our cats which was in the shop and had no right to be there, as they were not allowed, and was taking the animal to Peggy in the cash office, and seeing Bill carrying those eggs with both his hands full, tapped him on his shoulder, and when he turned his head to see who it was and what they wanted I held the cat close to his face. I thought I had committed a real 'faux pas' as Bill nearly passed out. He staggered and placed the eggs on the end of the counter, thank goodness, and sat down on a chair looking deathly white and breathing heavily.

"Are you okay?" I hastily asked, "what's the matter?" "What's the matter, what's the matter," Bill said labouring, "don't ever do anything like that again Dougie as I'm allergic to cats plus I thought it was a lion. Please don't ever do anything like that again." I know it frightened me and believe me I never did that trick again.

He was a good lad was Bill and came to work on a motorbike. We used to tease him a lot, such as saying things like "you only come to work on your bike as you haven't any soles on your shoes and your feet would get wet". It was true, half the time he did have holes in his shoes and couldn't afford to buy a new pair as he had a big family I remember. To make ends meet he used to work in the officers' mess on Catterick Camp serving at meal times and functions, and boasted that he regularly waited on the Duke of Kent who was in the army at this time.

There were changes in the staffing of shops at this time, as the chaps that had come back to work from being in the forces were either not happy with the way things were running, and would leave, or they were soon promoted to other branches. That was the case at our shop and the men were being replaced with girls. The wages were still poor and not many men would work for such poor money. My wages at this time were I think about £3 a week, which meant I could only go to the pictures about once a week, and spend the rest of the time with my friends going to the youth club. We also took part in a lot of church activities, like teaching at Sunday school and helping out at Junior Guild.

In those days the Methodist School held their anniversary concert in the church, and I remember rehearsing for weeks learning our lines off by heart. You weren't allowed to read the piece you were reciting or singing, you had to stand and talk loud enough for the congregation to the hear. The church was always packed full, with chairs having to be placed at the end of each row of pews. The day school concert was just one of those days when the church was full, another being the Harvest Festival.

As a child attending Sunday school it was always a big occasion, as we all had to take some fruit, veg or flowers, which would be received by the preacher and placed on a stepped platform at the back of the church. This made an attractive display when reorganised after the morning service ready for the evening service. The day after the service the produce was taken up stairs into the church hall where it would be auctioned. The money made was for the church funds but a proportion sometimes went to some other needy organisation, such as the National Childrens' Home. Our auctioneer was a local man who ran a saleroom in the town and it was always a joy to listen to a professional auctioneer accepting the bids.

All good and true Methodists enjoyed the Harvest Festival service, when the hymns were all well known, such as 'All is safely gathered in'. The country farmers would come in droves to hear the minister thank God for all the produce on display. I do believe the farmers interpreted the words thanking God meant them and went home feeling uplifted and righteous, and wouldn't mind working the land for another twelve months.

But on one occasion the leaders of the church in their wisdom had booked a well-known minister called Dr Charles Fozzard to conduct the Harvest Festival services. Now the trouble was they hadn't checked to see what sort of preacher the good doctor was. Dr Charles Fozzard was a nationally known evangelist and as an evangelist he was brilliant. The members of the youth club always went to sit in the balcony of the church and took up the two front pews. Before I left home that Sunday, I said to my dad "are you going to the Harvest Festival at church?" and he said "yes I am, but your mother is staying at home this morning to do the dinner, but we will all go tonight". Looking down into the church from the balcony I watched as my father took off his bowler hat and sat down on one of the chairs at the end of the pews. The church was full and the children brought their produce in and handed them to the person helping the minister, and all went well. After the service I heard some boys arguing about who had brought in the biggest marrow, so I discreetly moved away as it was getting a bit heated. That was the morning service.

But it was a different story at night. Mam wasn't feeling very well so she didn't go but dad did. It was my dad's usual practice on a Sunday evening after church to go to the Turf Hotel for half a beer, and then catch the 8.45 p.m. bus back home to Whitcliffe Terrace; I mention this because on this Sunday he nearly missed it.

It was like this. I, along with my friends Don and Tony, sat again up in the balcony front row this time, and again watched the church fill up. We saw little Mr Walker take his seat right under the pulpit at the wall end of the pews, as this was his usual place; I saw my dad come in and Don's dad, Mr Wood, all take their seats. The church was by now filled to overflowing capacity and in walks the good Dr Fozzard. He took the three steps up into the pulpit, said a short silent prayer, gazed at the congregation and shouted so loud that people walking outside I think could hear him say: "Good evening friends, I've got you now. I was told this morning that I hadn't to preach too long because you had dinner to make and like to be out before a quarter to twelve. So tonight you have no meal to cook, but if you have buses to catch, feel free to go, but I tell you this, you won't want to go because what I say tonight you will never forget."

The service started at 6.30 p.m. and after singing a couple of hymns and a lesson or two read he started his sermon. It was brilliant, a truly evangelistic service. He stirred all our emotions until we nearly stood up and shouted "Hallelujah" or "Praise be the Lord". By now he was in full swing and leaning over the pulpit and pointing his finger at Mr Walker shouted "you'll remember brother on numerous times". Now every week Mr Walker used to have half an hour's kip when the preacher gave his sermon but not tonight. Poor Mr Walker never got a minute's rest.

The time had now reached 8.15 and Dr Fozzard was still going at full stretch, and openly stated that if you had a bus to catch, go, don't be afraid. I knew who would take his words literally and the person who led the way by standing up was my father, followed by a few others. I knew dad would want a drink before catching the bus home so it came as no surprise to see him lead the way out. The service finished at about 9 p.m. and I'm sure everyone leaving the church that night felt exhausted but relieved and happy that it was over and finished. The good doctor was right when he said that we would not forget that night. I never have.

The following day I was back at work and out travelling again and I called at my usual calls, the first being on the way to Whashton. The lady was a true Methodist, who in her younger days led the Band of Hope, which was I suppose an evangelistic group for children. The words that greeted me were "what did you think of that episode yesterday?" I knew what she was getting at and not wanting to upset her in anyway, I replied: "Now Mrs Dinsdale you tell me what you thought of it." "Well," she said indignantly, "I've never been to a Harvest Festival like that, the man was a raving lunatic, did you see him going at poor Mr Walker, I thought it was dreadful. I'll tell you this Mr Shout (I always got my full title from her), "I'm not going to the auction tonight if he will be there." "I agree with you wholeheartedly," I said, "but he won't be there tonight as he is on tour and couldn't stay for tonight." "Your father did the right thing, bless him, I should have done the same but I daren't." All I said was that he should have preached about the harvest of food and not the harvest of man. It took me ages to get away from there and it wasn't the only house where I got stick about the service. For the following week I got remarks both in the shop and out travelling. I thought what a pity it had been a harvest service he had conducted, because the content had been beautiful and if it had been the following Sunday it would have done much more good. That evening the harvest was never mentioned and that was what hurt most people.

I said before that my mother enjoyed having a bet, well so did I, and so did Charlie Hodgson. One day after driving me around travelling, we called at his parents' home, which was on the edge of the moor at Richmond. This moor, as I have said, was used to train racehorses and at one time or another there could have been three or four trainers training their horses there. The main trainer was Harry Peacock who had as many as sixty to eighty horses in training at that time and was very successful with them too.

Now Charlie's dad used to look after the gallops for Mr Peacock by replacing the divots that the horses had kicked up when galloping. Calling this day, it would be in November because the flat racing season ended more or less with the Manchester Handicap, and H Peacock had a runner called Deredawa, and Charlie's dad said to his son "are you having a bet on the November Handicap lad?" "I am," said Charlie, "why do you want a bet putting on?" He said this because his dad very seldom gambled and he must have seen the horse on the gallops that day, and Harry Peacock must have said to Matt (that's Charlie's dad) you can have a bob on him he'll run well. That was a tip in itself, Matt having half a crown each way on this horse.

Saturday came and I put my bet on. I had five shillings each way on, and that was a good bet for me in those days. The horse won and my friends and me celebrated by going to the cinema. Strangely enough the same applied the following year and once again it won at eight to one.

Wednesday afternoon was our half day closing at the shop and Charlie and I would go rabbiting to Whitcliffe Woods area, sometimes with ferrets which Charlie kept and bred I think, and sometimes with guns. Chuck, as I sometimes called him, had two guns, a twelve-bore and a six-bore. He would use the twelve, leaving me with the six-bore. It was great standing on top of a set that we had put nets over all the holes we could find and then pop in the ferret and listen to it chasing the rabbits. Then one would bolt out straight into the net, where Charlie or I or whoever was nearest would get the rabbit out, neck it and reset the net in case another followed. If it was a big set, by that I mean six to ten holes to net, I've seen us get four or five rabbits out of that one set, and that would be enough caught for that day.

Mam made delicious rabbit pies; it's one meal I miss these days, as I can't force myself to eat rabbit after the myxomatosis exercise. It was the working man's chicken was rabbit in those days. Now it is reversed, there's more chicken in one form or another eaten today than any other meat or bird.

I will have to stop this rabbiting on as I am diversifying all the time. One day at work Mr Robinson came to me and asked if I knew where Fieldings Avenue was. "There's no such place in Richmond called Fieldings Avenue," I replied, "but there is a Fieldings Yard; why do you want to know that anyway?" I asked. "Well you know we could do with another girl in the shop and this letter is from a Hilda Cairns who had come to Richmond, and is looking for work". "What number Fieldings Yard is she living at?", the answer being number 3. "I know who lives at number 3, it's a Miss Wood, and it's only a cottage, hardly big enough I think to take a lodger." It was big enough, as later on I went out with, or should I say courted, a girl who was born in number 3, and she became my wife. So it was, Hilda was interviewed and started work in the shop. The boss also employed a man by the name of Les Harvey, and Les and I got on like a house on fire. We became good friends and one day he asked me if I knew where we could go horse riding. The only place that I knew which kept horses and allowed other people to ride them was a farm on the camp road, so Les went to see them and he became one of their customers for riding out work.

Then after a week or two he asked me if I would like to go riding with him. "We'll stay in the field," he said, "you needn't be worried, I'll teach you to ride and take care of you". "Okay," I said, "next Wednesday I'll come along with you." The day came, we left work at twelve and after having some dinner I met Les and we got the bus to Catterick Camp, getting off at Blythes Farm. We had to walk just a few yards to the farm and the farmer who said "Les I see you've got a pal with you this time, can he ride?" met us. "Oh yes," Les replied, "I'll see to him, you go and finish your dinner."

The farmer went inside the house, thank goodness, because I had never mounted a horse before. It was no great deal to Les, he just got hold of my leg and pushed me upwards towards the horse and before you could say 'Jack Frost' I was sitting on the animal, feeling as though I was sitting in the clouds. It seemed a long way to the ground when Les said "let's go" and go we did. Les led us to a field, and once inside the field he said "just follow me Doug you'll enjoy it". We just let the horses walk round the field and I was getting the hang of it when Les said "come on lets trot a bit". "You trot if you like," I said, "I am content to let this horse walk."

Someone should have told the horse that he had a learner on his back but no one did and when he saw his mate trotting he also started trotting. Now this was a new experience for me, and not a very pleasant one, as I was bouncing up and down on the horse's back, making my backside quite sore. My horse was following Les's horse, and he was getting quicker and quicker and so mine followed. The horse was now galloping and as I saw the ground from what appeared a great height below flashing past, I thought, good God, why did I say I would come with him to do this.

I never thought about shouting to the horse to stop, "woo woo" I think one is supposed to say to stop the horse, and then before I knew it I was in the air, the horse following the other one that had just jumped a hedge. I wish someone had been filming me because I'm sure when the horse jumped that fence when I was at least ten feet of the ground; it felt like that anyway. I only had one hand on the reins, the other in the air doing a John Wayne rodeo act. At last I came to my senses and pulled up the horse. "Les," I said walking bandy legged and with a very sore backside to catch the bus back to Richmond, "you can get stuffed if you think I will ever go with you again, you conned me, saying it would be nice and that I would enjoy it." It was the first and last time that I tried horse riding.

It took me about a week to get my bum and legs back to normal but nothing ventured nothing gained I said to myself, and then fell asleep in the chair.

Chapter Eight

The year was now 1950 and at work I was still very busy spending a lot of time on the grocery counter, getting to know more and more people, and getting faster at adding up one's groceries in my head. Without bragging or boasting, I was the fastest in the shop for doing that, and parcelling the goods up as well using large sheets of brown paper and tying up with string. The new girl, Hilda, was getting on fine and at closing time, or just before to be correct, a girl would come into the shop to wait for Hilda to walk home with. I knew this girl as she had at times been along to our house to a party, a birthday party for our Nancy, my youngest sister, on one or two occasions. Her name was Dorothy Wood, she lived at 49 Reeth Road and was sixteen years old. It wasn't long before Dorothy said to me "why don't you walk down the road with us?" That sounded all right to me and so from then on the three of us walked home together. Later when we got to know each other a bit more, Donald Wood and I would stand talking at the top of Reeth Road and often saw Dorothy being walked home by her boyfriend, who was a young soldier.

I would stare and possibly say "goodnight Dorothy" in a very seductive voice. I now know that she hated seeing Don and me at the road end, knowing full well that we were going to have some remark to say. Dorothy told me later that Bob, her boyfriend, had said to her "that chap", meaning me, "fancies you" and Dorothy replied "how do you know that?" I'm sure it made him feel uncomfortable but it was a bit of fun for us. We had more than likely been to the club and seen our girlfriends home and met on the way home.

Don was going with a girl called Steve, I think, and I was with Jean. Steve lived just across the road from Jean so that was how we always met up. Those were happy days, none of us had what is called a proper relationship with one person like they do nowadays. We went out in groups and spent the night having fun, then seeing the girls home, having a kiss and cuddle and saying goodnight.

About this time I was very interested in sport, as we played table tennis and badminton at the club and I enjoyed watching football. The team that I have always followed and still do is Middlesborough, and I must tell you about three of the many matches I went to at Ayresome Park. The three memorable matches were all cup-ties, and on two of those occasions the ground record was broken which made these memorable. The first one was against Blackpool, I think, and it was the second leg of the match, as then the cup-ties were played with home and away games and the team with the highest combined score won, much as in the UEFA cup today. I had gone to the Boro with some friends and when we got there we joined a very large queue outside the ground. Fortunately we had left ourselves plenty of time to get in, anticipating a long queue as we were winning 1-0 after the first match. I remember getting through the turnstile and was met with a wall of hundreds or people trying to get to the stands. We got to the top of the steps into the stands but couldn't get into the stand, it was chocker full. I then noticed some lads were climbing a ladder onto the roof of the stand, so I thought I'll have two pennyworth of that, as on the stand roof you would have an uninterrupted view of the match. I wished in hindsight that I hadn't seen those lads climbing onto the roof because when I got on the roof the only means of staying there was by getting your feet lodged behind the bolts holding the roof on. I couldn't find any of these bolts at first and kept moving down the roof. I was frightened then as people kept losing their grip at the bottom of the roof and were falling over into the crowd below.

I became more frightened when it came over the loud speakers "that if any more people were to get on to that roof it was liable to collapse". That did it for me, I was behind the chap on the front row and if he went over I would be next. Luckily I found two big bolt heads sticking up just behind this chap and believe me my shoes were stuck on those bolts as if they had been glued to them. It was a smashing match although we lost.

The problem now was how to get off the dammed roof; it proved easier than holding on to it. I must tell you that I walked bow-legged for two days but it did develop the muscles in my back.

The next match Charlie drove me to the Boro and we took a young lad called Ray Corbally with us. It was the first time either of them had ever been to a first class football match and it also proved memorable. Once again the ground was full to capacity but we managed to get into a standing area with crash barriers to lean on in normal times – but this was no normal time. I got behind one at the top of the stand, and trying to keep us three altogether, moved in front of the barrier, closely followed by Charlie. Ray was trying to keep with us and nearly slipped and stood on a man's foot. This man saw that Ray was trying to get to us and lifted him up to pass him to us but the others in the stand had different ideas. They just kept him in the air and passed him down over their heads and put him on the touchline. Ray had the best place of all of us, not crushed or shoved about, but sitting on the grass and with a perfect view of the game.

It was also at this match that once the game started, you moved with the crowd, and Charlie thought that he would light a cigarette. He pushed and shoved and eventually got a fag into his mouth and tried to light it but with the crowd swaying to and fro it was very difficult. Anyway he did get it lit but found he couldn't, no matter how hard he tried, get his lighter back into his pocket. Charlie's arm remained stuck up in the air or on someone's shoulder for the rest of the match. On our way back to his car I said to Charlie "that was a good match wasn't it?" Charlie looked at me, without a smile on his face, and replied "that was the first and it will be the last football match I'll go to, there's too much pushing and shoving for me, you can't even have a decent smoke".

The other match was memorable by it being tragic. It happened many years later but I will tell you about it now as I am writing about football. It was when our Hazel was courting a lad called Brian, so you can see that I have jumped a lot of years here, but never mind!. Brian was an avid Manchester United supporter and used to travel to see them each week by special coaches. A true supporter. Whenever Man U played the Boro at Ayresome Park I always got the tickets because: a) I liked a seat in the stand with the rest of the Boro fans, so Brian had to sit and endure the match silently, because if he had jumped up and cheered in this stand supporting Man U he would have been knocked to bits; and b) I've always liked to sit at matches under cover, whereas Brian liked to stand and cheer or jeer like a true fan.

Also I was working Middlesborough each week, so it was no hardship to call and get tickets. This time Brian said he had got tickets for us and I knew why, because I would be standing with the Man U fans and it was my turn to keep quiet. It was a good match and I must say being among the opposing team fans wasn't too bad. Although the language at times was a bit naughty it was all said in the right spirit. Man U won that night so I was in the happiest of company. We were about to leave when it came over the loud speakers "would all the Manchester United supporters remain in the ground until the Boro fans had got out". We walked to the top of the stand and down the steps on the other side into the ground road, which ran completely round the stadium, circled by the outside wall and exit gates.

This was a confined space stretching round one corner of the stadium and was enclosed by walls separating entry into the stands. This meant that inside the ground where we watched the game, which was allocated to the away teams and holding approximately 10,000 people were trying to be pushed into an enclosure holding around 2,000 people. It was the police that had told Middlesborough club to lock the fans in until the home fans had cleared. It proved to be a disaster, a tragic and fatal disaster, because as more and more fans came down the steps, they pushed the rest into the big double gates. The gates couldn't take the strain and in no time at all they came down under the pressure.

No sooner had the gates gone down than I found myself and Brian looking up a police horse's nostrils with the policeman holding his baton and saying stand still. Not only that, there were police dogs barking to be released at our legs. It was the most frightening experience I had ever had and I was never so pleased to get out of a crowd like that. I must say that the Man U fans were great and there was no trouble from them, it was just another police cock-up. If they had used their brains and let the fans out through even one gate then that would never have happened.

Brian and I got home and were shocked to hear that an old couple that had been walking past the gates when they were forced open had been killed. Needless to say, our families had been worried about us and had hoped that we were okay, and were pleased to see us home. I haven't been to another football match since then but I do still follow the Boro.

Still talking about football and the Boro in particular, it was when I was running the YMCA youth club that we had an evening's coaching and talk by two of Middlesborough FC's greats, George Hardwick who was a full back and also captain of the England team, and Mickey Fenton who was the centre forward for Boro and also England. Anyway more about that a little later; let me get back to the Co-op.

It was coming up to Christmas and getting very busy. The shop had two big windows to dress and it was my job to dress them if the boss didn't do it. I cast my eye back a few years when rationing was at its worst and Mr Robinson would dress the windows. He always had me to help him but when I had to dress the window I had to do it by myself. The trouble was the boss, who liked colourful windows, would put in such things as jellies, tea and coffee, and tins of fruit, all of which were very hard to get. Once anybody saw that the Co-op had jellies, etc, they made a beeline to get some. It was a rule that

Mr Robinson started that you do not take stuff out of the windows for customers. In theory this was a good idea, keeping the window dressed for the whole week or sometimes two. But when goods are in short supply you soon sell out and the customers got a bit irate when we told them that we couldn't take them out of the windows. "Who told you that?" would come the reply. "The boss," I said. "Well I'll see the boss if you don't mind." This is what really peeved all the staff – the customer would ask the boss why couldn't they have a jelly or a tin of fruit out of the window? They are there to sell aren't they, they would say quite sharply.

"I'm sorry," the boss would say and shout to one of the staff to get Mrs so and so what she wanted out of the window. It was galling to hear him say that. "Look," I said to the staff, "if anyone wants anything out of the window give them it and don't send them to see Mr Robinson as we now know what he will do."

The window always looked colourful with jellies, large and small tins of fruit, dried fruit in bowls, the raisins, sultanas and currants, and the different coloured packets of tea. At this time we had Red Label, Yellow Label (Eastern Tips) and Blue Label 'Indian Prince', the top quality tea. Combine all these colours – and this is what Mr Robinson did – and you have a beautiful coloured window.

When I dressed the window I didn't use half the amount of products that the boss used, and I didn't put in the window anything that was in short supply. What I tried to do was feature one or two products only and use other aids to make it a selling display. For example, the use of show cards, which were made to feature a product and crepe paper to highlight it, made the passers-by stop and look and hopefully come in and buy. Where as Mr Robinson's window, people would pass by, remark how colourful it was but didn't see a featured product.

I must have had a flare for this type of work, window dressing and shop interior displays, because our general manager, Mr Hall, awarded me a scholarship to Dalston Hall at Carlisle for a week's course on display and advertising with a diploma at the end if you passed the exams. Dalston Hall was an annexe of Loughborough College, which was sponsored by the Co-op. And I must say I was impressed not only with the building but also the tuition. I had an excellent week there, learning the finer arts of display and window dressing and getting my diploma with distinction. Mind you I thought no one could fail here as they had all the things imaginable for making a display – stands, wallpaper, bowls you name it – and it was there to use. "The only trouble was," I said to myself, "I haven't got all this at work and Mr Robinson wouldn't allow me to purchase any, it was a case of make do and mend and improvise."

Never mind, I learnt a lot and enjoyed a full week away from work and could always state to Mr Robinson that if he wouldn't sport buying a roll of decorative display paper he was losing out on sales by penny-pinching

It's only when you are away from home that you realise how much you miss doing your ordinary days things, in my case the youth club and the band practice and meeting with your friends. We had band practice two nights a week, Tuesdays and Thursdays, and although we enjoyed the actual band practices under Mr Woodhall it was the other nights that we used to meet in the band room that we had some good fun.

The band room at this time was in Victoria Road in a room above what used to be a motorcycle garage, owned by a Mr Bearpark. Four or five of us would meet there and play about with the instruments but mainly the drums. There was John on trombone, Arthur on euphonium, Bill and Punch on cornets, me on the B Flat Bass and Dennis on the drums, but we all liked knocking hell out of the drums. Anyway, some neighbours had complained about the noise we were making late at night and we were told that we could only play up till 9 p.m. Well we thought this was a bit of a raw deal, so we used to play as loud as we could from 8.30 till 9 p.m. prompt and then stop. We would then just sit and talk or play cards.

Christmas came and went in 1951 and a good time was had by all I think. Certainly nothing untoward happened as I would have remembered it if there was, but what did happen was this. I was back at work as usual and Dorothy had come into the shop as usual at closing time to wait for me and Hilda to walk home with her. I had got my coat on and was walking to Dorothy and I said: "Dorothy I haven't had my Christmas kiss off you yet" and went to give her a nice gentle kiss on the cheek. Dorothy was ahead of me in thinking on this and gave me a truly superb passionate kiss. I was stunned, as I never expected anything like that, but I was not complaining, as I had never been kissed like that before. All the way home I couldn't get it out of my mind – and that, my friends, was the beginning of a wonderful life for me.

Dorothy kept calling at the shop after she had left work and as I stated before we walked home together, only now it seemed a bit more interesting. She was still going out with this lad called Bob and when I used to see her getting walked home at night I began to wish it was me who was walking her home. A week or two passed and we gradually became friendlier, and a friend of Dorothy's, Ada she was called and she was also a friend of mine, as she was a member of the youth club. One night at the club Ada came dashing over to me and said "do you like Dorothy Wood?" "Of course I do," I said, "we walk home from work together every day, why?" "Well she's given Bob the elbow, so now's your chance to ask her out. Go on, she'd love it." After quite a bit of banter like "you're having me on, and I'll kill you Ada if you are setting me up".

Ada was a popular member of our club and got on well with everybody and took part in all the activities, so I said "okay I will ask her for a date". It rather spoilt my evening; I couldn't get it out of my mind and was wondering how I was going to get Dorothy on her own to ask her out. God moves in mysterious ways doesn't he? Because on the Monday following the Friday when we had all this dating game Hilda was off work sick. Oh wonderful, I thought, when Dorothy comes into the shop to walk home there'll only be me and that's when I can ask her out.

Dorothy, 1953

All the best-made plans come adrift is the saying and it was this day that Dorothy didn't call. She did call the next day and I was all keyed up about asking her out. What would I feel like if she said no? I wouldn't know where to put myself; things would never be the same again. Well I took two deep breaths and mustering all my courage up, I did ask her, and without any hesitation I got the reply that I had been waiting for. "Yes, yes," she said and gave me a quick peck on the cheek as we walked. I'm sure I felt that I was walking on air all the way home that night.

As I had band practice the following night, Dorothy said that she would meet me after it had finished and we could go for a walk before going home. I'll not forget that first night, it was lovely holding hands and talking whilst walking until it was dark and then we found ourselves at the bottom of Reeth Road standing at the gate of 49, which was where Dorothy lived. I felt so at ease with her and we kissed and kissed again saying goodnight. When I got home, which was just a hundred yards further along the road, I must have had an aura around me because my mother said: "What you feeling so happy about, you look as though you've lost a sixpence and found a shilling." All I said was that I'd had a wonderful night and left it at that. Let me say that from that first date we saw each other every day except for one for the next three years.

The day that we missed seeing each other was when there was a brass band concert at Manchester and naturally being in the band, and not knowing what time we would be back home, we decided not to make any arrangements. I'll not forget that contest either, as I was intrigued to see the adjudicator's box suspended (I think) from the ceiling of the Kings Hall in Belle Vue. Another reason was that Mr Woodhall changed who played the cadenza in the test piece, and this was in the boxing ring which was acting as the bandstand, with only two minutes to go before we started the piece. As it worked out it wasn't too bad a decision but I still think it was the wrong one. We came third to Bessers O' the Barn Band, and that band was third best in the country in that section.

Mr Woodhall was delighted as were we, and we travelled home in a very happy mood, arriving back home about eleven o clock. I couldn't wait to tell Dorothy when I met her the next morning, how I had missed seeing her and how well we had done in the contest. "Well done," she said happily, but the words weren't convincing. I'm sure poor Dorothy put up with me wittering on about the band and so on so as not to hurt my feelings. She was so full of life and vigour it was a joy to walk with her, although sometimes she got a little too carried away with herself.

We were on our way home one night and she was in one of those daredevil attitudes and we were walking up Victoria Road when she said: "What would you do if I knocked on one of these doors?" I said that I would just ignore it and when the person came to the door I would tell them it was a kid playing about. Nothing more was said, then Dorothy just let go of my hand and knocked on the nearest door, and fled and hid at the top of the road in the recess of a shop. I couldn't believe it but I just kept on walking very steadily until I got round the corner where Dorothy was laughing her hat off. Evidently there couldn't have been anyone at home that night in the house that

Dorothy had knocked on as no one answered, thank goodness. By now we were both in high spirits and played tricks on each other all the way home.

Before Dorothy started going out with me she used to go dancing every week, sometimes to the Civil Service Club at Catterick Camp or the town hall in Richmond, and I sometimes felt that she missed her dancing more than what she told me. My group of friends never went dancing so I never became a good dancer and to this day nothing has changed.

As time passed – and as I said we saw each other daily – we became more and more attached to each other. So, in 1953 we knew we loved each other and I asked her to marry me. We had been together for 18 months and we hardly ever had a wrong word to say to each other. "You will have to ask my dad and mam," said Dorothy then flung her arms around me and said "yes, yes, yes", showered me with kisses and said hurriedly "when are you going to ask them then, tomorrow?" "Oh I don't know about tomorrow, I'll have to build up my courage, I'll have to eat plenty of spinach like Popeye did to get his strength to ask them," I said jokingly.

To this day I don't know what made me say those words that night but it was right and I had no control of what I was saying, but all I knew was that I loved this girl and wanted to be with her all the time. I had proposed to Dorothy along Reeth Road, about three hundred yards from her house, and it took us about two hours to get there. We were both on cloud nine when we kissed again, this time goodnight. The words Dorothy left me with were: "I'll find a way for you to see my mam and dad tomorrow but I'm not being in the room when you ask them". She blew me a kiss and disappeared through her front door. I went home and never said a word to my mam and dad, although I think they guessed something was afoot by my actions and me being so happy. The next day dawned and I am sure that I'd had only one hour's sleep. I lay awake thinking about what I should say to Mr and Mrs Wood, never coming to anything definite. In the end, feeling mentally exhausted, I must have gone to sleep. I awoke and the first thing that came into my mind was what I had been thinking before I had gone to sleep, "what shall I say to Dorothy's mam and dad?"

My mam called me for breakfast and for the time being my mind was on something else. I went to work, but my mind wasn't on it as I kept making stupid mistakes. And to make matters worse, Dorothy called in to see me mid-morning and told me that she had told her parents that we were staying in tonight at her house. "So you can ask them then, I'll go and make a cuppa and leave you to it," she said. All I could say was "thanks a lot" then she hurried off.

We walked home that night after work and I hardly spoke a word but Dorothy was all excited and bubbling with joy. We got to her gate and I said "so long I'll see you later" and carried on walking. When I got in my mother had my tea ready as usual, so I sat down, ate it and never said a word. Mam naturally said "what's the matter with you tonight, have you and Dorothy been having words?" "No, no," I replied "just the opposite really, any way I'll tell you about it when I get in tonight" and left it at that.

I was longing to tell my mam how I felt and what I was going to do that night but daren't until I had spoken to Dorothy's mam and dad. I got changed and went along to Dorothy's, knocked on the door, and before you could say 'Jack Frost' the door opened and Dorothy gave me a quick kiss, before saying "come in" loud enough for her parents to hear. "What's up with you two, staying in tonight, nothing on the pictures you like?" "No not exactly," I stuttered, "I've got something to ask you." Me uttering those words, Dorothy made a quick exit as if she was going to the toilet or something, as she didn't want to be there when I asked for her hand in marriage. "Where are you going Dorothy?" asked her mam but she had gone and pretended not to hear that remark.

"What it is Mr and Mrs Wood, is that Dorothy doesn't want to be in the room when I ask you both if we can get married. As you know, we have been together for 18 months now and have fallen in love very deeply with each other and I thought it only right if I asked you if we can get engaged." "Oh dear, dear me she's too young, really too young," her mother said. Mr Wood, who was more forthright, said: "Norah (that's Mrs Woods' first name), "don't talk daft or get yourself in a tizz wozz – if they fall out, they fall out and there's nowt thee or me can do about it". With that, Mr Wood rose to his feet, came over to me and shook my hand saying "congratulations lad" quickly followed by the words "you can come in now Dorothy".

In walked Dorothy, looking I should say gleaming. "Well?" she said, and her mother went over to her and gave her and then me a big hug. It was very near Mrs Woods' birthday, so Dorothy said "let's get officially engaged on your birthday mam and we'll ask Dougie's mam and dad over for a bite to eat and a drink". So it was, and on October 1st which was Mrs Woods' birthday, we all gathered in Mr and Mrs Woods sitting room and enjoyed a nice buffet and a drink, plus an engagement cake was produced which was cut and offered around, and all present wished us all the best.

I have missed telling you what happened the night I had asked for Dorothy's hand when I got home. It wasn't late as I was excited and wanted to tell my mam and dad, so after saying goodnight to

Dorothy and her parents, I got home about ten-thirty and burst into the living room full of joy and sticking my chest out boldly said "listen all of you, you are now looking at an engaged man, for tonight I have just asked Dorothy to marry me, and she has said yes". In the room there was mam, dad, Denis, Fred and Nancy who were all talking or listening to the wireless until I burst in. After hearing my good news, they all jumped up and congratulated me. Mam came and gave me a kiss and a big hug and whispered emotionally in my ear "she's a nice girl, look after her". Dad came and shook my hand vigorously and wished me all the best. I told them that we would be getting engaged officially next week on Mrs Woods' birthday, and that mam and dad had to come with me to their house to celebrate.

It was late that night when we all went to bed and I lay thinking about the months that we had been going out with each other and that I wouldn't forget that first night that Dorothy met me from band practise and we went for a walk round. Coming down Reeth Road, Dorothy saw her dad waiting for her at their gate and said: "Oh heck, that's me dad and he looks cross, so I'll see you tomorrow so don't stop." I remember getting close to the gate where Mr Wood was waiting and heard him say to Dorothy "what time do you call this?" or words similar to that. He wasn't a happy chappy that night I thought, then fell asleep. From then on I walked on cloud nine, at work, at home, at the club, in fact everywhere I went.

Chapter Nine

Now that we were engaged, it was a matter of interest as to when we would get married and where would we live. At first with Christmas not far away and wondering what presents to buy for so and so, and most of all what to buy Dorothy, and to this day I can't remember what I did buy her, things just went along quite normally. But in the New Year we got more focused and concentrated on getting somewhere to live – and low and behold I persuaded my general manager to let me have the empty flat above the Co-op butchers and café in the market place.

The front of the flat overlooking the market place consisted of two large rooms with two big windows in each room. Looking out of these windows we gazed straight at the town clock on Trinity Tower. On the ground floor was the butcher's shop, the first floor the café, and our flat was on the second floor. It meant that we had to climb about forty stairs to get to our flat. Once you had climbed the stairs the two front rooms were straight across the landing, and if you turned left, down two stairs you came to the kitchen. This was a long narrow room about twenty-five feet long and six-feet wide, with the pantry and bathroom off it on the right. Those two rooms were also large, being ten feet square each. At the end of the kitchen was another room, which could only be described as being derelict, as the floor fell away by as much as fourteen inches away from the kitchen. The whole building had been neglected over the years and nothing had been done to keep it up to scratch.

However with help from my brothers, we got the flat into a nice place. Of course all the time we were working on it, or should I say the nights when my brothers weren't working on it, Dorothy and I had the place to ourselves. When we couldn't go walking because of the weather we made the excuse we would go and do a bit at the flat. There was no big hurry to get the flat ready, as we weren't getting married until March the next year, 1955, so we had plenty of time.

Mr Jennings, my general manager, had been very good to me because after he had seen the place and the condition it was in, he told me that I could rent it for seven shillings and sixpence a week, with no rates to pay, and that I needn't start to pay until we were married. He must have liked the look of my face, as it turned out that he and I got on very well over the years that followed. As we got the flat decorated it dawned on me that one would need furniture to put in it.

This is where my mother came to the rescue, as Dorothy or myself had had no experience in furnishing a house. Mam was well known by a manager of a furniture shop in Darlington called Sam Wilkes. I don't remember his name, even if I had heard it, but mother came to Darlington with us and introduced Dorothy and I to the manager. He was Mr Charming himself, and helped us every way he could. We had been promised by one of my brothers and sister that one would buy us a dining table and the other would buy us the sideboard, so all we had to do was buy the four chairs, and we would have a complete dining room suite.

Mother was delighted that we purchased something as the manager gave her a nice fireside rug for introducing us to Sam Wilkes. Besides being busy organising one thing and another, we still had our jobs to go to and also have fun at the club and band practice.

One Wednesday round about this time, Charlie suggested that we go rabbiting with the guns and not the nets. I agreed and off we went into Whitcliffe Woods. We never saw a single rabbit in the wood area and both of us were getting a bit sick, with not having had a shot between us. Just as we were leaving the wood, Charlie spotted two crows sitting on a branch of a tree, and said "look we can have a shot at them". "We both can't shoot together," I said, "so I'll shoot and aim for the one on the left". "Spoil sport," said Charlie, "but go on and get the big one on the left." I pushed the twelve-bore tightly into my shoulder, took aim and gently squeezed the trigger. I had forgotten how big a bang and how big the kick was when I picked myself up off the ground. "I thought you were aiming at the one on the left," I heard Charlie say. "I was," I said as I stumbled to my feet. "Well you hit the one on the right, you plonker." I'd never heard Charlie use that expression before. For the next hundred yards or so all I got was Charlie making remarks such as "you had better get your eyes tested tomorrow, or don't you know you're right from your left" and so on it went, until all of a sudden he stopped abruptly. "Look," he said as we came out of the wood into a field, "there's how many rabbits there?" He was looking at six rabbits pretty close together, just playing about and nibbling the grass.

If they get a bit closer together, I'll get the lot with one barrel. We stood perfectly still waiting for the rabbits to get closer together. We watched; at first there were five all together, only one more to get into the circle, but then instead of that one coming closer another would leap away and in the end I lost patience and said "for goodness sake have a shot now or you won't get any". "I will, I will," he replied, "just wait another minute and I tell you I'll get the lot." After more waiting I said "give me the gun and I'll surely get one". They must have heard me because all I saw was six white tails running like hell into their set. Another big bang and Charlie had fired at them. He managed to get one solitary rabbit after waiting for about forty minutes to try and get six. My comments to Charlie for the rest of the way home were similar to those that he had said to me for hitting the wrong bird, like "greed is one of the worse vices one can have" and "you didn't want to shoot all those rabbits really did you?" and so on.

The day of reckoning was getting nearer and we checked with Dorothy's mam and dad about arrangements for the wedding. I was told that my duties were to pay for the taxis, to get a best man and at the reception propose the toast to the bridesmaids. Mrs Wood had sent out the invitations and had received acceptances. The reception was held in the Methodist Hall at the back of the church and the food was provided by Dorothy's mam and dad and served and set up by the ladies of the Bright Hour. One big saving we had was that Dorothy's Uncle Bernie said that he would provide all the flowers for the wedding, from the bride and bridesmaid's bouquets and button holes for every one, and I must say he made a first class job of it. Mind you, Uncle Bernie was the parks superintendent for the city of Newcastle, so he knew a thing or two about arranging flowers.

Fixing all these arrangements and trying to keep everyone informed of what was going on tried me to a state of nearly having a heart attack, I think. That's exaggerating a bit but I also had my best man getting uptight and more nervous than me, I'm sure, as the big day drew nearer.

Donald Wood was my best man, naturally as he was my best friend. Dorothy's sister Sheila and her cousin's daughter Valerie were the young bridesmaids and my sister Nancy was chief bridesmaid. My brothers Denis and Fred were groomsmen and the minister was a friend, Mr Douglas Bourne. Stag nights and hen nights were not thought of in those days so the night before we were to be married I didn't see much of Dorothy as their house was a hive of activity, with our Nancy, Valerie and Sheila all there, I suppose trying their dresses on, etc. Our house wasn't much better, as people were calling wishing us well, staying for a cup of tea, so it was late when I got to bed that night. I remember because we sat up talking about tomorrow but I also remember waking up very early.

We were to be married at 2 p.m. and that morning to me was a very long one – as you know, every thing is done and what isn't doesn't matter now. Don came early to our house to keep both of us company and to comfort each other. I remember thinking that you say and think daft things whilst waiting to start the proceedings. Uncle Bernie, who was bringing the flowers, had said he would be at Dorothy's by 11 a.m. and would send the buttonholes for all my family along as soon as he arrived. It was 12-o-clock and no buttonholes had arrived and I was getting a bit agitated when a knock came to the door and there was someone with the buttonholes. A great sigh of relief came upon us all. We had a sandwich, I believe, and then waited for our taxi to come and take mam, dad, Denis and Fred to church. I can't remember precisely who went in the taxi first or last, all I know is that when David Espin came for Don and I we got in and went straight to the front of the church and sat down. David Espin who ran the taxi firm was also a good friend of mine and also a good club member, so it was only right that we had Dave as our taxi man.

Before I left Dorothy the night before, the last words she said to me were "I want you to turn round and watch me walk down the aisle, don't forget, turn right round". The church soon filled up and Don and I just talked gibberish, and I couldn't wait to get on with the proceedings. Don kept feeling to see if he still had the ring in his waistcoat pocket and I don't know what he would have done if he found it wasn't there. "It's still there," he said to me with a strained smile on his face. I just said "I hope it is or we'll be asking for a curtain ring as a substitute".

All of a sudden the organ struck up with the music 'Here comes the Bride' and Don and I stood up, or should I say jumped up out of fright. I remembered what Dorothy had told me to do when she started to walk down the aisle, so I turned round, right round, and watched her slowly walk arm-in-arm with her father down the aisle. I was stunned; I was going to marry this gorgeous blonde. Looking as radiant as can be and smiling at me all the way to the altar. My heart was beating like a big bass drum but at the same time I became more relaxed as the ceremony had now got started. When we stood up and I turned round it seemed as though the congregation were all looking at me, as though I was on show, until the bride approached them, then they turned and looked and gasped at how lovely Dorothy looked. The reason Dorothy told me to look at her coming down the aisle was that I would never see her all dolled up like that again and that was good enough reason for me. We now stood close together and Dorothy got hold of my hand and gave it a squeeze, and from then on all was well, except when I fluffed my lines a little, but I didn't worry about that.

Later in the vestry everybody was relaxed as we signed the register and had a laugh or two, about what I don't remember. Then Mr Bourne got us all lined up to parade through the church again, gave Norman Parker our organist the nod to play the wedding march, and off we went up the aisle, Dorothy and I leading the way, and all the congregation now looking at us both.

As we stood outside the church getting our photos taken, more and more people stopped and wished us all we would wish ourselves. I became aware just how well known we both were. It seemed ages to take the photos but the photographer that we had was spot on, getting the right people in the right groups. We knew him quite well as his daughter was friends with both of us. His name was Mr Stehens and he had a studio on Castle Hill. After a while he said "okay that's your lot" and we made our way round to the back of the church and upstairs into the hall.

Once again we lined up in military fashion to welcome our guests to the reception. The ladies of the Bright Hour had done us proud, as the tables looked absolutely lovely, with the three-tier wedding cake gracing the centre of the top table. Mrs Dobson had made and iced the cake as only a top professional can do. Mr and Mrs Dobson had a bakery business run from their home in Burrard Avenue, they had two children and they both attended the Methodist Youth Club, and that's how we came to get their parents to do our cake as we had seen a lot of their creations.

Everything went well, the speeches were good and at times humorous. The bridesmaids not only looked lovely but also enhanced the reception by their presence. Having the reception on the Methodist premises meant that no alcoholic drinks were allowed but Rev. Bourne had said that we could have a toast with sherry.

Then Dorothy and I mingled among the guests and had a great time meeting each others relations and friends until it was time to go and get changed ready to catch the train. We got changed at Dorothy's house and said our farewells to our parents there, then walked down the path waving to all the neighbours who had come out to see us go.

Let me say a few words about Dorothy's mother, before I go any further. Mrs Wood had been taken ill three weeks or more before the wedding was to take place, and at one stage had said that she couldn't make it to the church and reception, and also see to the arrangements that had to be done. Dorothy told her mam that if she couldn't make it we would postpone the wedding. Mrs Wood was having nothing to do with that and stated that she would be okay by the time of the wedding. Fortune smiles on the brave and it also happened that they had got a new doctor in their surgery, and as luck had it he attended to Mrs Wood. He fixed her up temporarily until after the wedding, when he would want her to go into hospital.

I remember Dorothy having to go to Darlington to buy her mam a new hat. In those days all travelling was done by bus. United buses ran to Darlington every half hour and the return was also every half hour – and this was how Dorothy had to go to Darlington to do the shopping.

Back to the wedding: We got to Richmond Railway Station, got on the train and the crowds that had come to see us off had spoken to the train guard and he came along and locked us in. The train had no corridor so we were in a compartment by ourselves all the way to Darlington. It wasn't until we got to Darlington and tried to get out that we realised we were locked in. Shouting to the guard to come and unlock the door made me feel a right Wally – and of course Darlington being a main line station there were scores of people about and they thought it very funny. You can't hide the fact that you've just been married, for example, we boarded the Edinburgh train, put our cases on the racks above our heads and sat down. This compartment catered for eight people and all the seats were taken. We tried to look like normal travellers but when the train jerked as it set off, confetti started trickling down onto the people sitting alongside us. I blushed, coughed and felt right embarrassed. What made things worse was there was a little old lady sat in the corner knitting and she said with a smile from ear to ear "someone always plays that trick, stuffing confetti into the cases, and no matter how often you try to get rid of it there's always some left".

The journey to the Scottish capital was uneventful after that and we arrived at Waverly station feeling happy but a little tired after all the day's emotions. It was dark when we came out of the station and we looked for a taxi to take us to our hotel. We joined a queue and strangely they were all young couples, and stranger than that we were all going to the same hotel.

When we arrived at our hotel, quickly followed by some of the other couples who had been in the same queue, we had to laugh, as there was a poor old man taking single beds out of the rooms and replacing them with doubles. All the time he was doing this he was muttering to himself "this isn't right, this should have been done by the day staff" and on and on he went. It wasn't a bad hotel, it was clean, the service turned out to be good and helpful and the food was great.

Breakfast was served between 7.30 and 9 a.m. officially but there was some fun when couples tried to creep in unobserved. When they were spotted a big cheer would go up and remarks such as "my you look tired, haven't you slept?" It was remarkable how many honeymooners there were at that hotel at the same time. After breakfast we had a discussion on what we should do that day, or should I say where should we go.

The weather was unkind to us, as it was misty and foggy, in fact you couldn't see the castle, and I often have wondered since how Dorothy persuaded me to go and visit the place. I think it was not only that I loved her but I wanted to please her as well. Anyway up the hill we climbed from Prince's Street. I remember thinking or might have remarked at the time that it was like doing a route march in the army! We should have chosen another day because once we got into the castle you couldn't see a thing below. It was like being above the clouds. "Never mind," I said, "lets look round the inside of the castle," which we did and enjoyed it but we didn't stop too long as it was a bit cold. We should have thought of that when we chose March to get married but that was the best month for tax purposes. I informed the income tax people and got the whole of the year's taxes I'd paid refunded.

We had ploughed our way up to the castle but we fair ran down, getting and feeling warmer with each step. At the bottom of the castle walk were the Royal residences and we had a walk around there and then went and explored the rest of the city, but not all on our first day of course.

Wherever we went we had to go by bus, as we had no car in those days, and it was an eye opener when we went to see the magnificent Forth Bridge. There was a tour guide to give us all the statistics like it's a continuing job painting it, no sooner do they get to one side of the bridge and then they have to start at the beginning again. It went through my mind that they deserve to be rewarded handsomely for doing such a dangerous and boring job. Dorothy and I were certainly enjoying our honeymoon and we went all over the place using the buses. Anyway as I say to the sheets each morning "the best of friends must part" and with a big sigh our week's holiday had come to an end and home we must go.

Believe it or not, all we had left was five pounds, which was to see us through the whole of next week. That was the total sum of money that we had between us, and that my friends, did buy all the groceries, etc, for the next week.

We arrived back in Richmond in the early afternoon and went straight to our own flat. It felt real strange once we had climbed the stairs and were gazing out onto the busy market place, it being a Saturday. We decided to just drop our luggage and go back downstairs and spend some of the five pounds that we had saved from our honeymoon. All we had to buy was fresh stuff, such as milk, vegetables and a bit of meat for Sunday's dinner, the total cost of which was about ten shillings, fifty pence in today's money.

After that little shopping spree, we went to see our families. The first call was Dorothy's, where we had our tea with them and talked about our holiday and our plans for the future. I was made most welcome and straight away felt like one of the family, especially by Sheila, Dorothy's sister, who was only thirteen years old.

From Dorothy's home we went along the road to see my parents, brothers and sister who were also pleased to see us and wanted to know if we wanted anything or help. We were pleased to say "no we're okay thank you" and after having spent a couple of hours with them, we returned to our very own love nest overlooking the market place and numbered 25a.

Things soon got back to normal I remember, with one exception, and that was when the youth club closed, six or seven members who were friends came back to our flat and had a cup of coffee or tea. We were really happy with our lot now and things only got better. Our flat became the meeting place for not only the families but friends as well. Dorothy's dad in particular would, after he had finished work, pop in and see us and it was also nice to see him.

Dad Wood, as I now called him, was chief ticket clerk for the United Bus Company and their office was just across the market place. From our flat we could get on to the roof, which was a flat one, with a three-foot high wall surrounding it. Dorothy had strung a washing line across it and dried our washing on it. It worked very well and being high up it always had a breeze blowing which dried the clothes. Then one day, Dad Wood saw this line of washing stretched right across the roof and blowing like flags in the wind. He went and saw Dorothy and asked her if she should be doing this, as I don't think he liked it very much. He must have had visions of knickers flying off the line into the market place or people standing in groups admiring Dorothy's underwear.

It was about this time that my boss advised me that if I wanted promotion I should study for some diplomas. Now the CWS ran correspondence courses through Loughborough College so I started with salesmanship, followed by human relations in management and bookkeeping. I passed all of the examinations and got distinction in human relations in management and bookkeeping, and high marks in both the practical and written paper in salesmanship. The ten-week course on management, for which the text book was Industrial Psychology, I only sent in two or three lessons, got very high marks and decided I was sending no more in to be marked as it was purely a matter of using common sense.

The practical side of the salesmanship exam was hard, as there were about twenty piles of cereals, pulses and legumes on a table, and all had to be identified; also a number of teas, dry and wet, and you had to distinguish which were tips and which were leaf. Harder than you think doing that, especially the fused tea. The practical also included boning and cutting bacon into joints. I found it very hard to study because I still liked the youth club and the band, and these two activities alone took up four nights a week. But Dorothy didn't mind that, as that allowed her to go and see her mam, dad and Sheila.

It wasn't long before I got promoted to first hand at our Leyburn branch, managed by a Mr F Laughlan. This meant that I had to catch the 7 a.m. bus each morning and I never missed it once. Although as time passed the bus conductor and driver got to know me well, as I was usually the only passenger on the bus leaving Richmond, and if I wasn't there before the bus was due to leave they would come across the market place and knock on the door for me. Those were the good old days when everyone helped each other and wouldn't do any one a bad turn if they couldn't do them a good one.

Frank the manager was a good chap, married with two children, a boy and a girl, and from the start we got on very well. He also had good staff who, although they maybe didn't realise it at the time, helped me an awful lot in what was my first managerial job. Being out in the country the Leyburn branch did some things that no other branch did, such as all the fruit and veg were bought locally from wholesalers and this was a skill I had to learn and which I enjoyed doing. It was only a small shop, with a manager, me, four girls, one man and a deliveryman.

I found it strange that I had to deal with a problem which I had once solved at Richmond in this my first managerial position. And that was to stop Frank pushing past the girls and pushing them onto the counter edge and so hurting their stomachs. So I told Frank what he was doing but he didn't believe that he was doing this. He said all he was doing was walking past them. We agreed to disagree on this subject and he continued to carry on as he always had. New measures had to be taken to put a stop to this, so I took it upon myself to change places with one of the girls on the counter. So that

when Frank started his run along the counter he would have to push
me. There was only one way to stop him and that was to trip him up
and send him sprawling. I told the girls what I was going to do and
they thought it was a bit naughty but after I said it was the only way,
they agreed to help. Help meant if I, or should I say he, missed my
leg, the next girl would put her leg out and so on right along the staff
line, until he be sent headlong in a dive. The plot worked first time I
am glad to say and after a few harsh words, from then on he moved
in a more civilised way.

I had only been in Leyburn a week when I met the owner of the
café in the market place and he had noticed that I got off the bus at
twenty-past-seven each morning and so he suggested that I go to the
café, help him set the tables and have a cuppa or two. In return I could
have a main course and a sweet at lunchtime for free. It was a good
deal because now I had a place to go if it was raining and I didn't
have to go to the shop early. It worked out well this arrangement and
once he knew that I liked the skin on the rice pudding I got it all, as
they didn't like serving rice pudding with a skin on the top.

Another thing that happened and surprised me whilst I was
at Leyburn was that on a Friday it was the farmers mart, and the
mart was held further up the road from the shop on higher ground.
One Friday on returning to work after lunch – we closed for lunch
from 12.30 to 1.45 p.m. – as we unlocked the front door, sewage
came flooding out. Oh it was terrible; it was filthy and stank to high
heavens. It was coming in through the back shop, where there was a
drain, and somewhere along the road the drains were blocked and it
was backing up through the drains. The sewage was coming from the
auction mart. We contacted the MOH who was fortunately at the mart
and he came down to see the state of things. Well, we had sacks of
potatoes standing in the mess along with other items. But he wouldn't
write off the spuds, as he said quite happily that they grow in it, but
condemned the bags of cabbages, etc, that were on the floor. We had
to close the shop for one hour while we washed all the floors and
sprayed disinfectant about. The customers weren't too upset about the
smell that lingered, as being country folk, what was a bit of a smell to
worry about. They smelt that all day long when they were fertilising
the crops.

Altogether I was at Leyburn nearly a year but after I had been there
about nine months, and the winter weather was getting worse, we
had a rare visit from the general manager, Mr Jennings. We had been
warned that he was on his way to Leyburn by the bush telegraph, i.e.
Richmond branch. So I decided to ask him for a move. I took him into
the back shop and asked him outright if I could have a move as I was

putting in a twelve-and-a-half hour day and in winter time it could only be funny getting here because of the weather at times.

Mr Jennings said that Frank had spoken to him and was very pleased with me and hoped that I could be persuaded to stay at Leyburn. He did not know that I was going to ask for a transfer. He went on to say that I had done well here and he would see what he could do but surprised me by going on to say "I can't remove Mr Robinson just yet Mr Shout". I thought a lot about that final sentence and came to the conclusion that he wanted Mr Robinson out. I didn't have to wait much longer for that move. Frank took a phone call from the GM who wanted to speak to me and handed me the phone, "Good morning, Mr Shout" (the G.M. taught all the buyers and departmental managers manners as he always greeted you with civility and courtesy). "I have got a move for you as from next Monday. I want you to take over the first hands job in Richmond, you know that this is the top branch outside the central one in Darlington, and I think you deserve it, don't let me down." "Thank you," I said, nearly shouting down the phone, and replaced the receiver.

Poor Frank was gutted; I know he would have liked to have kept me there as he admitted to me but that's being selfish he said and wished me all the best. I couldn't wait to tell Dorothy and as it happened on a Wednesday she would often catch the bus up to Leyburn, wait for me in the shop and we would travel back home together. Today was one of those Wednesdays and she guessed that I had some good news by the smile on my face when I greeted her. She was delighted, naturally, as now we could spend more time with each other.

It was nice on Monday morning not having to get up a 6 a.m. to catch the 7-o-clock bus. It felt quite strange going to work just round the corner and meeting all the old and new staff. But I soon settled in and got down to organising the staff as I had always wanted to but hadn't been able to as I hadn't been in a position to do so before. Mr Robinson gave me a free hand to do this, as he knew my ideas from before I left to go to Leyburn, but he hadn't wanted to implement them. The important ones were that I would control the counters, because by doing this I could see what was going on throughout the shop, and Amy would be in total control of getting the orders made up each day. Also the juniors and the warehouse boy would spend some time each day filling the fixtures and weighing up stock ready for use. This exercise would take place the latter part of the day, like two hours before we closed if we had that amount of time.

We were now running a happy shop, with all the staff pulling their weight, because now they all had set jobs to do and got on with them. Mr Robinson didn't bother us much at all. He sat in his office all day, occasionally coming out to help the staff weighing up sugar or anything in the back shop which was outside his office door. I always remember the little round burn marks on his desk top and the shelves beside the desk; they were cigarette burns, as Mr Robinson was a chain smoker and when he hadn't one in his mouth, it would be stood on end on the desk or the shelves and left to burn right down. Then he would blow away the ash that remained and light another one.

He came, opened the shop, opened the mail, asked me if there was anything that needed his attention and if not he would disappear until dinnertime at 12.30. He would give me the keys to open up after dinner at 1.50 but he didn't show his face till about three or later.

One of the jobs that he still did was to dress the windows and above the fixtures. From the top of the fixtures there was five feet of space up to the ceiling and no matter how many times I told him it was a waste of time decorating up there, he continued to do so. To do this he had to use a ladder, so you can imagine the trouble that caused for us behind the counter. It was a nightmare; even some of the customers remarked so as well. Well, one day the GM came about 2.30 and Mr Robinson wasn't back from his dinner, which was nothing new to us, and asked where he was. I covered up for him, saying he had gone to see a customer about something, I can't remember what. He continued looking round the shop, the GM and I stood in the middle of the shop, which was the customer space and he looked up at the top of the fixtures, and said: "Whose idea is it to dress all that, waving his arms and pointing around the two walls that got dressed." "Mr Robinson's," I said. Then waving his arms in the same direction as before, he said: "Take it down, take it down," he repeated, "no one looks up there." "Certainly," I said, thinking that's the best thing he's done today and it will give me great pleasure to tell Mr Robinson to do just that. Everything was fine with the shop and the GM went on his way. When the boss returned from dinner, he was mortified to learn that the GM had been but pleased that he had found everything okay. "Except," I said, "come with me" and I led him to the middle of the shop where Mr Jennings and I had stood and said "who dressed all up there" and I waved my arms just like the GM had done. "Take it down, take it down no one looks up there, pull it down." Mr Robinson thought I'd gone mad I think by the way he looked at me and then said in quite a casual manner. "He did, did he, leave it." And that was that. I thought "oh hell". I had hoped that we had at last got rid of having to dress those fixture tops. In fact we had; I think the boss was just proving a point to me but in fact again, he didn't dare to disobey the GM.

Dorothy and I were getting on fine in the flat living like any other married couple. We had many a laugh, especially when Dorothy had cooked a big dinner. The meat was lovely, the Yorkshire puddings lovely, the vegetables cooked to perfection but the gravy had Dorothy crying and me laughing my head off. Every time Dorothy made gravy it was lumpy, in fact very lumpy, and it had to be pressed through a sieve to make it edible. After many years of trying she did get it right. I joke when I say years, it just felt like years.

One night we had a couple of friends in for supper and we had had a good night chatting away to each other, but as I have said before all good things must come to an end. I must tell you at this stage that it was a very windy night outside and to get to our flat you had to go down a passage, and of course when the wind was so strong it made weird sounds like ghost's wailing. On our floor in the living room we had an army blanket, as we couldn't afford carpets at that time. This was on top of the lino. As our guests got up to go, we were stood talking by the doorway, when the wind howled again and at the same time blew under the door and lifted the lino and blanket a few inches off the floor. Our guests were called Sheila and Horace, and Sheila seeing this went deathly white and nearly fainted. Afterwards she said that she thought she was seeing a ghost and was terrified. I don't remember Sheila and Horace ever coming back to see us in that flat.

Also in the early days, we had another – I won't say frightening but interesting – experience. We had seen some mice dirt in the kitchen so I said I would get a trap to catch the little monster. I bought two from the hardware shop where Dorothy worked, and set them with a bit of cheese on the plate on the trap, put them under the sink in the cupboard, and went and sat down with Dorothy in the living room. We had been sat, I tell no lies, for no more than three minutes when I said to Dorothy "those dam traps have gone off, I'd better go and set them better this time". When I got to the cupboard the traps had certainly gone off but each one had a mouse in it. "Good God," I shouted to Dorothy, "we've caught two mice, so I'll set them up again." The same thing happened another seven times. Believe me, that night in a space of ninety minutes, we caught sixteen mice and for the rest of the time we lived there we never had another mouse.

We never had another mouse in the house but we were never short of visitors, what with our families, friends and youth club members we hardly ever had a night on our own, it was grand being married!. It was great at Whitsuntide when the fair would come into the market place, as our flat would become the meeting place for everybody, and you can imagine we were not short of company then.

What did worry us both a bit before the fair came into town was the noise it would make and in those days at the weekends it would stay open until there was no one left in the town, and we were both at work the next day. It only took one night to get used to it and after that we slept like babies.

Talking about babies, it was late in fifty-five that Dorothy found out that she was pregnant. It came as no shock really, because Dorothy was having morning sickness with a vengeance, but after she had been sick she felt as fit as a fiddle. We were invited to have Xmas dinner at mam and dad Woods' house and we gratefully accepted. It would have been criminal to spoil a dinner by the gravy Dorothy hadn't mastered making yet. We had, I distinctly remember, the best Xmas since being married and of course it was the first. In the evening we called at my family's and had some supper. All in all we had a great day and by the time we got home we were shattered and fell asleep as soon as our heads hit the pillow.

A few nights later we didn't have such a good night's sleep though. It had been snowing for a day or two and we had about four inches laying on our roof when we had gone to bed (not that I knew that at the time). Well, at about three in the morning, I was rudely awakened by water dripping on to my face. I thought for a moment I was in a Japanese POW camp being tortured (not really) but quickly got some clothes on and went on to the roof to see if I could stop it. The snow had blown onto the wall and was getting behind the lead facings and consequently thawing and coming into the bedroom. A quick sweep with the brush right along the wall soon stopped it. If anyone had seen me shovelling snow in the middle of the night they would have thought I had gone mad. I possibly was mad, I should have just got a blanket and gone into the living room for the rest of the night and shifted the snow in the morning.

As the months passed, we started to get things ready for the baby and Dorothy, I felt, loved buying all things needed when one is having a baby. I only paid for them but we did get a lot of goods bought and given to us by our parents and friends, who were thrilled to bits for us. Nearer the time that the baby was due, Dorothy's mam had suggested that we live at her house so that when she started in labour she wouldn't be on her own. The baby was due at the end of August or the beginning of September; well on Friday 3rd August, Dorothy's waters broke. After having a consultation with our doctor, we moved down to her mam's, as she wasn't in labour then.

On the Saturday evening, Dorothy and her mam were shelling peas ready for Sunday dinner and Dorothy was eating as many as she was putting in the basin. I don't know who it was that remarked "you'll be ill eating all those peas". "That's rubbish," Dorothy replied, "I've always liked fresh garden peas and they've never made me ill before." Well the inevitable happened, didn't it? We had just got into bed when Dorothy said she had tummy ache and me not being the least sympathetic said "I told you so, you shouldn't have eaten so many of those peas". It wasn't long before we realised it wasn't the peas but the baby was on its way.

Chapter Ten

Dorothy's mam and dad were in the bedroom next to ours, so I went and woke them up and said that I was going to the phone box to phone for the ambulance. I got back to find Dorothy being sick and really not feeling well at all. We hadn't long to wait for the ambulance and we knew the two crew on it. They had just come from seeing a prospective mother into hospital and she had been the same as Dorothy being sick. After a short while Dorothy stopped being sick long enough to get her into the ambulance and off we went to Northallerton.

The following morning, August Bank Holiday Sunday, Dorothy presented me with a beautiful baby girl weighing five pounds eight ounces, and doing very well. So much for the consultant who had said she wouldn't have the baby until the beginning of September – which goes to show that the patient should always be listened to, as Dorothy had told him he was wrong and that the baby would be born the first week in August. As she was. August Bank Holiday was always the first week in August in those days. After about ten days, Dorothy and baby came home and I was walking on cloud nine again.

It felt funny and I could hardly believe that I was a proud dad. I now had quite a few letters to write, one to the tax office to get my tax rebate and change my tax code, most important that, when you have little or no money, as the wrong code can make all the difference.

All our families were duly notified, mainly by our parents, and then we had to decide on a name. Dorothy and I thought that we would have names with no more than five letters and only have one forename. That was how we arrived at Hazel, who I called "my pride and joy". Hazel came into our lives little in weight but for the next nine months, for one being so tiny she made one hell of a noise crying. I blame spending a week or so at now nana and granddad Woods. When Dorothy and Hazel came out of hospital, she was never allowed to cry; as soon as she whimpered, granddad would be there

118

rocking the pram to soothe her, and this it did.

When we got back into our own home I thought things would be different but it wasn't. Bear in mind, I was working at Leyburn and catching the seven-o-clock bus each morning and by the time I had walked the floor trying to get Hazel to sleep, dawn was breaking. I've known times when I would get into bed and go flat out and then the door was being knocked down by the bus driver shouting "get yourself down here now if you're going to work". I must have had about two hours sleep and the worst thing was Dorothy would be out for the count and never heard a thing. Another annoying thing was when Dorothy looked after her during the day, Hazel slept. I thought "there's no justice in this world".

For all the trouble and upset, our Hazel really was "my pride and joy", and Dorothy and I loved every minute of it day and night. While I was at work, Dorothy had a lot of visitors popping in to see the new baby and have a cup of tea. Hazel wasn't getting any better at going to sleep and my mother said "you are bringing a rod to your own back; let her cry, she'll soon get the idea that when she cries she won't always get picked up". "Right," I said, "we'll try this" and at night-time when Dorothy put her in her cot we swore we would not lift her out tonight. As soon as she was put into her cot and covered up she cried. She cried and continued to cry and we felt terrible letting her. Dorothy went to her once after an hour's non-stop crying to see that she was okay and as soon as she put her arms around her she stopped crying. Hazel was just playing us up and let me say hear and now it was punishment to us letting her cry but it was the only way or else we would not be able to look after her during the day and I couldn't do my work properly. That night she cried for three solid hours and sobbed the rest of the night.

We felt proper pigs doing that but it had to be done. The next night we weren't looking forward to putting Hazel to bed but we had to and down she went at bedtime. The crying lasted only one and a half hours this time and the third night, as soon as Dorothy laid Hazel's head on the pillow and kissed her, she was asleep before she left the bedroom. We both felt that night that we had won the battle but it nearly crucified us doing so. I swore that if we had any more kids we would not make the same mistake again because it was cruel, not only to us but also to the baby. From then on things got better and we were enjoying our evenings together without the exercise of walking the floor.

I was enjoying my work and pleasure time at both the youth club and band practise. Moving on, nothing spectacular happened at work, except that I was sent to our Duke Street branch in Darlington to be the manager for a fortnight while the regular manager was on holiday. This was my first experience of managing a store and what an experience it turned out to be.

I got there by bus, leaving Richmond at seven-thirty and getting to Darlington at ten-past-eight. The shop was supposed to open at eight-thirty but at twenty-to-nine only the girl with the keys came. The rest of them, there were five, arrived at five-minute intervals and best of all three of them were heavily pregnant. I immediately laid down the law to them and told them if it happened again action would be taken. During the morning the grocery manager buyer, the boss of all grocery managers, phoned to see how I was getting on and I told him that he had asked me manage a harem of pregnant women who filed in at their leisure. Mr Gamble – that was his name – told me not to stand for this and if it happened again I had to send them down to his office in Priestgate and he would send replacements. It did happen the next morning so I told them they had been warned yesterday and sent them packing, or should I say waddling, down to the office. Alf Gamble was as good as his word and sent (thank goodness) three good girls. After that we all got on well and everything went smoothly. I enjoyed those two weeks, mainly because that branch's half day was Saturday and I thought it was my birthday having two Saturday afternoons off.

When Hazel was about seven months old I got promoted. The Co-op was opening a branch on a brand new estate called Cutpurse Lane Estate and I was to be the manager. The staff had been employed and I was told to take them to the shop and familiarise ourselves with the layout by filling the shelves, etc. It was lovely stocking a brand new shop the way I wanted. The staff I had were two young ladies and they turned out to be superb assistants. One was called Doni, the other Dorothy, and we worked as a team from day one.

On the day of the opening, Dorothy and I had a good laugh at the expense of the ladies of the local committee. Above the shop was a beautiful three-bedroom flat which we were given to live in at a rent of thirty shillings a week, with no rates to pay. It was tiled throughout and also had a window box and a veranda where Dorothy could put baby in the pram where she would get fresh air while sleeping and Dorothy was working.

Well on the day of the official opening, I warned the people living next door to us to lock their flat as we could possibly get some nosy old parkers of the committee wanting to see our flat. We were locking ours as they had no right to look at our private abode. Dorothy had been downstairs to see the GM open the shop and chat to some friends and was on her way back when she came face to face with two of the committee ladies. "My, you've soon got your flat looking nice Dorothy," they said, and Dorothy gave them a lovely smile and said: "But you haven't been round my flat, you have just been in Mr and Mrs Kipling's, good morning." Dorothy told me later on that I should have seen their faces and that they had scuttled off as fast as they could.

Let me tell you of another incident while I was at Cutpurse Lane branch. This being a new estate, the majority of tenants were young couples like Dorothy and I, and we had a lot of close friends living on the estate. Well one day I was serving some of these friends and we were having a bit of a banter and the language wasn't all it should have been in the shop, but there was only us in, when in walked my GM accompanied by the company secretary. "That's it," I said to my pals, "that's me out of a job" because he must have heard us. He had heard us and after the formal "good morning Mr Shout" he remarked "are you that familiar with all your customers Mr Shout?" My mind was in turmoil and I thought "oh hell, tell the truth" so I did. "Yes Mr Jennings, I am, especially to that lot out there. If I was polite to them they would think there's something wrong with me." I waited for the reply with baited breath. "Good," he said, "I like someone who knows his or her customers well, carry on".

Later that day I saw some of the friends that had been in and the first thing they wanted to know was how did the GM treat me after hearing all that banter.

Dorothy was finding it handy living at Cutpurse as we were near to one of my sisters who lived at Earl Edwin Drive, which was about four hundred yards away, and she would go to our Norah's for coffee and a chat or Norah would call on her. Also the bus stopped right outside our flat if she wanted to go into town. One of the drawbacks was that she had to leave the baby in the pram in the flat if she needed to go into the garden to hang out washing. Dorothy didn't like doing this, so she used to put a line across the balcony and would hang it there.

We stayed in this flat above the shop at Cutpurse for eighteen months, in which time Dorothy fell pregnant again. At this time I should say that my sister Norah had got cancer and was very very ill and it was only a matter of time before she would leave us. It was very upsetting to see her deteriorate so quickly, so much so, that Dorothy had been to see her and it so upset her blood pressure, etc, that the nurse attending Dorothy told her not to go and see Norah again. That was the sad part of time then, the good part was my youngest sister Nancy was getting married very shortly. Well to cut the story short, we had a birth, a marriage and a death in that order on three consecutive weekends. Moira was our second child and the birth was at home. When it got near to the time of the birth, our neighbours Ernie and Doris told us they would leave their door unlocked and when Dorothy started I could go into their flat and phone the midwife, because we had no phone in our flat.

It was sod's law that the night that Dorothy started having the baby, Ernie had forgotten to leave the door unlocked, so I had to knock them up. Both Ernie and Doris were most apologetic and came into our flat to keep us company. On reflection, I wished Ernie hadn't come in to us as he was a nervous wreck and when the midwife came and saw that Dorothy was just about to give birth he got worse. He was making me nearly as bad as he was, so I suggested he light the fire. Poor Ernie was all fingers and thumbs but did eventually get the fire lit. I was meant to see the baby being born but she came so quickly that the nurse didn't have time to shout to me until Moira was born. What a lovely moment that was, when I walked into the bedroom seconds after Moira was born and gave Dorothy and baby a big kiss.

Those moments one never forgets, like when Ernie and Doris came in to see them both, Ernie had all his water on to stop himself from crying. This birthday was March 18th 1958. The next Saturday our Nancy was married to Dr John Hilton, a plant manager at ICI, and their wedding was a real happy occasion, with John and my dad dressed in top hat and tails. I still think that my father looked the smartest man present dressed in all his tails. The doctors and nurses that were attending our Norah had arranged to give her just enough morphine so she could see Nancy in her wedding dress when they called to see her. It seemed that she had hung on to life to see Nancy married, because the next Sunday morning my brother Denis came up to tell us that Norah had died that night, and that's how we got a birth, marriage and death in so short a time.

It was an eventful year 1958, as not only was Moira born but also my younger brother Fred went to Canada to teach in a one-teacher school. This made him headmaster, janitor and general dogsbody, but being all this, the pay was good, as I think no Canadians wanted such a position.

At work we had another chap join the staff called Frank Grievson who in his spare time was a hypnotist. Frank and I got on okay and he suggested one day that I go with him to a venue and help him put on a show of hypnotism. I jumped at this chance as I had never seen a hypnotist work before. The venue where he was doing his demonstration was at Dalton Young Farmer's meeting in the village hall. On the way to Dalton, Frank told me what he was going to do and what I had to do. He was going to get them under, as the saying goes, and then hand them over to me to do some simple things.

The hall was packed with young farmers, men and women, from around the area all eager to see and wondering what was going to happen. Frank got the whole of the audience to take part in a simple exercise to see who would be the easiest to hypnotise. He chose eight, five lads and three girls, and with these eight we had a smashing night. Without going into the whole sequence of events, we had them marching round the room, each one playing a different instrument which they thought they had, to smoking and the cigarette tasting like burnt socks, and others, every time they saw a certain playing card, had to stand up and shout Hallelujah and then drop off back to sleep. Not only did I enjoy it but also the audience went mad and loved it, so much that they kept us there till the hall keeper chucked us out at eleven-o-clock.

I got better the more the more shows we did and soon we were in demand all over the area. We went to another demo in Richmond and were the guests of the Round Table, and among the members were two doctors who were very interested in the subject, so we had to put on a special show. We did all the usual things to start with and then we stretched one lad between two chairs about two feet apart. We then asked another member to come and sit on the middle of the outstretched volunteer. Everyone was very impressed by this and we were asked all sorts of questions about what could and could not be done by hypnotism. Frank explained that everyone could be hypnotised except the insane. But you always get one clever so and so in every audience and this night was no exception.

One cocky gentleman said: "I'm not insane but I bet you can't hypnotise me." Now we had noticed when doing our first exercise that he was one of the best to be hypnotised so Frank said to him, words to the effect of "okay maybe I can't, but have you a vivid imagination?" "I think so," came the reply. So Frank went over to him, placed his thumb in the middle of his scalp and said: "Can you, for instance, imagine that where I have my thumb there is a hole in your head, and try and look through that hole."

Before two minutes had passed, Frank had him under his control, hypnotised, and of course the audience wanted us to make him do something stupid. Frank did; he made him act like a baby when he awoke him and when he put him back to sleep he told him that all he would remember when he brought him out of the deep sleep would be just that. Well he acted like a baby and he knew it, and it took quite a while before he realised that he had been hypnotised, much to the delight of the rest of the meeting.

We did a lot of demos while Frank worked with me at the Co-op, right up to when he went away to take up a manager's job. When Dorothy had been in hospital having Hazel, she had made friends with a girl called Marjorie, who had given birth to her first child, a little girl called Linda. And she and her husband Ron became our friends and still are up to this day.

In those early days we used to go to Thirsk where they lived or they would come through to our house. I shan't forget one time that we had gone through to see them and had got on talking about hypnotism and Marjorie asked me to hypnotise her. Well Marjorie was a giggly sort of person and no way could I get her to concentrate and in the end Ron told her to get a hold of herself and listen to me. I was stood behind her and Ron was sitting next to her and listening intently to what I was saying, and after a few minutes, I hadn't got Marjorie under control but I had Ron.

This made my day as now I could have some real fun under these conditions. First I told Ron he would hear only my voice and he would do whatever I told him. This was lovely, the first thing I told him was, as he was sitting next to a real sweet good looking lady, would I introduce her to him, as she was a complete stranger and really fancied her. I clicked my fingers and he came alive to us and straight away he said "hello" to Marge. "Who are you, you are lovely. Doug, do you know who this lovely lady is?" "Yes," I replied, "it's Mary Ann from across the road, she's on holiday." Ron really did us proud as he started chatting up his own wife. Marg kept saying to him to stop being so stupid, you are not hypnotised but Ron was having none of it; he carried on saying things like I've not seen you around here and so on. I asked him to do other things for around half an hour before I woke him up. Marjorie was relieved when she got her Ron back to herself. We had a really great evening.

Also this year, 1958, my brother Fred had gone to Canada and my younger sister Francis (Nancy) had got married on March 22nd. Late in the year Dorothy fell pregnant again and on July 3rd 1959 she presented me with twin girls.

Let me tell you about this pregnancy. Dorothy never felt one hundred per cent as she had done carrying the first two but carried on gamely with the nurse calling frequently. Every time the nurse examined Dorothy she had difficulty finding the heartbeat and/or finding a heartbeat in two places. Dorothy was piling on the weight and not feeling too good, so she went to see the doctor, Dr Mac. He put her in hospital, as he was frightened about her high blood pressure and toxaemia.

She was sent in for a rest, as Dr Mac knew she wouldn't rest at home, and she still had another two months to go. Well I went visiting as one good husband does, plus the fact it was fathers only at that time, and we were given visiting cards which were collected off us as we went in.

On July 3rd when I went to visit, all the fathers were in the waiting room waiting until a man would come in and say we could go in now and see our spouses. Well this day as he collected the cards off us he was looking at each one as we handed them in and I wondered what on earth was he doing that for, as it was slowing up the process. When he got to me, and I handed him the card he said: "Oh, Mr Shout will you call at the sister's office before you go to the ward." He stopped looking at the cards now that he had seen me so I wondered what was so special that I had to see the sister before I saw Dorothy.

I knocked on the sister's office door and went in. The sister said: "Oh, Mr Shout isn't it?" "Yes," I said, "what's up?" "Well your wife's got it over with" or words similar to that. "What do you mean?" I remember saying and before I could say another word she said, pushing me into a chair, "you had better sit down". I'd better sit down, I thought. I was pushed down really and I began to worry that something had happened to Dorothy. Had she died? All sorts of things were running through my brain. The sister went on: "Mrs Shout has just given birth to twins." Now I knew what the sit down business was all about. I honestly think the sister thought that I would pass out or have a heart attack. I'm made of sterner stuff than that I think, I hasten to add, but I was delighted to say the least.

The sister went on to tell me that Dorothy had just gone back to the ward and the babies were in incubators and that one of them was having difficulty breathing. "This does happen sometimes," she said, "as the lungs weren't fully expanded and it takes a few hours to get them back to normal," or something like that was said. She took me to see the babies and I had to put on a hat, mask and gown. When I saw them I knew what she meant, because the larger baby was heaving as though she was breathing from her stomach. Her little chest was going up and down and I didn't like the look of her at all but sister said she could be okay shortly and that the doctor was coming back in a few minutes.

After losing half a stone being in the premature baby room, dressed in cap and gown, and it also being the hottest day of the year, I went to see my lovely wife. Poor Dorothy, after all the hard work of giving birth to twins and them not knowing that there were twins there, the nurses had just rushed Dorothy back to bed without a wash or clean up, as visiting was due. It was Dorothy that had held up the proceedings, so I told her so with a huge smile on my face and gave her a big hug and kiss and told her how much I loved her.

The next day Dorothy had to give the baby girls names, as one was in difficulty, but also this was practice when twins were born. Dorothy had all the ward suggesting names with only five letters in them as this is what we had agreed earlier, that all our children, even if we had a football team, their names would be short with no more than five letters in each. So we came to Paula and Carol. I've got a bit ahead of myself telling you that information, so let me go back to after visiting on the day they were born. Going home I felt on top of the world, me being the proud father of twin girls, and wondered what would our parents say. As I walked up the path to Dorothy's parents house I pondered on how I could tell them, or how should I tell them. I didn't have time to work it out, as before I reached their front door I was nearly running and burst into their sitting room where mam and dad Wood were sitting.

As they saw me come running into the house they jumped up and looking startled asked what was wrong. "You had better sit down," I seem to remember saying to them. "I've got such superb news for you." "Well spit it out," dad Wood said, getting more and more agitated with the suspense. "Well," I said, "you are the grandparents of twins." I was really glad that I had told mam to sit down because she was so overcome by the news that she didn't know whether to laugh or cry. Instead she got up out of her chair and came over to me and hugged me for, it seemed, an hour. "Is Dorothy all right?" she said in my ear, not letting me out of her hug. "Yes," I replied, "Dorothy's fine but one of the babies is having difficulty in breathing." "Oh dear, is she going to be all right"?."The sister said this does happen now and again until the lungs start functioning properly," I said.

When they had settled down, I went along the road to tell my mam and dad. I got just about the same reaction there, as my mother said: "How are you going to manage now with four girls and the oldest isn't three yet? You'll have your work cut out now my boy." On the whole, everybody was delighted, no one more than my father who said "well that calls for a drink or two" and two or maybe three he had.

I slept very little that night, with my thoughts working overtime. My mother's words kept coming back to me, how were we going to manage? Mixed with the excitement and joy I was feeling, no wonder when I awoke the next day I felt as if I had never been to bed. Anyway the day dawned and off I went to see my super mum Dorothy again. When I got to her bedside she told me that she had had to have the babies christened Paula and Carol and that the doctors were seeing to Carol at this moment because she hadn't improved and was not responding to treatment.

I hadn't been at Dorothy's bedside long when the doctor came in and told us that Carol had died. From utter joy one minute to acute sadness the next. All I could do was comfort Dorothy the best I could and she was comforting me at the same time. I left the hospital that night the saddest man alive, as I knew when I got home I had to tell both our parents and I wasn't looking forward to that. Well without going into a great deal of the events at that time, we all got over it to a larger or lesser extent, and all that remained was the funeral.

Again I'm not reliving all that again, sufficient to say that that was the most heartbreaking experience that I have ever had to endure. Carrying Carol in a white satin covered coffin was about as much as I could endure.

Going back to our own home in Cutpurse Lane we learned to settle down again and get on with our lives. One thing that did start to bug us was that we were feeling a bit cramped in the flat, what with having to lift the pram up and down the stairs, and managing the kids while we did this was no mean feat.

Luck was on our side for a change and as the saying goes "it's not what you know, but who you know that counts". A friend of ours was a councillor and we had a talk with her and she agreed that it was nearly impossible to cope with three children under three years old in an upstairs flat and that she would push our case to the council to get a house. Joyce, our councillor friend, not only got us a house but also got us one on the same estate, for which I was grateful.

The year now was 1960 and we got settled in No 13 Norman Road, a three-bedroom house with gardens at front and back. The garden at the back was a nice size and getting it planted up kept me busy. It also meant that Dorothy could hang her washing out and also put baby to sleep in the pram and keep an eye on her as well.

Also this year I was running two youth clubs for which I got a small remuneration. I, along with another friend, started the YMCA Youth Club, and we had some real lads in that youth club. The other club that I was asked to form and run was the Melsonby and Aldborough Youth Club. This was a different type of membership, being mainly lads that worked on the land in the two villages. I should say that we also had girls in that youth club.

At the YMCA we only had boys and some were big boys not averse to looking after themselves. Knowing the lads like I did, Fred my partner and I made only one rule and kept to it. That was, that there was to be no fighting on the club premises and they honoured that rule. We also allowed young servicemen into the club and made them very welcome. But one night three came in and were walking up to the coffee bar, which incidentally we built, when one noticed that one of our lads had a pony tail hair style and said to his mates: "I wonder where his handbag his?" Fortunately, I heard this and immediately looked across at our three members to see if they had heard it. They had and they saw me looking at them, knowing what my rule was. I told the three soldiers that I had heard the remark and warned them any more of that and they would be out but they denied making any remark so I left it at that knowing full well that my lads wouldn't leave it at that. When the three soldiers left, the whole club membership left with them. Fred and I couldn't do anything about it but they abided by the club rules that there was to be no fighting in the club – and there wasn't. I'll leave it to your imagination as to what happened.

One thing that we did shine at was our quiz team, who reached the national final of the Youth Club Quiz competition. Unfortunately, we couldn't attend the final due to many circumstances and had to settle for a semi-final position. We enjoyed travelling all over the place to take part in it and made many more friends too.

The Melsonby and Aldorough YC was the brainchild of a Major Reynolds who lived in Melsonby and it was he who approached me about starting a club. The major was a good man but he thought he was still in the army and the kids resented this so much that I had to tell him to cool it. He tried but couldn't get over the kids not jumping when he shouted. To raise funds for us, the major would hold a garden party at his home and all the villagers would be invited. He had a large garden perfect for these occasions and in these activities he was brilliant, using all his army training to get people involved in the games and nearly forcing money from them. The garden party would be a huge success and he in particular would be so pleased.

Let me tell you about what happened to our family on the way to the party. I got Dorothy, Hazel, Moira and Paula into the car at home and set off. We had to come round a sharp corner on the estate and as I turned the corner our Paula fell out of the car, hurting her wrist, which turned out to be a green stick fracture. It never stopped us going to the garden party, though, and even Paula enjoyed all the fuss that was made of her. That event made Paula and the others always check that the car door was shut properly.

In the autumn of this year, I was down town banking the shops takings and called in to see Mr Robinson at the big branch and was surprised to learn from him that he was leaving to retire. Now this was a shock to the system, as I never thought of Mr Robinson retiring, although I don't know why I should have thought this. When I finished work that night, I pondered on this and tried to work out who would fill his position, bearing in mind that Richmond grocery branch was the top branch in the society, with only the central branch being higher in prestige. It also carried the highest wages of all the managers, including the central branch, I was to find out later on.

I went through all the names of the fellas that had left Richmond and were managing good shops in Darlington and other towns and villages in the society. In the end I came to the conclusion that I would get this, the best job in the grocery department. Mr Robinson had told me many years earlier that I was going to be the last manager he trained and hoped that I would be the best. He must have been thinking along the same lines as me, because the next time I saw him he took me into the office and said "you will get this job". He had worked this out the same way that I had. One man wouldn't leave his shop at Leyburn because of his children who were at critical stages in their schooling; another wouldn't leave Darlington to come back to Richmond; and others had similar reasons – and all of them because they didn't know what the wages were. They thought that being in the country the wages wouldn't be as good as they were getting in town. They forgot that Richmond was the largest branch.

I was working away in my shop one day just before Mr Robinson was due to leave, and in walked my GM and department manager. After the usual formalities, the GM asked me if I would like to be promoted to Leyburn branch, this being a lot bigger shop and a big rise in wages for me. He knew I had worked there and done a good job and went on to say a cartload of bull about being the manager there. How you were a pillar of society and would be well respected as the present manager was. I knew all this but Frank the manager had lived there all his life and I knew, but the GM didn't, that Frank wouldn't uproot from all his friends for just a few quid more. The GM went on: "We have to ask you if you would be prepared to move to Leyburn before we ask Mr Laughlan if he will take the manager's job at Richmond. We know that you would require housing and thought that we would buy his house which would put you up for the time being." I said that I would be delighted to manage Leyburn providing that what he had said about the housing was okay with my wife, and I was sure that it would be.

After hearing what he had wanted to hear, he departed to go to Leyburn and ask Frank to be the big branch manager. As soon as he had got into his car, I was on the phone to Frank to tell him the good news that he was about to receive. Frank didn't give the GM an answer one way or another that day but he did ring me and told me all I wanted to know – for instance, the wages that he had been offered. It was, as I thought; the GM hadn't offered Frank the wages that I knew Mr Robinson was being paid, only I knew that. The one thing that Mr Robinson had told me before he left was "don't let the GM reduce your wages, as he will certainly try". Because the wage that he was getting was made up because he was doing the work that the general office did at Darlington. His words came true when Frank told me what he had been offered. Me being a shrewd man and a gentleman didn't make him any the wiser, as it was now every man for himself. I knew that my friend who was managing Barnard Castle branch thought he stood a good chance of getting this top shop and once again I made him no wiser.

Anyway, a decision was to be made at the next weekly board meeting, which was on a Monday evening, so for that week a lot of speculation was bounding around, and me saying nothing at all. On the Tuesday morning after the board meeting, I got my staff together at 8.30 a.m. as soon as we opened the shop and told them that the phone would ring at approximately ten-past-nine and they were not to answer it, as it would be the GM for me. The mentioning of the GM was enough for my staff to stay clear of the phone all day. At ten-past-nine the phone did ring and I answered it in my usual calm and polite manner: "Cutpurse Lane, how can I help you?" I said down the phone, my heart beating like a bass drum. "Congratulations Mr Shout, I have pleasure in informing you that at the board meeting last night the board selected you to manage Richmond Grocery. You are a big boss now Mr Shout and I want you to go down and take over from Mr Robinson today. You are the best man for the job and I know that you won't let me down, good day" and the phone went dead. "Yes, yes, yes," I shouted so loud that I think they could have heard me a mile away.

My staff, who had known that I had been fighting for this top job, were delighted for me and Doni and Dot said that I had better go and let my wife know about it. I ran out of the shop and up to Norman Road flat out and told Dorothy the good news. I think we did a quick waltz round the living room and then I left to go down town the other shop. I went straight into the office and found Mr Robinson doing some paper work and told him that I was to take over from him today.

I didn't like doing it this way as he and I had got on famously and being the perfect gentleman he offered me his congratulations and best wishes. He said: "Doug, there is nothing I can show you about running this shop. As I told you years ago, you were going to be the best one I have turned out, so for the rest of the week you can resume where you left off eighteen months ago and I can take it easy."

We collected for a leaving present, which I presented to him on the

Saturday. For the life of me I can't remember what it was we bought him but he was feeling very emotional when he thanked everybody and said a lot of kind words about me. Then I was emotional and to be honest I was glad when I locked the shop for the weekend.

The years passed and we were very happy both at work and at home. At work I made good progress both with sales and the staff. I was complimented on managing the store so well and getting excellent reports each time an official made a visit.

At home our Hazel was now eight years old, Moira seven and Paula six, and I remember one Christmas stands out about this time. On Christmas Eve we put the girls to bed and told them to go straight to sleep as Father Christmas was on his way. Well being excited and being children they couldn't go to sleep straight away, could they, I never did when I was a child. Once they had got over to sleep we started getting all the presents out that we had hidden from them and put them into piles on chairs. One chair for each girl and, to make things look good, one for mam and dad. This little exercise took a bit of time and by the time we had finished we were ready for bed.

Now in previous years, the girls always woke up too early and rushed downstairs to see if the great man had been and finding all the presents there we couldn't send them back to bed could we? So we just had to stay up and open the parcels. This made it one long day, not only for the kids but for the parents as well. So this year I said to Dorothy to stop them going into the living room too early I suggested we write a note saying 'Do not enter, Father Christmas in room' and pinned it on the living room door. It worked a treat, we heard them go down the stairs, and saw the note. "What does it say Hazel," our Paula said, and Hazel, after reading it, said most urgently to the other two "get back, get back upstairs, he's in there now, Father Christmas is in our living room, get back to bed". We heard them scuttle back up stairs, really worried and dashed into bed, being as quiet as they could be trying not to wake us up. Dorothy and I were cracking our sides, laughing our heads off under the sheets trying not to make a noise. We gave them a minute or two to calm down, then Dorothy went in to see them and told them to go back to sleep so Father Christmas could leave in peace. It worked, they went back to sleep and didn't wake up till half past six, which was a lot better than half past four.

Every Christmas was special in one way or another and all of us looked forward to it for weeks before. I took the girls to buy a present for their mam and Dorothy would take them to buy one for me, all very secret you know. The girls would come out saying things like: "You don't know where we've been today dad do you, and I'm not telling you." Usually, one of them would accidentally let it slip that they had been shopping to buy me a present. The best years of your life are when your young innocent children are around you.

We were down at my mam's house one day and my dad was putting his boots on whilst sitting in a chair and Paula was watching him. After he had got them on and laced up he saw Paula looking at his boots. I don't think she had seen boots before and I heard him say to her "did you see that fly go into there?" pointing at one of the lace holes. Paula replied "no I didn't, did it go right in?" Dad had Paula right agitated as she hadn't seen any flies going into granddad's boots and in the end she said "oh granddad you are telling lies" and walked away in disgust. Dad said in return "you are too clever for your own good" and left it at that.

A similar thing happened when our friends from Thirsk were staying with us for a holiday. The side wall of our living room was eighteen-foot long with no windows; so to brighten it up we papered an eight-foot mural of Lake Mount Shasta in Canada on it. Actually it was two four-foot ones as a mirror image and lining the lake there were fir trees. It was a beautiful picture and I made it look like a large window. I put a pelmet above it with a strip light set into it and curtains down the side of it. Along the bottom I made a windowsill to complete the picture and make it look like a window. It was fun at night time when we lit it up and people on the buses passing by would turn their heads so to see as much as possible of it. It was a talking point amongst our neighbours.

Anyway I digress, back to Paula again. One afternoon we were sat in the living room talking away and Ron, our friend from Thirsk, started looking intently at the mural and the kids asked him what was he looking at? "Didn't you see that man go behind those trees?" he said. "What man, what trees?" said Paula and Tony, Tony being Ron's son. "There, look," Ron replied pointing to a bunch of trees on the mural. They were baffled because they didn't see any man go behind the trees. This kept all the kids intent on catching the man going behind the trees all afternoon, until our Hazel the eldest came in and spoilt the illusion and told them that Uncle Ron was having them on.

It was also about this time that Moira took ill and we had to get the doctor to see her. She frightened us, as she was delirious, having illusions and didn't always know us, as well as running a high temperature. So we were more than pleased when the doc arrived. It was a locum doctor who diagnosed scarlet fever, the doctor was an old man and he frightened Dorothy and I by his remarks. He was obviously one of the old school and would have had us putting up damp sheets around the bed along with other daft ideas.

It was hard work bringing up the three children in those years and it was going to get harder. Hazel was now nine years old and Dorothy did the dirty on me by becoming pregnant again. It was good luck and best wishes from everyone and I can't forget mother's words to me when she remarked: "Well I hope it's a boy this time, to carry on the family name." It didn't bother me in the least, as I always said that I would like daughters in preference to boys and I got my wish again. Sonia was born on September 19th 1965 and I was there at the birth. Oh what a night that was, I repeat what a night. Dorothy had started in labour at 6.30 in the morning and her mother came up to sit with her and keep her company. The nurse had called and said that she would be back later to see how she was getting on. I took the children down to Sunday school and Dorothy's sister Sheila took them to her house for dinner and then brought them back at bedtime. I put them to bed, kissed them after they had kissed their mam and told them to go straight to sleep.

At 7 p.m. Nurse Reed called again and after a short while things began to happen, and at ten-twenty Sonia was born. Dorothy had been in labour for sixteen hours and was not only excited but also exhausted, bless her. Sheila had just left and was going to catch the bus home, when she heard the baby cry being born and returned to see if she was all right. Of course she was and she stayed a while longer before getting a taxi home to tell her father.

Another friend of ours was there as well, and that was Joan, who had said that she would come and look after the children while Dorothy was in bed. So much went on that week and everyone was most helpful and considerate. It would take me a month to tell you all that went on but Dorothy's mam was a gem, helping us and running her own home as well.

Leaving all that excitement for a while, let me say I still had to go to work and still run the youth club. At work the company ran a window dressing competition and I put a lot of thought into the design. Whether to do a modern window or an old fashioned colourful one? If I knew who was going to judge it would have been much easier to decide but we didn't know. I put on a modern design using little product but elegant lines of design. I am proud to say that I won that competition as I was the only one that dressed using a modern design. My winnings were a week's course at Dalton Hall Carlisle an annex of Loughborough College, sponsored by the CWS. I had to wait quite a time before I could get there but the waiting was well worth it. The hall was marvellous, as were the facilities there, anything you needed to create a display was at hand, and I gained my Diploma in

Display and Advertising with excellent marks.

It was always a great pleasure to return home and be greeted by Dorothy and the girls. One never knows how much you miss them until you go away. This year was also a sad one as my father was taken into Scorton Hospital with lung cancer and after being in a week or two he died. The memories of him I still cherish, how strong he was for such a little man. One never forgets loving parents.

Let me go on to a more happy memory. Charlie our deliveryman used to come up to our house every morning to take me to work. As I've said before, Charlie wasn't just one of my staff, he was a good friend too. On the mornings when the kids weren't dressed he would dress them. His intentions were good but on a lot of occasions Dorothy would have to re-dress them as he had put some of the clothes on the wrong child, and others he would have put on back to front and so on. The trouble was that as soon as the girls saw him they would want him to dress them. "I want Uncle Charlie to dress me" was the favourite statement and we couldn't do a thing about it then. Other times he would recite little poems or rhymes to them while Dorothy was doing their hair. One of his favourite verses was:

"Little fly upon the wall, aint you got no clothes at all,
Aint you got a shimmy shirty, cor blimey aint you dirty."

The girls always liked that one so they got it plenty of times.

Chapter Eleven

Getting back to the goings on at work, on Saturday afternoons the local committee would have their board meetings at the shop and a member of the main board always used to come and I would always have a chat with them. This particular Saturday the main board member was one of my favourite members, as he would discuss what was happening within the society. On this occasion we got on talking about the dividend we were paying and I told him quite calmly that in my opinion we had got away from the principle of the Rochdale Pioneers, that the company should sell at the cheapest possible price, and at the end of each quarter if there was any profit left after all expenses and costs, it should be paid back to the members as dividend. I went on (I was in full swing now, on my soap box) that we weren't doing this but that we were budgeting to pay a dividend. We carried on chatting and I never gave it another thought.

But on the following Tuesday morning I had a phone call from the GM asking me what I was doing lecturing his member of the board. Well I was flabbergasted and I told him so and went on to tell him what had gone on. He rather surprised me when he replied in a nice quiet voice, "please (and he used the word 'please') don't say too much to any of them; it's taken me all this time to get them to do what I want them to do and it only takes a wrong word from a manager and they think that they are no longer in control". I put the phone down and chuckled to myself. I would have loved to bring up that subject again the next time that member of the board came but I didn't dare.

Everything was going along quite nicely at work though, until after stocktaking one half-year end, after all the figures had been worked out, I found that I had a big leakage, which was very unusual as I had always had a little surplus. Leakage is another word for discrepancy. This turned out most peculiar as all the branches – and I mean all the branches – had a leakage and going through my figures again and again I couldn't find out where the problem was. At the same time as the half-year end results were circulated, I was attending a course on the treatment of bacon.

All the managers attended the course, half going in the morning, the other half in the afternoon, and I was in that group. What took place during these lessons was that the GM had two managers in to see him one at a time and he wiped the floor with them over their leakages. One of my group was our trade union representative, Arthur. Now Arthur was an old guy but a nice chap, the only thing was, he was the nervous type and used to shake a little. Now when he came out of the GM's office he was in one hell of a state. After the lesson had finished I spoke to Arthur and asked him what had been said. "He practically inferred that I had been pinching or doing something, meaning that I got the blooming money." Jokingly I said: "Have you then Arthur?" "Look," I said to him, "if you haven't got any idea where it's gone then you are no different to the rest of us, why didn't you throw the shop keys at him?" "It's all right for you," Arthur replied, "but I haven't got long to go before I retire on pension." By this time a lot more of the managers were listening when I said "well I would have". The GM really did scare a lot of my colleagues because like Arthur they were thinking of their pensions.

Three weeks later there were only two of us left to go to the slaughter when the GM's personal assistant came into the room and said "Mr Shout, Mr Jennings wants to see you". All of us in the meeting were friends and when my name came up they gave me a real cheering send-off to see the GM. Before I went to that meeting that day I had said to my first hand Ruby "I'm taking the keys with me today and if the boss starts on me I'll throw them at him". As soon as I got into the GM's office, I got the feeling that he meant business with me as I had the worst result of all. "Sit down," he said and I was a bit surprised by his manner when he said that, because he was always polite and civil whenever he spoke to anyone. "You know what you are here for Mr Shout," he said, and I replied "not really". This took him by surprise, me being so cocky. "It's this leakage, you've got the worst in the company, what have you got to say to that?" His PA was stood by his side. He was a young man, very qualified, and with me very amiable, we had never had a wrong word between us. Now feeling very comfortable with myself I replied: "Every instruction that you sent out and every visit of inspection that he has carried out has been carried out to the letter. If you look at his reports on my shop you will not find one bad one and I have carried out useful procedures of my own which I have gained from experience." "How many numbers do you have Mr Shout?", the numbers being the ones for getting the dividend. I couldn't believe what I had just heard coming from him, as each person could only have one dividend number. So I told him. I got the impression that he didn't like that remark. I gave him my number, 37188. He then told his PA to go and get the voucher for that number. The voucher was a sheet of paper showing how much had been spent on that number and how much dividend would be paid on it.

The PA brought the voucher and gave it to the GM. He studied it and his face (I think) had a wry smile on it, because it showed that I had only spent thirty-seven pounds in the last quarter. "Where do you do your shopping?" was the GM's next question. I knew what he was getting at and that was how I had spent so little when we did all our shopping at the Co-op; it wasn't anywhere near what it should have been. "We do all our shopping at the Co-op," I replied. I was now beginning to enjoy this interview, knowing what he was going to say next. "Well for a man and wife with four children this doesn't run true Mr Shout does it?" I think he detected a little smirk on my face then, so I replied: "That voucher shows the amount that I have spent Mr Jennings, me only. I buy my cigarettes and coal and the odd personal thing but that isn't our main shopping account. What you want to look at if you think I'm on the fiddle is my wife's number, that's 49653." And with that I saw his jaw drop six inches and he then sent his PA to get that voucher. He returned with the voucher, handed it to the boss and from then on the atmosphere cleared and from being at each other's throats we got back to being civil again. As Dorothy's voucher declared she had spent one hundred and fifty seven pounds, this making a total of one hundred and ninety four pounds. This was a considerable sum in those days and the GM realised this and soon we were talking about anything but the leakage and I departed with a "good day Mr Jennings" and the shop keys still in my pocket.

I didn't realise what time it was until I was walking with Mr G, the PA, along through the main general offices and there was no one there. Mr Graney said to me as we were walking out that I was the luckiest man alive. "How do you get that?" I said. He replied: "Every manager has been rollicked by Mr Jennings and you get away Scot free." "Hold on a minute," I said and stopped him in his tracks. "He tried to wipe the floor with me but it didn't come off because I'm not like you or the rest of them that let him spout off, I'm not frightened of him. I've always found Mr J to be the person to talk to if I want anything doing, as I know then it gets done, so don't you ever think that I'll bow down to you or anyone if I think I'm right. I call a spade a spade and that's me." I wished him good night and left the office at 6.15 p.m.

The next day at work I knew that a lot of my fellow managers would want to know if I was still in a job and how I had got on. We all had a good laugh and soon forgot all about it.

Time passed and in 1966 we had the chance to move from Norman Road to Whitcliffe Grange by doing a swap with a couple who couldn't get away with the gas central heating because of their health. We jumped at the chance as this was a new estate with central heating and a toilet upstairs and one downstairs; also we would only be a hundred or so yards away from our parents' homes.

It was an eventful year this and I'll not forget a trick or dirty trick that was played on me at work. Ruby got up to all sorts of tricks with me and this time she had hid some kippers in my office and after a few days they began to stink something terrible. I searched the office with Ruby, trying to find out what was causing the terrible smell. I realised later why she had helped me search, that was so I didn't find the damn things. It was unfortunate that day as the GM called and was not very happy with the smell in my office. It got me told off and we had to move into the back shop to talk. His final words before departing were "get that smell out of your office today Mr Shout" and he left. I think he couldn't get out quick enough. That was the final straw; I got Ruby and promised to throttle her if she didn't remove that smell from the office. When she brought out those kippers I chased her round the shop but she got away and ran into the toilet and I think the kippers went down the pan.

On another occasion Dorothy's father called in to see me but Ruby got to him before he got to me. She told him that I wasn't in a very good mood and that I was being spiteful to the staff. She said to him that she wanted to go to the Market Place for something and would he keep me busy talking in the office while she popped out for five minutes. Dad was always willing to oblige a lady and he duly kept me in my office until he saw Ruby return. Ruby gave my father in law the thumbs up sign and a big wink; I saw this and asked what it was all about. He told me and we just had a laugh. She was the best first hand I had, was Ruby. We worked extremely well together and I could leave her in charge knowing that all would be okay. I was very sad the day she handed in her notice to leave; I was losing not only an excellent under manager but a close friend as well.

The shop staff were a happy lot and we had numerous exciting things happen, too many to mention all or even some but I will relate one episode that took place. One of our customers was shoplifting and try as we might we couldn't prove it until one day she came into the shop and I was immediately informed. I put the usual procedures

Whitcliffe Grange Estate, built on this site, 1966

What a snowy day! Entrance to Cutpure Lane Est.

in to practice – that was that one of the staff must keep an eye on her all the way round the shop. As it happened I was sat in my office at the time, with the door partly opened, and by chance with the door being half glass and partly open, it reflected on to the fridge so that I saw this lady just by sheer luck come to the fridge and handle some packs of pre-packed bacon joints. I had a superb view and watched intently and saw her put a joint of bacon under her coat and under her armpit. I couldn't believe my eyes when I saw her continuing with her shopping but keeping her left arm down by her side, her right arm moving quite normally. She got to the checkout and went out. I said to Greta, a lovely girl, to go and bring her back as she had just pinched a joint of bacon. Greta said "are you sure, Mary didn't see her?", Mary being the one that was supposed to have been watching her round the shop. I said: "Don't argue, go and get her." Well Greta ran out of the shop chasing this lady into the Market Place and eventually caught her and brought her back. I would have loved to have had a camera to film Greta running down the street and marching this shoplifter back. We all had a good laugh when Greta was relating what she did.

I seem to be writing a lot about work and what went on there but I did enjoy work and never felt fed up with having to go. It is strange that since I started writing these memories I find that I have missed out quite a lot of happenings and experiences but I have made notes and will either relay them later on or write a new book called something like 'Shout's missed little gems'.

One such happening that I should mention here though, is that we replaced the old delivery lorry with a travelling shop. Good old Charlie was to manage this and he soon got the hang of selling instead of just delivering. Charlie became one of the shop staff now and had to phone his order in each day of what he required for the next day. We in the shop would then make up his order and check it ready for him to load the next morning. The only thing that was made up on the morning was the amount of bacon he required, which was cut fresh each day. Of course this replaced putting up orders, which was fine except that on Saturdays instead of delivering I had to stock-take the travelling shop and work out the result. It worked out fine each week with Charlie but the problems arose when he was on holiday and getting a relief to be as honest as him. Charlie had a girl assistant Charlotte to help him and in these circumstances she was invaluable. On one occasion I had a relief driver on the mobile shop, Fred by name, and after taking stock I found that he was two hundred pounds short. This was a new experience for me, as I always trusted everybody. I went over the figures again and got the same result each time. So I asked Fred to explain to me where the discrepancy was. He as much as blamed me and asked me or told me in as many words to check the stock sheets. I told him that they had been checked not only by me but also by another member of staff. To cut the story short I was instructed by the GM to call in the police. The detective that came had at one time been a neighbour of mine, a Sgt Tommy Armstrong. After grilling him for about two hours and getting nowhere I helped him. By chance we had changed the colour of milk tokens, which he carried on the shop, and after proving that he had stolen a few tokens that was all that was needed. He was duly prosecuted and fined two pounds and ordered to pay restitution of £6-5-0 (six pounds five shillings), which was the cost of 200 tokens at 7 ½d each. Milk tokens could be purchased at the shop and you got your divi on them; you then paid the milkman in tokens and not cash.

I did not enjoy that day at court although it did have a funny side to it. I had to attend to ask for restitution of the money involved and entering the court I was assured by the police that I had to wait until the next case was heard but that wouldn't take long, the constable told me, as the man charged was pleading guilty. Now I knew the man that was 'up before' the magistrate before me and I knew that Tarry – that was the name that he went by – never ever pleaded guilty. He was a regular up at court but was also a likeable chap. This day when asked what he was pleading guilty or not guilty, he stood proud and said "not guilty sir". This was not what the police had come to expect and they were not ready for that plea. It didn't do me any good either as my stomach was getting more and more churned up. The magistrates were not very pleased with the police and neither was I as it put an extra half hour on my waiting time.

When we were eventually called and the case was heard the magistrate stunned me by what he said to Fred. "You look a very dejected figure stood there Johnson." I must admit he did. Fred had played a blinder; he stood there with a grubby overcoat on that was nearly touching the floor and with head bowed and shoulders slumped he said to the magistrate "my wife's dying of cancer sir" and along with other woeful untruths asked if he could have time to pay the fine. As I have said he only admitted to £6-5-0 and that was the amount he had asked for time to pay, along with the fine of £2-0-0. Great balls of fire – I couldn't believe what I heard next from the magistrates. "Under your circumstances Johnson, you can have four weeks to pay."

When I got back to the shop I had to phone the GM and tell him what had taken place. He didn't believe it and shouted down the phone that we were a load of crooks here. I reminded him that it was the grocery departmental manager that had started him not me. I also informed him that two years earlier he had been sacked from another employer for the same thing and that the court had fined him £200 and put him on probation for a year.

The travelling shops were becoming harder and harder to manage and later in the year I was told to take over another mobile shop at Catterick. Well I must have woke up that morning feeling a bit fed up as when I was told to take over this mobile I replied "no I am not". "What do you mean?" said the GM's PA. "You have no option here." I looked at the poor guy and politely told him "but I have you see, I am still entitled to a week's holiday" and handing him the shop keys I said "that's one week's notice to you, I quit" and duly picked up my coat and walked out. That was the best days work that I had done for a long time.

Before I had set out for work that morning, Dorothy had told me that she was going to her mother's for the day, so I made my way down Reeth Road to tell her what I had done. "What are you doing here this time of day?" was what her father greeted me with. We went into the sitting room and I told him along with Dorothy and her mam who were already there that I had resigned and walked out. I don't know what reaction I expected but I was pleasantly surprised when dad said: "You did right son." Dorothy looked a bit worried, as did her mother, but if it was all right with her dad it was all right with her.

Word soon spread round the town that Dougie Shout had left the Co-op. It was a surprise to me that when we got home that the manager of the Fine Fare Supermarket called and offered me a job as manager designate, with a salary of twice the amount that I was getting at the Co-op. I told that I was flattered but had to refuse his offer for the time being. The real reason being, now that I was out of the retail side, I didn't want to go down that line again, preferring to be a rep (a company representative). I was sent my superannuation that I had paid and we lived on that for a while, as I couldn't claim dole because I had left work on my own accord.

Then one day I saw in the situations vacant in my local paper a representative was required for a salesman. The salary was £1,000 per year, plus commission, and the company was called Satinex G B Ltd. I did not know what they sold, except that it was paper, so I sent in an application and in due time got an interview.

This was held in the Rex Hotel at Whitley Bay and I must say I enjoyed it. Three gentlemen, the regional sales manager and two area managers, interviewed me. I won't go into a lot of detail about the interview, which was the usual type that I applied when interviewing for staff for myself. When asked if there was anything I would like to know, I replied: "Only one thing, would you please let me know as soon as possible, as I can not be out of work for very much longer?" They agreed to this request and I left feeling that it had been a very good interview. I then made my way down the coast and through the Tyne Tunnel to home.

I had applied for other jobs which I knew that I stood a good chance of getting but they were for retail managers, the job that I had just left, and I didn't want to go down that line again if I could help it. One such job was for a managerial position with L and N Stores, the full name being The London & Newcastle Tea Company. I went for an interview with them in their shop in Darlington. Once again I had a good interview and they offered me the job. But when they told me of the salary I had to refuse the job as it was not as good as I got at the Co-op. They evidently wanted me and were prepared to meet my demands but it would have meant moving to a larger store away from the area. I thanked them very much for the interview after turning down their last offer and left them after agreeing to be kept on their books in case another vacancy came up nearby.

I had now been out of work for four weeks, give or take a day or two, and was beginning to feel the pinch financially. So I thought that I had better look into the offer from Fine Fare which was in the market place. So once again I got dressed up in my best suit and went to see the manager about the job that he was offering me. Once in his office we got down to the nitty gritties about the job. With knowing each other, so be it by sight only, the talk was informal and light-hearted. I nearly fainted when he quoted me what the starting salary would be. The position of manager designate carried a salary of £3,000 pa, plus commission, plus all the other fringe benefits such as healthcare and pension. This proposition on the face of it, sounded too good to be true, and so it was. Going deeper into what the job required, I found out that Garfield Weston, the man who owned and ran the grocery chain, expected his managers to work at least eighty-four hours a week. I was shocked to hear this, as this was more than twice the hours that I had been doing at the Co-op, but the salary wasn't. After a while I told him that I would give it some thought and get back to him.

Six weeks had now passed and I was feeling a bit depressed with not working, so I decided I would give the Fine Fare job a go. I arranged to see their regional manager on Saturday morning at 11.30. At this time I was not on the phone but always gave my sister's number to anyone who required it. It was this number that I had given at my interview for the Satinex job and thought that this job had been lost to me. On this particular Saturday morning I walked to town and called in at my sister's before I went for the Fine Fare interview. I was told that Ron Hamnette from Satinex had phoned and would I return the call as soon as possible. This I did straight away and was told that I had got the job and it would be confirmed in writing by post which I should get by Monday or Tuesday. Talk about eleventh hour decisions. I now had to go to Fine Fare and apologise for bringing their regional manager all the way from Newcastle to say that I didn't want the job after all. I met him and explained what had happened and to be honest he was very kind about it and understood my reasons for taking the Satinex job.

That's not the end of the tale, though I now had a job as a sales executive with Satinex and I still didn't know what I was going to be selling. It was only when I was walking back home that I happened to look in the window of a hardware shop in the market place that I saw a display of Satinex man-size tissues. So that was what I would be selling in the near future – paper tissues, regular 150, man-size, toilet rolls and kitchen towels. Ron had given me a date to start, along with a travel voucher to get me to the head office at Hawarden near Chester, where we were to spend the next two weeks training. An awful lot was going on at the same time as this, as we had been approached by a couple living on the new estate down Reeth Road called Whitcliffe Grange and asked if we would like to swap houses. This was because both of them were asthma sufferers and found that the central heating in the new house didn't agree with them. Dorothy and I gave this a lot of thought and in the end came to the conclusion that it would be a good move for us.

Firstly, it was a new and better built house; it had a central heating system of blown air run by gas; we would be near both our parents; and if we could get Sonia into the school on Reeth Road this would be a bonus. As Sonia was four now it was a deciding factor. The only drawback about that was we are Methodists and the other girls all went to the Methodist school and this school was Catholic. Anyway, Dorothy went to see the headmaster and discussed it and he agreed to take Sonia into the school when the time arrived, subject to there being spare places, as he must give first priority to Catholic children. This we thought was fair. We met Mr and Mrs Macey and agreed to a swap, both parties were delighted. The only trouble now was I had to go away for two weeks with my new job and this left an awful lot of work for Dorothy. There's always an answer to a problem and Dorothy soon saw the answer to this problem. She got her sister Sheila to give her a helping hand and by jingo, the two of them worked like slaves. By the time I had finished my training, the two ladies had packed everything and cleared up and even arranged for the removal vans to pick up at the same time at each house, so as to avoid stacking furniture outside until the other house was cleared. This was most important had it been raining.

I got home on the Friday evening, never bothered to unpack my car, and we did a joint removal that you would think was done with military precision. We left our house, thanks to Dorothy and Sheila all nice and clean, and although they had done the same, with both of them being heavy smokers the smell of nicotine seemed to be every where you went. Being a new house all the walls were emulsioned and not papered, so we set about papering one room at a time to get rid of the nicotine smell. I could never come to terms with how asthmatics could smoke like they did and blame the central heating. Never mind, they did us a good turn.

We worked very hard that weekend and at ten-o-clock on the Sunday night I said that I must get myself ready for work the next day. So while Dorothy tidied up and looked in on the girls who were fast asleep and oblivious to what was going on, I emptied my car of stuff that I had brought from the office and loaded it up with Monday's work. That night I slept like a baby, being so exhausted, but woke up fit and raring to go.

Chapter Twelve

There were four of us on this induction course and we were billeted in a flat adjoining the factory which slept just four people. We had our meals in the factory canteen, which proved to be very good indeed. At night after we had completed our homework we went into the city of Chester for a drink or to go the pictures, or even just walking exploring the city. During the day we learnt from various books and area managers who would act out situations of the art of selling. I called this playing charades. We learnt about all the paperwork, forms, etc, and often went into the factory for practical experience. Needless to say, we got some ribbings from the girls whilst we were going around.

It came to our notice that the flat was used by other personnel in the factory when no one else was training for other purposes – I'll leave you to guess what. This was also the year that the flu jab became available to all factory staff and of course us being there at the right time got one too. I've had one every year since from my own doctor. Another medical practice was also available at the factory and that was that the birth pill was given free to any girl who wanted it. I think all the ladies in our factory were on the pill. We were also introduced to the girls in the office. Two of these girls were also telesales girls and were super. All the time I was at Modo those girls were the most helpful, not only to me but all the area. I called it Modo just then because after eighteen months a company called Modo bought out Satinex G B Ltd.

Let me first tell you about an experience or two with Satinex. At this time, 1966, salesman or travellers, as we were commonly called, wore bowler hats and carried an umbrella, so while we were training at Chester one day we were marched down to the city and measured for bowlers. Fortunately, we never got them, as I would have been the laughing stock of all my mates at home. But quietly I would have liked one as I thought I looked good in it, just like my dad did. At the end of our fortnight's training we were given our brand new Vauxhall Nova car – my number plate was TFM 178F, the first new car I'd ever had. It felt great driving away in a brand new car but also frightening; I don't think I reached fifty miles per hour all the way home.

Before we left we were told to load up our cars with samples of stock. All four of us weren't sure how much we should take but Ron came along and showed us how to fill our cars. Cases of all the products, until we couldn't see much out of the back window, were stuffed into the car and Ron told us we would be delivered a case of each product once a month. Two of us were to join the North East Area under John Milner who was area manager. I met John briefly while down at Hawarden and was pleased that he was to be my area manager, as we seemed to get on very well together.

One man, a Mr Walter Shaw, owned Satinex and he had very few rules but one had to obey those rules to the letter. Let me explain. For example, we were told to sell at least one gross of product each day. That was fine, it didn't seem a lot to me and I soon found out this was the case generally speaking.

On my first day on the road I met John at Leeming Bar Motel at 9 a.m. and supped tea and ate toasted teacakes until about 11 a.m., swapping notes about the company, as he was also a new starter at Satinex. Anyway we decided that we would give it a go and see how the jolly old goods sold. Me knowing this area better than John, as he lived in Upper Batley, I suggested we go to the nearest town which was Northallerton. We left his car at the motel and he came with me to Northallerton. The first place we saw was Northallerton Co-op Society, so we decided to try our hands in there.

As far as we were concerned it was all cold canvas, as we had not been given any record cards at this time. It was at this very first call that I found out that John Milner was a pure professional and skilled in every detail of selling. We came out of that call with fifteen gross of product on the sheet. I must say that John did most of the selling at that call but we called at other shops, mainly Spar and V.G. grocers, and I did the selling and did very well thank you. I continued to work by myself from then on and got well over my one gross of product each day that was required of me.

Then one day I was one case, I repeat one case, short of my gross that was expected of me and two days later I got a telegram from Mr Shaw asking what had gone wrong, why hadn't I sold one gross of product that day. That was what Mr Shaw had meant when he said "I'm not asking a lot of you, but, you must sell one gross per day". I learnt a lot that day; first if ever I had sold over two gross of product

I would keep one until tomorrow. I would not have another telegram from Walter Shaw.

Over the next few years once Modo had got settled in, we had so many meetings that I'm sure I must have been in every big hotel in every major town and city in this country. I was enjoying my job, meeting and making new friends all the time. Meanwhile at home Dorothy was fed up with me having to attend meetings nearly every two weeks and stopping overnight at the hotel. It was nice at weekends though, with a nice new car we could go to the seaside, Scarborough usually, and spend the day on the beach with the girls. We would stay until it was dark and then go to our Denis and Ruby's flat, have something to eat, and then Denis would take us all down to Peasholm Park to go round the tree walk. We all loved this and we did it for years. After going round the tree walk, Uncle Denis, who the kids loved, would then buy the fish and chips for supper, which we would eat at their home, and then off we would go back home.

I always used to say let's have a sing-song once we were on our way and would all join in singing 'Ten Green Bottles Hanging on the Wall' and Cliff College choruses such as 'Wide Wide as the Ocean' and so on. Before we had gone three miles, all the girls, including Dorothy, would be fast asleep, leaving me to talk to myself for the seventy-odd miles left to travel. Of course it was very late, about midnight many a time, before we got home. Those weekends I shall never forget because we all had such a good time.

Wherever we went in the car, I would always give the girls a competition to take part in. For example if we were nearing the coast, I would say to them: "There's sixpence to the first one that sees the sea." This would keep them quiet for a while, except they kept seeing the horizon and not the sea and it was a hard job to convince them that it was not the sea. In the end if we were anywhere near the sea I used to say to myself that the next one that says she can see the sea I'll agree and give her the sixpence. This would happen and there would be such uproar that I would give them all money just to keep the piece.

Our Hazel, the eldest daughter, was now twelve or thereabouts, Moira eleven, Paula ten and Sonia three, and all were growing up so fast I couldn't believe it. I remember one day when we were at Dorothy's parents and the kids were playing with a ball. Now Sonia, being only three, liked this and kept throwing the ball on to the garden for granddad Wood to go and get it. But granddad was lame, being injured in the first world war, losing a hand and suffering from having a piece of shrapnel in his hip, and soon got tired of this and told Sonia that if she threw the ball on to the garden again he would smack her bum. I had been sitting in a deck chair and was watching and heard dad say this, so I said to him "see that you do, if she throws it on the garden again". The girls' granddad loved them so much I knew he would never smack any of them and I wondered what he would do. I didn't have to wait long, as he picked up the ball and said: "That's all for today kids, come and have a bar of chocolate!"

On another occasion he and I were walking up his garden path and I suggested to him that his rose bushes needed de-budding if he wanted some decent blooms. "No, no, they're all right as they are, they flower every year so why touch them," came the reply. I couldn't and wouldn't argue with him but I had to laugh a few days later when his brother came from Newcastle to see him. The brother was Dorothy's Uncle Bernie, a lovely chap, who was the parks superintendent at Newcastle for the city council. Dad and I were at the gate when he arrived and started to walk up the garden path. As he walked and talked he said to Arthur (dad) "de-budding these roses should have been done by now Arthur" and he continued de-budding them right up to the house. I had a quiet chuckle to myself and left it at that.

There was such a lot going on now that the girls were growing up. Birthday parties seemed to come along every week. If it wasn't one of our girls birthday, one of ours would be going to a friend's party and I had to be the one to see that they got there and back because we were the only parents that had a car.

In 1969 our Moira wanted to go in the Whitsuntide fancy dress parade along with her friend Julie, so Dorothy dressed them up as Quakers and they won first prize. It was always fun at Whitsun, what with the fair being in town and the girls wanting rides on the bumper cars and goes on the side shows. It always ended up that one of them would win a goldfish and then we would have to find a bowl to keep it in until it died but it was all great fun.

At this time I was still in the brass band and we always led the parade. I played the Bb bass, and my brother Fred played the Eb bass and we were on the front rank when marching and leading the parade. It was great lining up in Wellington Place and then marching along Quaker's Lane into Queens Road, spreading right across the road, stopping occasionally to let all the rest of the parade catch up. One year, I don't remember which, I couldn't play my bass as I had recently had my appendix out, and with it being the heaviest instrument it was too hard for me to carry and play at the same time, so I played the symbols. I thought this was grand for a change, bashing these two pieces of metal against each other. Well on this parade we always tried to play the most rousing march up King Street as the buildings echoed the sound, and I gave the symbols one hell of a bang to make it even better but one of them split a little and instead of a nice clean, sharp sound, out came a ring like an alarm clock going off. I could hardly continue for laughing but our bandmaster didn't see the funny side of it at all.

While I'm thinking about it, let me tell you another story of banding. When the town band disbanded, our bandmaster, Mr Fred Woodhall, was asked to form a T A band for the 50 DIV Royal Signals at Darlington and naturally most of us lads joined. This meant that we were in the army, the territorial army so be it, but we got paid of course for attending practices as well as doing parades and concerts. The band was made up of our old band and some chaps from Darlington area. These others that we recruited were older men but good company and good musicians. On the concert platform they were great but when it came to marching that was a different kettle of fish. On the front rank, once again we had the four basses, Fred and I and two from Darlington. One of these from Darlington was a little deaf and only had one eye, so when we were marching it was very difficult for him to march with us. Let me explain a little better. The army ran band contests for the TA's in regions and we entered into the North East one. The contest was in two parts, marching and counter marching being one part, and the other was a half-hour concert of pieces of music of your own choice. The concert part was fine but I didn't like the idea of counter marching with the one eyed player called Benny. I said to the bandmaster that he would be better letting the trombones be in the front rank and then Benny would be able to follow the man in front of him. "No it will be all right," came the reply from Mr Woodhall, "he knows the drill", and so it was left at that. The day came for the contest and off we went, where to I can't remember, but there was a large parade ground and large drill hall where we were to give the concert. Six bands were competing and we drew the band to play last on both parts. We watched the other five bands marching on the parade ground and most were pretty good. This was because they had ex-army bandsmen in their ranks and they knew what went on.

Our turn came at last and my worst fears were to happen. "By the left, quick march" came the order and off we went marching like guardsmen. I'm sure at first everything went fine until we came to counter marching and Benny, the one-eyed bass player, instead of turning about carried on forward, with the trombone player behind him running after him and bringing him back to his right place. Talk about being embarrassed, I was gutted, but saw the funny side of it and so did all the people that were watching. There were shouts of "Dads' Army on parade". We did not get good marks for that performance; in fact we were last, about twenty points behind the rest. "Never mind," said our bandmaster, "we will make it up on the concert."

He had taken some stick from the other bandmasters but being an ex-army bandmaster he could take it. We listened to the others play their concert pieces and then we went on to the stage to play ours. The pieces that we played were much more demanding than those that the other bands had played and to be honest God must have played with us that day because the sounds that we produced were a pleasure to the ear, they were superb. We got the biggest claps of the day for that concert. I knew we had done well on stage but I didn't think that we could make up that many points. To my and all our astonishment, when we heard that we had won the overall contest by one point, you could have heard the cheers back in Richmond. For winning this contest the bandmaster was given a silver baton and I think we got a weekend's pay.

I enjoyed playing in the TA band but I didn't like the rules as one had to put in so many hours and drills to stay in. It was like playing soldiers again.

The TA band also played at the top brass functions. One such function that happened regularly was a banquet in the drill hall and there were more generals down to lieutenants, all with their wives and all dressed to kill. The food was out of this world and we ate after the dinner was finished and the dance band took over. While we played for dinner, we played the game of who was the first one to notice which officer's wife was wearing the same dress that she wore for the last dinner.

I came out of the TA when they said that we had to attend W/E camps, I think at least six a year, and I was not prepared to do this. The band soon disbanded because all were not interested in playing soldiers again; they had done all that and got the t-shirt.

I was now enjoying my work more, as I was my own boss, working out my journeys, like where I was to start and where I would finish working for that day. The weeks passed and so did the months and before I knew it we were getting our girls sorted for the Whitsuntide fancy dress parade again. On TV at this time was a very popular advert for flour, with two people dressed up as flour graders, and we thought it would be a good idea to dress our kids up the same. Well that's not quite true, as it was Moira and her friend Joy Ferguson that we dressed up as flour graders, and Paula as a Hawaiian dancer and Sonia as a sailor.

They all looked smashing and couldn't wait to get in the parade.

Moira and Joy's dress was, starting at the top, bowler hats; Moira's was white and Joy's black. In fact Moira was all in white, white top and white trousers and Joy was all black. Each carried a sack with the words 'ordinary flour' on Joy's in a paper sack and Moira's we painted the same colour as Homepride flour bags were. They carried the slogan 'Before and after the Flour Graders', the same as the telly advert showed.

Chapter Thirteen

The same year, 1970, we went on holiday to Butlins Holiday Camp at Filey after we had had a shocking car accident. What happened was, we set off to go to Filey in a new car, only a few weeks old. We had got one mile out of Richmond when a young couple driving a big Ford car got into a spin, couldn't correct it and smashed head on into our little 1360 Triumph Herald car. Dorothy and Sonia landed in Catterick Hospital, Dorothy with head and chest wounds, and Sonia with a cut head.

What was strange was that Dorothy's head smashed the windscreen and sent her glasses twenty yards along the road, when we found them there was not a scratch on them, but mine remained on my face and were broken and twisted to hell leaving them no good at all.

Another little story about the accident was, I got my garage man to come and tow my car back to his garage and he parked it temporarily on the forecourt. It was about lunch time when one of Hazel's friends, Heather, was being driven home for lunch by her father and said to him: "That's Hazel's dad's car there all smashed up." Her dad replied: "Don't be so daft, they've gone on holiday haven't they." Heather replied: "Yes, they were going on holiday but that's their car because it has the Richmond sticker on the back window." Of course she was right and I am told she never let her father forget that she was more observant than he was.

I had to phone Butlins and tell them what had happened and would they let our friends know who we were meeting there, that was Marjorie and Ron and their two children Linda and Tony who were from Thirsk. They did this and offered us a new date for our holiday when we were all well again, which I thought was very nice of them. Meanwhile Dorothy and Sonia spent the night in hospital and then I went and brought them home in a car which I had borrowed from my

153

friend Bob Hall.

We did go to Butlins in the September and I remember parking the car in the big car park and saying "that's it for a week, I don't want to see it until we go home". I did not expect what happened when we had got loaded up and ready to leave after having such a lovely time. We were all in the car and I automatically turned the ignition key to start the engine. I did this but nothing happened, after turning the engine over once or twice more and still it didn't start, our poor little Sonia got really frightened and burst into tears crying. I think she was thinking that the car was going to crash again. Eventually it did start but it took us a long time to settle Sonia and get on our way home. In actual fact it took a long time altogether for Sonia to come to terms with getting into the car.

It also took a long time for one of my friend's father to come to terms with his Christian beliefs or convictions. There were two brothers, Keith and Peter Blades, and it was their father I'm talking about. His name was Bert; well that was what he was always called. Now Bert had seen the light about a year ago and had turned into a local Methodist preacher and had given up all his drinking and gambling habits then. Well on this particular day I had been to the bookies to put a bet on for myself and was walking back into the town when I stopped to talk to Bert, who was painting part of the Zetland Cinema.

After the usual greetings of how are you, etc, Bert seemed agitated so I said to him "what's up Bert, you're not your usual happy go lucky chappie". This is what he said to me in reply: "Dougie, I had a dream last night, in fact it seemed to keep me awake all night, and I woke up thinking about a sugar bowl. All this morning it's been on my mind and in the end when I was having my ten-o-clocks I succumbed and looked at the racing pages in the paper. I haven't done that for over a year and I feel quite guilty about it but the trouble is there is a horse running today in the big handicap called Sugar Bowl and I have two hundred pounds in my pocket here and I'm in turmoil whether to put it on this horse. On the other hand it might be the good Lord putting temptation in front of me to see if I can resist it. What do I do?" "Bert," I said, "I can't tell you what to do but what I do know is if you give in to this temptation you have to live with yourself for the rest of your life.".

I had to leave him in his quandary because I wanted to look in the paper and see if this horse had a chance of winning, or should I just back it on the strength of Bert's premonition or dream. I looked in the paper at this horse and it was about 50 to 1 in the paper with no chance at all. I'm not sure if the odds I quote are correct or if it was another horse I had been given some time later. Never mind, I did not back it, nor did Bert give in to his temptation, but I wish I had backed it because the damn horse won at good odds. The next time I saw Bert he was all smiles and happy because by not backing the horse, he said, meant that he could walk tall and hold his head high and thank God for giving him the strength to resist any more temptation.

I was acting like a taxi driver these days, what with running Hazel to her friends and Moira to hers, as well as running her down to Catterick village to take horse-riding lessons. That was a twofold run, having to take her there and then go back for her in an hour's time. It was also a costly pastime, as we had to buy her a riding helmet as well as paying the learning fees.

One thing that really pleased Dorothy and I was that all the girls had made friends with nice people and didn't give us any cause for complaint.

Getting back to my work, which I was enjoying more and more now that we weren't having so many meetings, and even more so when I heard and was told to get my passport in order as our national conference was being held in Portugal. The conference was being held in the town of Estoril and we were staying in one of the two very large hotels. It was strange how things happen, as when I was in Estoril and staying at one of these hotels, my brother-in-law John, our Nancy's husband, was staying at the other one and we didn't know this until we were back home. We found out that my hotel was far better than his for comfort and décor but his was far better than mine for food. I'll go as far as to say that the food in my hotel was atrocious, being mainly fish which was usually cold, but John had a marvellous menu.

Our conference was to launch a new product, which was Fashion Toilet Rolls, and along with all our other products this was to form the backcloth on the stage. A half container load was shipped off to reach our hotel in good time but unfortunately never arrived and we were left with a few show cards, etc, to show us what the new product looked like. As far as I can remember that container never showed up, so we presumed it had been stolen.

One day we were taking a break from the conference and had gone outside for a breath of fresh air and were enjoying a cigarette, when a large van pulled up and out got a man and woman and started showing us goods that we could buy. I looked at some shawls and purchased one for very little money for the quality of the shawl and thought it would be a nice present for Dorothy. We were looking and examining these shawls when the man from the van shouted something to his wife, which meant get back in the van here's the police. His wife started to take the goods off the lads before getting back in to the van but my mate and I put our shawls over the wall as we had paid for ours. The poor woman didn't make it back to the van as her husband just shut the doors and drove off. The police car screeched to a halt and out got two policemen, one grabbed the woman, the other drew his gun and fired two or three shots at the van. "Good Lord," I said to myself, "it's like gangland with all guns blazing"; what an experience that was.

The best of it was, after the police had taken the woman away after collecting the goods off the lads, Jim my mate and I went down on to the beach below and picked up our shawls. We were the only two who had kept their purchases.

It was an eventful year, 1973, because besides going to Portugal, my brother Fred brought the brass band that he had formed at school in Canada over for two weeks. This meant that there was a lot of organising to do beforehand, such as all the children in the band and the chaperones had to be given lodgings. This was done by members of our band and friends sharing their houses and hospitality. Our bandmaster, Fred Woodhall, worked very hard making all the arrangements for the two-week stay.

Our Fred had arranged concerts for the band to play at, such as schools, and one of the sponsors over in Canada – a timber company I think it was – had arranged for them to play at their factory over here. The whole two weeks were a huge success, bar the odd hiccup. Our Fred had very strict rules and if they strayed from obeying these rules they would be sent back home on the next plane – and he meant it. But on one occasion a member of ours held a party in their garage inviting some of the visiting band and of course there was a little alcohol floating about. In fact there was too much and the boy that was in Dorothy and mine's care got a little drunk. Kim was his name and he was a grand lad really. When he came home that night he was obviously the worse for wear and Dorothy had to put him to bed.

The trouble here was that although he was staying with us, he had to sleep at Dorothy's mam's, as us having four girls meant we had no spare bedroom, but he came along to us for all his meals, etc. Dorothy and I had a chat about this behaviour and realised if we told our Fred he would have no hesitation in informing his parents and sending him back home. So being loving and understanding parents ourselves, we decided not to say a word and asked the other parents to do the same. The funny side of all this was that when he came round for breakfast the following day after being drunk, he was ashamed of himself, stood to attention, called me sir and begged me not to tell my brother. It took me all my time not to laugh and in the end after assuring me that this would not happen again, I said to him "okay, now let's forget it and enjoy your stay".

In the July of this year we had another happy event and that was my nephew Colin got married to Irene and that also was a very happy day. Colin was my sister Norah's only child. Norah had died after suffering for a long time with cancer at the age of 39 and this left Dick her husband to bring up Colin who was I think only nine at that time. Thinking about Dick, he and I used to go to bingo every Saturday night and that was a nice night out which we did for years. By going regularly and sitting in the same seats, one got to know and enjoy a bit of fun with the others, who also sat in the same seats around us. Well one night Dick and I thought we would have a laugh with a young lady by saying that I would drop her off at her house before I took Dick home. I was the only one in the group that had a car. "Thanks," she said, and at the end of the bingo session we said our goodnights to the others in our group and Dick, Sheila (that was her name) and myself got into my car. The fun started once we got on the road. She noticed that I wasn't going in the direction of her house and said: "Where are you going, I don't live this way." Dick and I looked at each other and then at Sheila and I said "to the woods, to the woods". Poor Sheila was panic stricken, wondering what we were going to do to her. "No, no, take me home," she yelled and was getting quite upset so we had to put her out of her misery telling her it was only a joke. She didn't know whether to laugh or cry but in the end she just had a good laugh with us before we dropped her off on her doorstep. The following Saturday she couldn't wait to tell our friends about us and what a pair of sods Dick and I were but we all had a good laugh.

I had to give up running the youth clubs now because I was away so much and also had quite a bit of preparation to do at night ready for the next day and found that it was proving too much of a headache to get someone to cover for me. So reluctantly I gave up all three clubs but kept on with the band.

I had one big celebration this year 1972, and that was my mother's 80th birthday. My elder sister Daisy arranged a lovely tea party in my mother's own home in Victoria Road and nearly all the family gathered to sing happy birthday dear mother. I had never known my mother get emotional but on this occasion she was overwhelmed with joy. These sorts of celebrations one never forgets, nor does one want to.

Over the next couple of years nothing of any importance happened that I can remember. But in saying that, there was one exception, and that was on November 16th 1974 our eldest daughter married Brian

Dawson, a local lad from Catterick village. Hazel looked absolutely gorgeous dressed in a beautiful wedding dress and train. She had six bridesmaids all dressed in purple, with skullcaps and carrying dolly bags. That's what I called a colourful set of girls and I remember taking their photos on the grass outside our front door, with all the neighbours gasping "aren't they lovely".

My greatest joy was when Hazel and I got in the bridal car to take us to the church and we were on our own, and more so when I walked her down the aisle of the church. Then there was the reception at the Kings Head Hotel and the speeches. Talking about speeches, I realised that this was the first of four I would have to give in due time and as much as I enjoyed the atmosphere of the whole day, I never relaxed until I had delivered my words of wisdom.

We really went to town with Hazel's wedding, having the reception at the Kings Head Hotel, the largest and best hotel in the town. I remember looking across at the people on the top table and thinking how wonderful everyone looked. The bride and groom in the centre and three bridesmaids each side of them dressed in their purple dresses, and the parents of the happy couple along with the best man completed the layout. One little item made me chuckle and I don't mean to be disrespectful in any shape or manner, but all the menfolk were dressed in their Sunday best suits and Mr Dawson was in his too, but he was wearing a cardigan as well. Needless to say we had one hell of a good day. The year of 1974 was what one would call a good year for weddings, as earlier in the year my niece Barbara got married to a lad called Chris, and they were married in the June. Also Hazel's friend Jackie got wed to Terry Pinning in October. Jackie had been living with us for quite a time before she got married, as her parents had moved away and Jackie didn't want to go with them, so she asked if she could stay with us. Her parents organised all her arrangements and once again we had another grand day. I digress with the memories of these weddings so I will go back to Hazel's wedding. If my memory serves me right, the management of the Kings Head Hotel gave Hazel and Brian a weekend's accommodation for their anniversary free of charge but I can't remember if they took it up.

After a hectic weekend, I had to find the strength to go to work on the Monday morning. By good journey planning I had arranged an easy day and by midday I was home again. The area that I covered was North Yorkshire and Durham and it proved a very lucrative one too. I used to love to go to the Hartlepool area, as I had made a good contact with a wholesaler there and I transferred a lot of orders through his warehouse. By doing this I used to get one big order, which helped me and my commission on payday.

It wasn't long before I knew all the towns and even the villages in my area, which was great if we went for a ride out in the car, as I knew where all the toilets were situated in cases of emergency. I don't remember where we went on our holiday this year but I do the following year.

Our family went with Sheila and Jim, Dorothy's sister and brother-in-law, to Berwick-on-Tweed, to Feather's Holiday Park. It was mainly a caravan site but there were entertainment halls, games hall and everything one needed for a perfect holiday. We had a smashing time there, as we could leave the girls at night and know they were being looked after, while we went out for a drink and some adult entertainment. The first part of the evening was devoted to family entertainment, where all the families along with the kids took part in games, etc. On one such night there was a competition for the title of Miss Feathers 1974 and low and behold Sheila won it. I don't remember fully what the prize was but I know we didn't have many drinks to buy that night.

Our girls, along with Sheila and Jim's two, Shelley and Joanna, had a great time on that holiday. It was while we were there that we upped sticks and spent the day in Edinburgh. I think it was that day that we went to see the Chillingham Wild Cattle on our way to Edinburgh and by jingo they were worth seeing.

In January the following year my work held a national conference at the Chateau Impney at Droitwich which was memorable because it was built as a chateau and was smashing. Everything about our stay there was good; the food was magnificent, the rooms great and the grounds were great too. This was the hotel used in the series of Crossroads Motel if any of you can remember that soap.

It was this year that my great friend Charlie Hodgson died of a heart attack. We had been good friends since I had left school and started work at the Co-op. There are so many memories of Charlie that I could write a book of them. His sense of humour and understanding were a credit for all to follow. I shall not forget the words he said to Dorothy as he drove his little car up Reeth Road. He had seen Dorothy walking up Reeth Road, he stopped his car and said: "Do you want a lift into town, or are you in a hurry?" That was the sort of man he was. He loved his wife Betty and all his family. It was a very sad day when Dorothy and I went to his funeral at St Mary's Church and were asked by Betty and Margaret, his eldest daughter, if we would accompany them to the crematorium in their car.

On a happier note, our Moira was in the dancing group of our local amateur operatic society's pantomime and she looked and danced superbly. Our Paula was also rehearsing for the show but she accidentally scalded herself and landed in the Victoria Hospital. It was touch and go whether or not to transfer her to the burns unit at Middlesborough but our own doctor was sure he could treat her, and treat her he did, and he did it well. The sister in the hospital was telling Dorothy on one visit that Paula was bell-happy, as she kept ringing for attention. This remark upset Dorothy so the next time she went to see Paula she would be ready to reply to any such remark like that from the sister again. As it happened, I was with Dorothy the next time she visited and while we were talking to Paula, the sister came along and I got the impression that she was going to have another go at Dorothy regarding Paula ringing the bell. But when she saw me her whole attitude changed, as she said to me: "I nearly didn't recognise you with your clothes on Dougie, how are you?" Well, Dorothy didn't know how to take this last remark but I told her that she was learning to swim and was at the lessons with me. After that Paula could do no wrong – it's a true saying "it's not what you know, but who you know". I got into trouble when learning to swim thanks to a cousin of Dorothy's, Pat, who was the wife of John who I used to pick up and go to the swimming classes with. We were late home one night and Pat came out of their house and gave me such a rollicking, saying I was leading John astray because we had stayed back at the baths and had a cup of Bovril or coffee with the other girls in our class, and she thought we were having a date with them.

We did have some fun with the girls, though, for example one night when we were circling round close to each other, one of the girls got the top of her bikini pulled off by the person following her. Of course it was an accident but the cheers that went up were deafening. It was a good laugh as we were all mature students and all wanted to help to replace the bikini.

On another occasion I had taken a new towel to the baths; it was the one that I had won at work for my sales increase and it was maroon in colour. I didn't think anything of this as it was new and had never been washed but I should have as when I got dried after being in the bath I didn't notice that I was all reddy. This didn't show up when we were having a cuppa because of the light but when I got home Dorothy said: "Are you all right, you look flushed?" It wasn't until I got under the shower that it dawned on me it was the new towel. At first I was worried when I saw the red water running off me but then I wondered why my friends hadn't noticed how red I was.

Our family was growing up, as they do, and I found myself playing

Father Xmas, not to our kids but to some friends of ours. It happened like this: Our friend Ruby and her friend Diane were having an Xmas party at Diane's house and they wanted a Father Xmas to come and give Diane's two children and Ruby's child some presents, so I was asked if I would oblige. Ruby knew that I had played Father Xmas before, so I agreed. At the pre-arranged time I arrived and did my "ho, ho, ho" bit and sat down with the kids. Diane had stuffed a cushion up my front to make me look fatter, more like a proper Father Xmas, and as I sat down this cushion began to show so Ruby, I think it was, pushed me down on the chair and at the same time lifted the cushion above my costume belt. All the adults were laughing at this exercise and me trying to carry on with the kids. The next thing that happened was Ronnie, Diane's husband, offered me a drink, to which I said "thanks very much". But when I tried to drink the damn thing, my moustache and beard got in the way. The more I tried the worse it got and in the finish I said to Ronnie and the girls "I'll leave it for now and have it later". They were cracking their sides laughing at me trying to get a drink. We all had a great time and I must have played the part well because Ruby and Ken's lad Michael didn't recognise me at all. I often borrowed that Father Xmas costume after that and enjoyed every minute wearing it.

At home Paula started going out with a soldier called Eddie and after a while he started staying at our house. Eddie enjoyed making models and kept his model kits and part-finished models under his bed. For a Londoner, we liked him and before too long they asked if they could get married. Well it was nice to be asked but if push came to shove we couldn't stop them, so I said "I would be delighted to welcome you into the Shout household Eddie". So now I had two daughters who were engaged, as Moira had previously moved in to Ken's flat to live and have a trial living together. Ken's a wonderful lad who was divorced and he thought the world of our Moira and the next year 1979 Moira and Ken got married.

I thought this was going to be easy to organise, having had the experience gained arranging Hazel's, but no, Moira didn't want a church wedding and didn't want any big do at all. All Moira wanted was to get married and go on their honeymoon. We had talks and talks until we were blue in the face and finally agreed on a registry office marriage and the reception we would have at the Terrace House Hotel.

So on September 22nd 1979, Moira and Ken got married, everything went well, right up to the time when there was only Moira and I left in the house waiting for the taxi to return from taking Dorothy and her mother to the registry office. Moira started to get upset and didn't know if she could go through with it; all she wanted, was for her and Ken to get the certificate and go their own way. After a while I got her settled. I did say to her that it wasn't too late to change her mind but she assured me it wasn't that that was bothering her; it was all the fuss and festivities. Before that it was me that had been nervous and sweating under the collar, thinking that I was going to have to call it off.

Like a real trooper, I managed to get her into the car and got her to the office, where the cheering only made her worse, but somehow Ken took over and into the office we all went. That done, and the confetti thrown, we made our way to the reception. Once again I had a speech to make and I remember very little of what I said except for one sentence and that was welcoming and thanking all for coming, and that we had friends from the three Cs – Colburn, Coventry and Canada.

After the speeches and the meal, we went outside into the gardens for the photos. Looking now at the photos, they were certainly unique as Hazel was pregnant and Paula had her legs in plaster after having had her bunions removed. The owners of the hotel were Mike Hollingworth and his wife, who we could not fault for their attention and services of the whole reception. Now Mike was a presenter of a programme on Radio Cleveland each morning and he knew I was a listener so he said that he would give us a mention on Monday morning and he sure did. I still have a tape recording of his kind words.

I seem to be relating about nothing else but weddings and sure enough the next year our Paula and Eddie got married. I was now suffering from severe dropsy, as my hand seemed to do nothing but pay out for weddings. Eddie was a serving soldier and was married in full dress uniform. I must say he looked like a general and with Paula in a superb dress and long train they made a handsome couple. The date was November 1st 1980 and it was, to say the least, cold. They got married in the Methodist Church and after the service went across the road into the Friary Gardens for the photos. The Friary Gardens made a great backcloth for the photos but the only thing was the photographer was a bit slow and all the girls, and boys for that matter, were getting goose pimples with the cold. Fortunately we didn't have far to go for the reception, which was in the Fleece Hotel across the road. Once in the Fleece and a drink down my throat I soon thawed out. We had a lovely day and I know our Paula loved every minute of it being the centre of attraction. Just the opposite of how Moira had felt.

These last two or three years had drained me physically and

financially, so I was pleased to be able to help Ken with his pigeons. His partner had let him down so often and he was fed up and wanted a new partner, as it was too expensive to do on his own. I said that I would love to be a partner, providing that I could be an active one and the partnership be on a fifty-fifty basis. Ken would have to train me, as well as the pigeons to start with, and this he did.

In both the clubs that Ken raced the birds, Richmond H.S. and Colburn H.S., the partnership of Malton and Shout was accepted, and that was how a successful partnership started and lasted nearly twenty years, without one row between us. As far as I was concerned, Ken was the master and me the helper, and if he said black was white, I didn't argue, it was right. We soon worked out how to work together but not necessarily be together, as Ken worked shifts. We were a very successful team, Ken and I, and won many prizes, and being in the top three fanciers in both clubs. In fact in Colburn Club we were often the top flyers.

In the meantime, our Paula was living on Catterick Camp and it wasn't long before Eddie's regiment was posted to Germany. I remember Dorothy and I going up to the camp to see Paula off on her way to Fallingbostle in Germany. Coaches had been laid on to take the wives to the airfield where they would be flown to Germany, and there were a few tears amongst the whole congregation of people, gathered there to see their loved ones leave.

The following year, 1982, Paula gave birth to our first grandson, Paul. We couldn't wait to see both him and Paula and Eddy. We had another happy event in April of 82, as our Moira gave us a girl grandchild, Gillian, and she was christened in the May. It seemed life was getting better and better, as there was something happening all the time. I was happy at work and having my hobby with the pigeons made our daily life a pleasure to be alive.

It was to continue in the next year but not before we had some upsets with Hazel and Brian, and to cut the story down to size, without going into detail, Brian left Hazel. He was most thoughtless, as when he left, the girls had whooping cough and weren't very well at all. But all problems have to be solved and Hazel soon came to terms with it and started to build a new life for herself.

After Brian left her, she got the chance to move to a flat on the same estate as we were, and started to live again. One of her friends got her to go on a blind date to meet a chap who was a friend of her friend's partner and was in the same situation as Hazel, being divorced recently. This was how she met Dave, who was a soldier, still serving at that time. Well things developed between the two of them and they decided they would marry and that the date would be on Hazel's nanna's birthday, October 1st 1983.

Naturally we were all excited and none more than Dorothy's mam, whose birthday it was. They got married in the registry office and the reception was held in the Town Hall Hotel. It's always nice to meet your new relations and this was no exception. Dave's brother Rick and his wife travelled up on the day and came to our house before going to the registry office. Not knowing the town, he did not know where to park, so I took him to my sister Daisy's area and got him parked there. Walking back from parking the car I was greeted or just spoke to nearly everybody that we passed, and Rick couldn't get over how everybody spoke or just said "how do, how are you?" to me. "Do you know everybody?" he said.

The Town Hall did us proud and after all the festivities were over, all the Bransby members came back to our house where we got to know each other better. Jean, Dave's mam, a lovely gentle lady, said how nice everything had been and hoped that we would see more of each other. Over the years we have seen a lot of each other as the good lady often goes on holiday to Hazel and Dave's.

Dave was a keen photographer and I'll never forget one day he said that he would take a photo of Dorothy's mother. Living just four doors away it was no hassle for him to bring his camera down to our house. We were all in our living room, Nanna Wood the subject, Dorothy, me and some of the children, when Dave came armed not only with his camera as we thought he would but with numerous attachments to go with it. Dorothy's mam was fascinated with all this gear, just to have one's photo taken. There were spotlights, floodlights, umbrellas and I don't know what, all this to take a photo of Nanna Wood. When all this was set up and Dave said "say cheese", I think we all said cheese and had a good laugh. I would like to say that to this day, that photo was the best one ever taken of Mam Wood.

Dave came out of the army but found living as a civilian hard. But gradually he overcame the problems and settled into a normal husband, and may I say a good husband to Hazel and dad to her two girls, Helen and Elaine, by Brian. The next thing that happened was Hazel became pregnant and Anne was born on October 10th 1984. She was christened on December 30th 1984 in the Methodist Church. Hazel now had three girls and I wondered if she was trying to outdo her mam, who had had four. I'm only joking of course but one never knows, does one?

It was also this year that my swimming mate John died. He was very good to us, was John, as he was trained as an electrician and also a TV mechanic. Not only did he keep our electrics right but he saved us a fortune in television repairs. A good friend and sadly missed.

Over in Fallingbostle, Germany, Paula informed us that she was pregnant and in March 85 our Suzanne was born. This was nice for Paula and Eddie as now they had a boy and a girl, and it was nicer still for us when they came over for a holiday. Not satisfied with that, we went over to Germany in 1985 and for the first time set foot in that country. We went by ferry from Hull to Rotterdam, where Eddie was to meet us and take us back to their home back in Fallingbostle. After getting off the ferry and going through the custom sheds, we looked for Eddie but he was not there. After half an hour had passed I was just going to say to Dorothy "we'll get back on that boat because I'm not being stranded here", when a car came speeding along the road and came to a grinding halt right beside us. It was Eddie and his mate Frenchie. "Thank goodness," I said, "I was just thinking about getting back on board."

Eddie was full of apologies and told us that he had got about two miles from his home when his car had broken down. Fortunately Frenchie had come to the rescue and that's why they were a little bit late. It was a long drive, having to go through Holland and to the other side of Germany. However, we had a good tour of the countries before pulling up outside an enormous block of flats. Paula's was on the first floor and had a little balcony. It was lovely to see Paula again and to see the two children. We had a great time there; Eddie drove us around the tourist spots, including going to Hanover, which we liked very much.

Every morning while Paula and Dorothy were getting the children dressed, etc, I would go walking. On one of these walks I came across a lovely park, with a swimming pool and diving boards. We could bring the children here I thought and spend a pleasant hour or two but Paula not liking to walk anywhere, I never got back there. Eddie took us to a safari park one day and you are not supposed to open your car windows whilst going through the park because of the animals. This was okay to start with, except that it was a very hot day. We had just more or less started our trip when two monkeys jumped on to the bonnet of the car. As you know the animals always have right of way and after pulling faces at them, and in return they pulled funny faces at us through the windscreen for fifteen minutes, the car was getting hotter and hotter, and by the time they had jumped off, we were glad that Eddie opened his window to let a bit of fresh air circulate. We noticed some llamas in the distance and Eddie had just remarked how he hated them. What we hadn't noticed, though, was while Eddie was telling us this, one came from behind and put his head – or tried to put his head – through the open window next to Eddie. Well when it breathed down his neck, he shouted "bloody hell", went six shades of white and at the same time was trying to close the window and accelerate. All of us in the car burst into fits of laughter but poor Eddie was not amused. Altogether we had a smashing time and said our good byes at Rotterdam again after Paula and Eddie drove us there.

Arriving back in Hull, my friend and work colleague Tony had, as previously arranged, left my car in the car park. I should have said that at the beginning of this trip I drove down to Hull, met Tony who took my car away and would return it on the due date. This he did. Today we still meet and have pleasant weekends together. He brings his partner Jean and this makes up a nice party of four wherever we go. Tony and I worked very close to each other at Modo and we never had a wrong word to say to each other.

It was back to normal for the next few months, doing my DIY bit at home, training the pigeons with Ken, as well as doing a full time job. Being a sales executive meant that I did a lot of travelling and usually on average I clocked up about 50,000 miles a year for the company and another six or seven thousand private miles in our own car. So by the time August 1986 came along I was ready for another holiday.

This time I said that I was not driving anywhere; we would go on a coach tour, and this we did. We chose a local operator, Westways of Bedale, as he was offering a tour of Newquay taking in Lands End, Penzance, Mevagissey, Padstow and other places of interest. Ruby and Ken joined us on this holiday and it was a scream. The hotel was good, the food good and the tours good. One of the highlights was looking round Truro Cathedral and having our photo taken at Lands End under a signpost showing Scotch Corner being so many miles and New York 2,827 miles, Berlin 730, and John O Groats 874 miles. We all had a great time.

Unfortunately, later on in the year I took ill with pains in my chest that turned out to be a heart attack. What happened was I got these pains on the Thursday but didn't think much about them then as I thought it was only indigestion. But by Friday I had to go to the doctor's as they were getting worse. The doctor gave me a good examination and wanted to see me the next day. I went on the Saturday feeling quite poorly again. The doctor said he thought it was indigestion but wanted to see me on Monday.

On Sunday the pains got much worse and I said to Dorothy that I had better have the doctor down to see me. The doctor that came examined me and gave me two squirts of the GTM spray under my tongue. When this didn't do anything he stood pondering. While he was standing there in front of me I remembered what my good friend had said to me about pains in the chest, and that was, if you are having a heart attack the pains are not near your heart but in the middle of your chest. I said to the doctor "I think I'm having a heart attack" and looked him straight in the face to see what reaction I would get. "You're right," he said, "I'll phone for an ambulance right away on your phone if I may." He did and the ambulance came and took me to Catterick Military Hospital. I remember going into the hospital but that's all until a week later when I was taken from the intensive care unit to Ward Three.

After being there for a few days, I was allowed to get out of bed and have a wash and shave in the washbasin next to my bed. I thought this was lovely, as my chest was beginning to itch and I thought it was because I hadn't had a good wash, never mind a shower. Anyway, I gingerly stepped out of my bed and on to my feet, and gently stood up. It felt very strange and I felt very weak but I stood up, stretched and proceeded to take off my pyjama jacket. What a surprise I got when I eventually got my jacket off. I looked in the mirror and to my astonishment saw six red circle patches, three down each side. That was what was making me feel itchy I thought, but didn't realise until minutes later what those red patches were caused by.

Of course when I had entered the hospital, I arrested, and they had to put the jump leads on me to get my heart started again. I nearly had another heart attack until I got to terms with seeing that. It's a known fact that you do not remember your time spent in intensive care and I can confirm that.

After I had got out of hospital after spending ten days or so there, and a week or two at home, Dorothy took me to town for a change from just walking round the house. We met a chap who Dorothy spoke to. I didn't know him and Dorothy said to me: "You don't know this man do you?" Naturally I said "No, should I?" "You should," she said, "he was the nurse looking after you all the time you were in intensive care." It was he that told us that no one remembers being in ITU. We had a chat and I learnt more from him, and later on from Dorothy, what I had been like in there.

From all accounts I must have been a bit of a naughty boy, as I kept pulling off all the leads that were fastened to me monitoring my condition. This of course brought all the nurses running to my bedside, thinking that I was in trouble. Evidently they used to give me a mouthful of abuse, which I didn't care about. In the end they gave me some Valium to calm me down. I can't say what happened really, as I have said one doesn't remember being in there. I can only repeat what Dorothy has told me.

What I do remember, though, is that when I was in the ward, I had a load of visitors, which was smashing, and the staff in the hospital were superb. In particular, my doctor, Colonel Bradford. I had to see the colonel before I was discharged and he gave me what I considered some very sound advice, and that was he said: "I want you to walk two or three miles a day, two or three times a week, and then I won't have to see you again in that condition." He has been right as I have tried to keep to that exercise and I haven't had to go and see him again.

At home Dorothy looked after me with all the love, care and attention that only she could administer. Since my heart attack I had not had a cigarette, so Dorothy made our house a 'no smoking' area which meant even our girls and their husbands had to go outside for a smoke. This helped me a lot to get over not smoking but what helped me more was the amount of sweets I got through. I've always liked sweets and even to this day I still eat too many. Dorothy used to see that I was comfortable and then she would dash up town to Woolworth's and buy a cartload. Pick and Mix were just being introduced at this time, I think, and it cost us a fortune, but it stopped me smoking.

With eating all those sweets, and in the early days not being able to walk far, I didn't realise how much weight I had put on until one morning I took a look in the mirror and saw that my face was twice the size it should be. After that I cut down on the sweets and started walking in earnest and soon got into shape again. It was six weeks before I could drive the car and that couldn't come soon enough.

It was unfortunate that when I was in hospital not one of our girls could drive. I had a brand new car only a few weeks old stood in the garage. My friend and colleague Tony Drury who came to see me as soon as he was told, had been in touch with the office and arranged for our Moira to drive the car, so as to help all going to the hospital.

Moira, as I've said, couldn't drive and she vowed as soon as I got fit that she would learn to drive, so if any other unfortunate thing happened, there would be herself and me to drive. We did this and after a few lessons she sat her test and passed first time. I'll never forget seeing her face as she came home to tell us; it was a picture of happiness and great achievement. As she came in the back door of our house, Dorothy and I were sitting in the kitchen, and she thumped the air with her hands and shouted "I've bloody well done it, passed first time". No one was happier than Dorothy and me.

In recognition for teaching her to drive and getting her through her test, she bought a toy Dinky car and mounted it on a plinth, wrote an L plate on it and gave it to me.

Talking about cars, for the first few years I ran one of my brother-in-law's cars, a Vauxhall Velux. Vic, our Daisy's husband, had two cars and it was he who said I should drive one, rather than let it stand. His other vehicle was a Morris pick-up van, which he used for work, and if he and Daisy were going out for the day we would swap over vehicles. Well on one such day when we had swapped cars and I had the Morris I thought I would take our family for a trip up the Dales. Off we went up Swaledale and thoroughly enjoyed our day out. A few days later Vic saw me and told me what a workmate had said to him, and that was that he, Vic, was giving the Morris some welly on Sunday and into the wind at that. Now Vic never abused a motor and he didn't like driving into a head wind, bless him, but he thought that I had been belting the hell out of the Morris, which I hastily say I wasn't.

We found out a strange thing whilst running these cars; our Hazel used to get car sick when we went for a drive in good cars. But when we were in the boneshaker Morris, she was never sick. After a lot of thought I decided that the majority of our family enjoyed riding in the better cars so we wouldn't go out in the Morris just to please Hazel. It was a matter of 'pull up the drawbridge Doug, I'm on the inside'.

Our own first car was a Hillman Minx, which we bought by selling some unit trusts that I had bought some years earlier. I thought it was super, until I took the family for a day out to Scarborough. Travelling from Richmond to Scarborough you had to go via Helmsley and this meant that you had to go up Sutton Bank, which is a one in four incline. Dorothy didn't like the idea and wasn't sure if the car with all the kids in would get up this bank. So she and the kids got out of the car and proceeded to walk up. It was a good job she did, because half way up the hill the engine began to boil. The sound that it made going up the hill was just like a foghorn and I felt like Fred Flintstone driving the thing. When I eventually got to the top of the hill, Dorothy and the girls, along with what looked like hundreds to me, were all staring and wondering if it was going to explode.

I stopped, well I had to didn't I, to let the engine cool down before I decided it was okay to carry on. Being all down hill to Helmsley I coasted most of the way and stopped at a house where I knew the occupant to fill up with water again. We had a lovely day on the beach and fairground and then called at our Denis and Ruby's house for tea. Denis was the managing director of a laundry and dry cleaning business in Scarborough and loved our children, and every year we made a point to visit them.

It was Denis who started the annual trip round the Tree Walk in Peasholm Park once it was dark. All of us really did enjoy ourselves and when Denis bought the fish and chips on the way back to his house, it was a bonus. The girls thought it was grand being out so late at night when we finally left Scarborough for home. I always chuckled to myself when we left Scarborough, as all were jolly and bright when they got in the car but after about two or three minutes all were asleep, including Dorothy, leaving me to talk to myself.

We all loved Scarborough and naturally we went there a lot. We always called at Denis and Ruby's and they always provided us with a meal, sometimes two. On one occasion Denis would take us for a trip out to sea in his boat. That was an experience and a half because none of the girls had ever been in a boat and they thought it was super. It was great when a wave would splash over us and give us a shower; this brought at first fear then pure enjoyment when we all got wet.

It was after one of these trips out and we had gone back to Denis's for tea that a major catastrophe happened. Ruby had set the table for tea and we all sat down to some lovely sandwiches that Ruby had made. Denis didn't sit down with us straight away as he was looking for something. "What are you looking for?" said Ruby. "That lobster I brought in at lunchtime, I thought I'd have it for my tea." The conversation flowed back and forth between them and it was getting more irate by the second. "I wrapped it in some newspaper," said Denis. "I threw a lot of papers in to the dustbin this morning," Ruby replied. "Bloody hell," said Denis, "I bet that's what you've done with my lobster" and immediately ran out and searched in the bin. Denis returned with a smile on his face and clutching a pile of newspapers proceeded to find his lobster. It was all there; all wrapped up like a baby in a shawl. The smile and relief on his face had to be seen to be believed. He promptly put it on a plate and brought it to the table to eat. A chorus rang out. "You're not eating that, it's been in the bin," said Ruby and the girls. "I am," replied Denis, "it's been wrapped up all the time and is as clean as one can get it; you don't think I'm throwing away two quid, or whatever it cost," he went on. We all watched as he ate that lobster with gusto and I'm sure he enjoyed every mouthful.

We continued being one happy family, with all the girls working and doing well and we thought happily married, but we got a shock when Paula phoned to say that her and Eddie were going to get a divorce. She came home from Germany and went into married quarters on the garrison and in 1987 she got her divorce. Now I don't like dwelling on sad happenings so I'll pass on to our holidays the following year.

We chose Whitby because of not having loads of money to throw about and Hazel suggested it. We had a hectic week, going out to a different place each day. At the same time that we were at Hazel and Dave's, so was Jean, Dave's mother, and this made for a better holiday, what with having more company. Our first day out was to Flamingo Land. This was a lovely day out except for one thing, and that was seeing a panther parading back and forth, back and forth, like a demented soul. None of us liked that as we all thought it was cruel. It wasn't cruel though when I put Dorothy in the stocks; it was hilarious. All that was missing was the soft fruit to throw at her!. The hours sped by and soon it was time to go back to Whitby. We were all feeling tired but happy after a strenuous day out.

Being Regatta week, there was something happening every day, so we never had a minute to spare. On another day out we went to Hornsea and looked round the pottery factory and also the lakeside. I remember on the way to Hornsea, we stopped at North Landing, Flamborough Head, and I must say that the view from there was magnificent.

Whilst we were at Hazel's, she invited Florrie and Walter over for tea one day and this proved to be a great success, as the conversation naturally turned to art, in particular to painting. Both Florrie and Walter were very good artists and regularly had paintings hung in various exhibitions. Listening to them telling us about the places they had been, and in most cases painted, was a great joy. Needless to say we had one heck of a good week's holiday.

Our car at this time was an Austin and it was playing up a bit so I decided to change it. I was filling up with petrol one day at my garage, Marwoods, and the owner Peter Marwood came across to me and said that it was time I changed my car. I told him that I was thinking about it and would consider anything in my price range. He said that he had a Citroen GSA Special for sale and told me the price he was asking. It was just above my limit and I told him so. His reply was "everything negotiable Dougie, come and have a look at it". Now I know Peter well enough to be able to talk to him openly and to cut the story short, I bought it at my price. To me it was like riding in a Rolls Royce, compared to the basic Austin I had had.

Peter had sold me the Austin and it was hard for people to grasp when I told them the age of the car and the mileage that it had done. When I had got the car, Peter told me that it had belonged to an old lady, who used it two or three times a week to travel from her house to the market place and back. If she was going to Darlington, that's twelve miles away, she would get the bus. The car was twelve years old and had only 17,000 miles on the clock.

It was round about this year of 89 that Sonia bought her first car and that was a Citroen 2 C V 6 painted blue with red wheel arches. Thank goodness they no longer produce them, as I thought they were death traps.

The same year, our next-door neighbour's son-in-law, Steve Peary, produced the world's only eight-foot poster bed. It went on display all over the country and was eventually auctioned off for charity.

We continued happily passing the days away but it was always nice when some of the family called. It was one of these days when Hazel and Dave called and being a warm and sunny day I suggested, or maybe Dave suggested, that we christen the BBQ that I had built in the back garden. All agreed that that was a good idea. Without any more thought, in the car I got and went straight to my butchers and bought the meat that we wanted to BBQ. In the meantime, Dorothy and Hazel made the salads, etc, to go with it. Dave was in his element playing head chef and was doing a great job, when all of a sudden the rains came down. We all scuttled into the kitchen but not Dave. He just said "pass me an umbrella" and without any more ado he continued to cook the sausages singing '"cooking in the rain". He thought he was Gene Kelly; instead of dancing in the rain, he was cooking in the rain.

Chapter Fourteen

All of the 1980s were a busy time – as well as work, I was actively busy with the pigeons and I must say by the end of the 80s Ken and I had been very successful in both Richmond and Colburn Clubs. Some of the major prizes we won were: In 83 we won the Championship Club Trophy; 84 the First Beawats National race; 85, 86 and 87 we won the longest race, which was the most prestigious race at 555 miles; in 87 we won the most races for young birds and that meant that we won the young bird average for that year; and in 88 we topped the federation, that's the Stockton and District Fed which took in Ripon and Thirsk from Chermont in France. Thinking about pigeons, I remember how our grandchildren used to love to come with me when I used to take the birds down the A1 to Ripon roundabout. I would lay the baskets in a line – there were usually two or three – and whoever was with me, be it Paul or Suzy or whoever, when I said "go" they would open the baskets and let the pigeons out.

While I'm on about racing, this time I'm referring to horse racing. I'll not forget the day Dorothy and I and my friend Noel Richardson went to Catterick Races. It was the first time that Dorothy had stepped on the hallowed turf and what a time we had; this was in 1954. Let me explain; two or three races had been run and I don't think we had backed any winners. Anyway, we had picked out our selections for the next race and I had put the money on the tote for them.

It was two shillings win and place for all of us but on different horses that meant it cost us four shillings each. That was the amount that Dorothy had said that she could afford on each race. I had put the bets on and was walking back to Dorothy and Noel and at the same time was reading the race card and noticed a horse called Gazelle was running in this race. I ran back to Noel and said: "We've backed the wrong horse in this race, Gazelle will win." I had been tipped this horse months ago, that when it ran in a five furlong race to back it. I had been watching it as I've said for months previously and it was always six furlongs it was running in. But today it was the five furlongs it needed.

I looked at the price that the bookies were offering and it was 33 to 1. "Good God," I said, "I'm backing this", and took the 33 to 1 offered from one bookie. A pound was a lot of money for me to gamble those days, as it was for Noel. I can still picture the three of us debating how much to put on this horse. In the end Dorothy said: "Well if you're sure, I'll have another two shilling each way on the tote and that's me broke, so it had better win." "No sweat," I said, "it will go so fast that the others will only see its backside". Noel was a bit more adventurous and had four shillings each way on it.

We weren't in the stands or anything like that; we were just on the course, which had cost us the outrageous sum of four bob to get in. Looking round for a decent spot to watch the race from, we found a slightly raised bit of grass where we were able to see the whole five furlongs. "I hope you are right about this horse" I kept hearing from both my partners but I ignored these remarks, although I must say I began to sweat a little myself.

The three of us stood on this little raised bit of grass, looking as though we had spent our last penny and were ready for the workhouse, when we heard those famous words over the loud speaker system "they're off". My heart jumped and thumped like it never had before as I saw Gazelle jump away from the start straight into the lead. I can still hear the course commentator saying "Gazelle goes straight into the lead" and after two furlongs she still lead the main bunch. Noel looked at me and I looked at him, as we both had seen so many times before that the horse in front early very seldom wins. But Dorothy was jumping up and down, liking what she saw. The three of us were watching intently as Gazelle wasn't tiring at the three-furlong pole but starting to pull away from the rest. There were only three people cheering like mad when Gazelle went past the winning post and won us a fortune. What a pleasure it was to go and pick up our winnings.

Getting back to the year 1989, our Sonia was with us when we were over at Whitby and she met Dave's brother Ric. Straight away she liked Ric as she said he made her laugh. This relationship turned into a full-blown courtship and the following year they got married. We had fun and games trying to get the minister to marry them in the church. To cut a long story short, the Rev Parr finally consented. So on January 6th 1990, Sonia and Ric tied the knot and became man and wife. Sonia looked beautiful in her wedding dress. As bridesmaids she had Helen, Elaine and Gillian and they too looked gorgeous. Not to be vain, but to be honest the best photo that I have ever had taken of me was with Sonia on her wedding day in the back of the Daimler car going to the church. Two lovely people in a lovely vintage car, so say I.

If this year was a happy one with Sonia getting married, the next wasn't, as we had two most unhappy things happen. First, at the end of March, Dorothy's mother died. This came as a great shock, as only the day before she had been her usual happy self. The next day she had a heart attack and died in her bed. Poor mam died on Suzanne's birthday, March 27th, and was buried on my birthday, April 3rd. These dates one never forgets. It took us a long time to get over mam's departing, as she was always the heart and soul of the party, good humoured and couldn't be cross for too long, even if she tried.

The other tragic happening was at Paula's house. Paula's children, Paul and Suzy, were staying with us because Paula was taken into hospital with quinsy and was very poorly. However, after a few days we got her home, that's to our house, where she started to recover, when she asked me to run her up to Colburn to her house for a change of clothing for Paul and Suzy. Now Paula was still quite poorly and it was an effort to get her there but what greeted us when we did, one couldn't describe the horror that be fronted us. While Paula was unlocking the door, we heard water running and when she opened the door all we saw was a waterfall running down the stairs and filling all the ground floor. The water was up over our shoes as we stepped in and I immediately went to turn the water off. This was the last thing that Paula needed. Bless her, she was broken-hearted but with the help of her next-door neighbour we gradually got things sorted out. I can't describe the state that that house was in. In Paula's bedroom the ceiling had come down on to the bed; if Paula had been in the bed it would have killed her, as it must have weighed half a ton. What had happened was, with a night or two of frost the tank had frozen in the loft, and of course when it had thawed the inevitable happened. The living room ceiling was also down and all the ground floor flooded. I've never in all my life seen such devastation. The only cupboard in the house that was not affected was the one that Paula had hidden the children's Christmas presents in, and we thanked God for that. "Never mind," I said to Paula, "we'll sort all this lot out, don't worry," and after doing all we could at that time, we got what we came for plus the Christmas presents and came home.

It took quite a time to get that house habitable again and when eventually Paula and family returned it was like a new house. Thank God for having good insurance I thought. Thank goodness I had

Moira also, as she helped us to paper and paint. She was a brick and we couldn't have got it done so quickly without her help.

Before this horror at Paula's though, we were honoured by an American couple to celebrate Thanksgiving Day on November 26th with them. Anne and Mitch they were called, and they were Hazel and Dave's friends. Mitch, being a top sergeant in the American Air Force, was working at Fylingdales early warning station. This was commonly called the Golf Balls because the buildings resembled golf balls.

Anne had made a beautiful meal with turkey, etc, and Pecan pie, which I had for the first time and thought it was superb. A lovely couple who gave us our first Thanksgiving celebration and one that I'll never forget. In return, Hazel put on a leaving party when Mitch's tour of duty had been completed and they were returning to the States and we were invited to that grand night.

Dorothy and I never had a dull moment and we were always doing something or going somewhere. I should have said earlier that after I had had my heart attack, one day when visiting Whitby our Florrie suggested I should take up another hobby to keep me focussed and active. "Such as what?", I said, and she replied "why not do what I do, and make some greeting cards".

Florrie used to press flowers out of the garden and wild flowers which she got whilst out walking and turn them into lovely cards. For birthdays or just a note, they looked and were appreciated by all who received one. That was how I got started making cards. I didn't stop at cards, though, because people who we had sent them to had framed them, turning them into pictures. That's when I decided that I would make pictures as well as cards.

After I had sold a few pictures, I thought of other products to make with pressed flowers, such as door fingerplates, decorate crockery in particular plain white plates, and other items such as lampshades and paperweights. I started making all these sorts of things when I decided to do the craft fairs around this area. I had to make some display units to use on the tables that were provided and after about six months I was fully equipped to display on any size table.

Dorothy usually accompanied me and we became one of the craft fair set. We became friends with some lovely people and always looked for them whenever we were at a craft fair. When we weren't busy, we would go to each other's stalls and have a chat or tell a joke or two, besides passing on information about other venues and whether they were worth going to or whether it was best to avoid them. But like all businesses, one has good days and also bad days. On a good day, especially in the beginning when I was doing parchment cards, that

Richmond Market Place

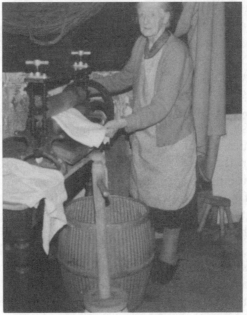

My mother aged 89-90.
She wouldn't let any of us do this for her.

was called Pergamano, as I was the only one doing it on the craft fair circuit, I could take up to one hundred pounds. But as more and more people started doing them, it was hard to make thirty pounds.

I continued doing the craft fairs, though, because I enjoyed meeting people from all walks of life and also enjoyed going to all the different venues. It also gave me something to do, making the cards, etc. It was always nice on a summer's day to go for a ride out, stop and pick some wild flowers for pressing. This I would do as soon as we arrived home. One of the presses I have was made by my brother Fred in Canada; this is a metal one.

It came about like this. Once when we were talking about my craft, I remarked that I could do with a heavy press. "I'll make you one," he said without any hesitation, and after giving him some rough measurements of the size, he set about making me one.

He had gone down to the foundry near by where he lives and got them to cut him the pieces of iron. He then duly took them home and started making the press. He got it finished, parcelled it up, or should I say boxed it up, and took it to the Post Office. Surprise, surprise, they couldn't send it by post, as it was too heavy. Fred took it back home and worked out how to make it lighter. What he did was drill out hundreds of holes on the plates, all different sizes to make a design, and this lightened it to make it to the weight required. When he took it back to the Post Office, they had to cover the whole of the parcel with stamps to get the value required. I remember taking photos of all the stamps. Needless to say that press is in constant use even as I write these memories.

I was enjoying my forced retirement doing what we wanted to do and when we wanted too with only ourselves to please. One night I remember us just lounging about, talking and reflecting on life, and remarked how nice it was to be on our own at times, and how all our family had flown the nest. As your family leaves you, one thinks that the family is reducing in size; not a bit of it, as I can prove.

We started off having four daughters. That's grand as it stands but then four daughters got married and now we have eight in the family. It doesn't stop there either, as those couples have children. At present we have, at the last count, four daughters with husbands and eight grandchildren. So you can see by having just four in the family it has now reached sixteen and may still rise with great grandchildren, God help us. I'll be taking out a bank loan before then to cover the cost of birthdays and Christmas. At the same time let me say, I love every one of them and I don't care. In fact, I'd love to have another eight of them as they all in turn have given both Dorothy and I enormous pleasure seeing them grow up into lovely people. That is looking into the future and before I get there, let us get back to reality in 1993.

One thing in particular stands out in this year and that is, councillors Roy and Pam Cross were out walking and stopped to talk to me, as I was in the garden doing a bit of weeding. I stopped what I was doing and went over to them. Pam spoke first and said: "Roy and I walked round here the other day and thought that this embankment would look nice with some daffodils planted on it." I must say at this time the embankment was all grass and I had been thinking that I would fill it full of shrubs and perennials in due course. If I saw a shrub or plant that I liked I would cut out a square in the grass and plant it. In time, I was in no hurry, but what is grass now would be a beautiful herbaceous border. That is what it is today in 2004.

"Well," Pam said, "Roy has some bulbs if you would like them and could use them, he can drop them of next time he is round here in the car." I thought to myself: "Why does he need the car to drop off a few daffodil bulbs? I could have called and picked them up when I was on one of my walks." Roy called a day or two later and dropped off a sack full of bulbs. No wonder he needed the car, I thought, as I wouldn't have liked to carry that sack from his house to mine, be it only sixty to eighty yards away.

If my memory serves me right, I think Roy was in charge of the 'Britain in Bloom' arrangement at that time and the bulbs that he gave me were some that were left over after planting some areas of the town, as the borough was entering the 'Britain in Bloom' competition. After a bit of thought I said to myself: "Why don't I put into being my plan of having the border a perennial one?"

"Good idea," I said to myself, "I'll get Ken to come and give me a hand to remove all the grass." No sooner said than done, Ken came and worked like a Trojan until all the grass had been lifted. The next item on the agenda was to get rid of it, so I got a friend of mine in the pigeon club to bring his car and trailer. We loaded it up a couple of times and took it to the tip. I planted all the bulbs, or at least most of them, and also some shrubs and plants that I had scrounged off friends, until the embankment looked as though it was fully planted. It looked pretty awful really that summer but in spring it was a bed of yellow daffodils. "By you've got a good garden there Doug," the neighbours and passers by would remark, and from that day to this the garden has got better each year, as I am told by friends and neighbours.

Writing about Roy and Pam Cross, I've just remembered something that Roy did for us. Our Sonia and Ric were living in Dunstable at this time and had planned to go to the Himalayas for their holiday but changed their minds and decided to use their mountain bikes and head north to our house. Sonia had a good idea, and that was to make it a sponsored ride, so she got all her workmates and friends to sponsor her, even the bank where she worked added to the fund. In all, she raised £600 for charity. The charity she chose was the British Heart Foundation and said she would give it to Roy Cross when she eventually arrived in Richmond. I mentioned this to Roy and he was delighted and said that he would officially meet them on Maison Due with the mayor complete with chain of office.

The day arrived and the mayor, along with Dorothy and I, waited for them along Maison Due at the expected time of arrival. True to form, about ten minutes late two very weary cyclists appeared and were greeted by Roy and the Mayor. It was a nice gesture from Roy, and Sonia duly sent him the £600 for the British Heart Foundation of which he was the area representative. I must say that the mayor, John Benkion, was only too pleased to do this, as we are natives of Richmond.

We thanked Roy for all his help with the arrangements regarding this presentation; which we all thought was extremely grand. Roy even presented Sonia and Ric with British Heart Foundation t-shirts with the words "It's great to be alive" printed on the front of them.

Chapter Fifteen

In 1994, our Fred and Audrey, along with their daughters, came over from Canada for a holiday. This was in September/October of that year and Fred, Heather and Linda, his two daughters, stayed at our house and Audrey stayed with her two sisters, Olive and Dorothy, at their house. It was lovely having Fred and the girls staying with us, as it meant there was always some activity or good conversation going on.

It was on one of these holidays that Dorothy and I took Fred and Audrey to Preston Park Museum at Eaglescliffe to see the reconstructed street in which they had transferred all the interior fixtures and fittings of the chemist shop where both he and our Denis, my older brother, had worked. The shop front was the one that they had taken off the shop in the market place and the interior was filled with all the jars, bottles and drawers with glass knobs on just like it had been. When we got there some school children were being shown around and while Fred was looking in another shop, I went into Newton Clarkson & Son, the chemist shop where Fred had worked.

As I went through the door into the shop itself, there was a teacher telling the children about the different items in the shop, like all the blue bottles were for one thing and the brown bottles for something else, and so on. I listened for quite a while, waiting for Fred to come in, and I thought it should be Fred doing all this talking and demonstrating, so I said to the teacher: "Excuse me, I can't help hearing you telling the children all about this shop and I thought, would you like someone who worked in this shop in Richmond for years to tell you all the actual facts about it." The teacher looked at me and said: "That would be great but were only here for an hour." "That's all right," I said, "my brother is that person and he's on holiday from Canada and he'll be coming through that door any minute now". "Oh good," she replied, "that will be a special treat for the children." With that, our Fred came marching through the door and I introduced him to the teacher. On introducing him, I mentioned that he was used to this sort of thing, as he was the principal of a high school in Canada. I was chuckling to myself, all the time I was talking to the teacher, thinking that our Fred will kill me for dropping him in it like this. The truth was, of course, I think he enjoyed it and that it made his day.

Heather and Linda weren't keen to come with us; they liked doing their own thing, like looking in all the charity shops for bargains. Let me say this; they got some very good buys in those shops.

Our Paula was now running the 'Scallywags' playschool for children from the age of three to five. At Christmas, the helpers put on or gave the children a party and Paula asked me if I would play Father Christmas to them. I did, and loved it. Paula got all the kids to sit in a circle and they sang some carols before I handed out the presents. I always had a present of a bottle of wine for Paula, Bridie and the other helpers to make things look real. I did this lovely job all the time Paula was at Scallywags and enjoyed it more each year.

That Christmas, Dorothy and I spent Christmas at Whitby with Hazel, Dave and family; we had, as usual, a great time. Our Florrie came over to Hazel's on Boxing Day for tea and all in all a good time was had by all. On New Year's Eve, it was our turn to have a party, even if it was all family. Hazel, Dave and family came over from Whitby, as did Sonia, Ric and Sam, Moira, Ken and family, and also Paula and family. We had a photo taken of the grandchildren with only Sam missing from it as he was in bed. Once again, one could say that a happy time was had by all. Our house was very quiet once they had all departed by Jan 2nd.

It's in these winter months that I had all the pigeon club meetings and presentations to go to. I remember one year that I was asked to present the prizes at Staindrop club and I got the surprise of my life when Dorothy and I went into the hotel where it was being held. Staindrop is a large village and the club hadn't what you would call a big membership, so you can imagine our feelings when we entered the hall upstairs in the pub and saw what I'm sure was the whole population of Staindrop had turned out. The top flyer of the club, Les Woofe, and his wife greeted us very warmly. We had a smashing time there and left about 11 p.m. but I understand the night's activities went on for a long time after that.

For presenting the prizes, I was given four silver goblets on a tray, which was a nice present indeed. Whenever I was asked to present prizes I always got a present of some kind or Dorothy would get a

Our pigeon loft.
I was in partnership with my son-in-law Ken as Malton and Shout

My craft stall at a craft fair in Market Hall Richmond.
Pressed flower cars, pictures, book marks. Also pergamano (parchment) cards)

beautiful bunch of flowers.

Ken and I were still being very successful in our pigeon racing and in 1995 we had the best bird in the Stockton and District Federation. The bird, a lovely chequer, won the Federation Trophy by winning three firsts, one second and one fourth in the Fed. In the club it did even better, even winning for us the channel averages.

This year was also our ruby wedding anniversary and we received many lovely presents. The only thing is now, I can't remember what they were and who gave us them. I must be getting old and losing my memory. The only one I do know and what it was is a wall clock, which our Fred made for us. It is made out of a circular saw blade and has ruby coloured beads encased in a wonderful wooden frame. We have this hung in our lounge, so you can see I can't forget that present. From March 5th 1995 to this day in 2004, it has never stopped and has also kept good time.

Later on this year, Dorothy and I spent our holidays in Scotland. We went on a tour run by Shearings and the main stop was at Pitlochry in Fishers Hotel. It was a nice hotel and we had a ground floor room, which proved very useful. Across the road was an off licence and we bought our drinks from there, after buying our first drink in the hotel to get the glasses. I remember going on the Whiskey Trail and of course sampling the drink after we had toured the distillery; in this instance it was the Edradour, the smallest in Scotland I'm told. Now I don't drink whiskey, so one can imagine the state of Dorothy by the end of the day, after she had drunk mine as well as that of anybody else who didn't like the fire water.

It was a good tour that one, as we travelled all over the place. Another day we went to see the Waltzing Waters and I must say that I had never seen anything like it; it was marvellousOn another day after visiting some castle or other, we stopped for a break at the Spittal of Glenshee, a little complex of shops, etc, including a restaurant, and after digesting what the name meant, and where it came from, I remember seeing their motto or words of wisdom at the bottom of the board. It read: 'A stranger ye come, a friend you'll depart.'.Nice words, I thought, and you could tell they meant it as it showed by their hospitality.

Another nice thing that happened this year was that our Moira and Ken's daughters, Gillian and Fiona, were bridesmaids for their stepbrother Garry's wedding, Garry being the second child of Ken from a previous marriage. The girls looked beautiful in their lilac-coloured dresses and a great day was had by all.

Getting away from weddings, my daily work involved seeing to the

Richmond from N.E. (Maison due)

Victoria Road, Richmond

pigeons and the garden, amongst other duties. I do believe a man's work is never done, as I never seemed to have a minute to spare. It's all worth it, though, when you learn that you have won a prize in the council's garden competition. This I did and to this day I've won seconds and thirds but never won first prize yet. As the school reports say, 'Must try harder next year'.

Well in 1999 I would try my hand at topiary to add a bit of interest to the garden. At the time our youngest grandson was 'into' Thomas the Tank stories and in it was a character called the Fat Controller, so I thought for my first try at topiary I would turn a bush I had in the garden into him. After clipping away for a couple of days, I managed to turn my bush into something looking like a human. It wasn't until I gave him a flat cap, like that the station master wears, that he resembled anything like the Fat Controller.

I had great fun doing this topiary and up to now I have a large pineapple, an animal with a horn, a round ball, a chair and a five-headed alien. I never realised just how much interest all these topiary subjects created for all who passed by – friends, neighbours, tourists and our own family. At first it was the kids but soon it was the adults as well who showed more interest. Some called my Fat Controller a teddy bear, others called it a snow man, and neighbours would bring their company to see it. It was of such interest that in 2003 a book was published about all the streets in Richmond and lo and behold who should be photographed in the book but my Fat Controller, saying that I had created it earlier. I am sure that it was the Fat Controller that got me a 2nd prize in the garden competition.

This year, 1999, we had our holiday with our very good friends Ruby and Ken and we went to the Cheddar Gorge. It was the first time that any of us had been that far down the West side of the country and we all loved it immensely. Not only were the caves fabulous but we also took in the city of Bath, Stratford, Wells and Bourton on the Water. Both Dorothy and I remarked that Wells Cathedral was the highlight of that day's tour. I've never seen such a lovely church in all my life. Looking around Bath and the Royal Baths, and also the Crescent, were places that I'll never forget. I won't forget that on the first day. I had come without headwear, so the first thing that I had to do was to look for a flat cap as it was so hot that I couldn't have gone without one. Once I had got one and it was on my head I was as happy as a lark.

The next year started off really lovely because on May 20th 2000 our Paula re-married. The man she loved and married was Colin Addison, a local lad who she had been going out with for over a year. It was best bib and tucker for the groom and best man, and for Paul who pigeons and the garden, amongst other duties. I do believe a man's work is never done, as I never seemed to have a minute to spare. It's all worth it, though, when you learn that you have won a prize in the council's garden competition. This I did and to this day I've won seconds and thirds but never won first prize yet. As the school reports say, 'Must try harder next year'.

Well in 1999 I would try my hand at topiary to add a bit of interest to the garden. At the time our youngest grandson was 'into' Thomas the Tank stories and in it was a character called the Fat Controller, so I thought for my first try at topiary I would turn a bush I had in the garden into him. After clipping away for a couple of days, I managed to turn my bush into something looking like a human. It wasn't until I gave him a flat cap, like that the station master wears, that he resembled anything like the Fat Controller.

I had great fun doing this topiary and up to now I have a large pineapple, an animal with a horn, a round ball, a chair and a five-headed alien. I never realised just how much interest all these topiary subjects created for all who passed by – friends, neighbours, tourists and our own family. At first it was the kids but soon it was the adults as well who showed more interest. Some called my Fat Controller a teddy bear, others called it a snow man, and neighbours would bring their company to see it. It was of such interest that in 2003 a book was published about all the streets in Richmond and lo and behold who should be photographed in the book but my Fat Controller, saying that I had created it earlier. I am sure that it was the Fat Controller that got me a 2nd prize in the garden competition.

This year, 1999, we had our holiday with our very good friends Ruby and Ken and we went to the Cheddar Gorge. It was the first time that any of us had been that far down the West side of the country and we all loved it immensely. Not only were the caves fabulous but we also took in the city of Bath, Stratford, Wells and Bourton on the Water. Both Dorothy and I remarked that Wells Cathedral was the highlight of that day's tour. I've never seen such a lovely church in all my life. Looking around Bath and the Royal Baths, and also the Crescent, were places that I'll never forget. I won't forget that on the first day. I had come without headwear, so the first thing that I had to do was to look for a flat cap as it was so hot that I couldn't have gone without one. Once I had got one and it was on my head I was as happy as a lark.

The next year started off really lovely because on May 20th 2000 our Paula re-married. The man she loved and married was Colin Addison, a local lad who she had been going out with for over a year. It was best bib and tucker for the groom and best man, and for Paul who gave his mam away at church. Paula looked a million dollars, as did her bridesmaids, who were the ladies that she worked with, Bridie, Josephine and her daughter Leanne and of course our Suzanne.

Dorothy and Sheila decorated the church with flowers and when finished it looked superb. The reception was held at Dalesway Lodge at Scotch Corner, which was also very nice. From leaving her house to the end of the reception, one of Colin's uncles was recording all the time, and I must say, when Paula and Colin gave us a videotape of the whole of the wedding, it was grand. I think Paula still likes to play her tape when she has nothing pressing to do.

Before this happy occasion though, we had a shocking event that took place. On Sunday February 18th we had just gone, or were going, to bed when I saw out of our bedroom window a red glow in the sky. I said to Dorothy "get dressed, I'm sure that the old convent is on fire" and I must say that I have never seen such a fire before or since then. The middle of the main building had flames reaching out to the sky and it wasn't long before the floors collapsed.

There were four or five fire engines there but they were making no progress in putting out the fire. I remember saying to a neighbour that what they needed here was a Simon Snorkel to get on top of this fire. He agreed with me after seeing one engine on the road outside trying to squirt water into the building and the damn thing wouldn't reach right across the road. My friend said: "Look at that, I could pee further than that." Before long, the Simon Snorkel, which came from Darlington, arrived and then there was progress. After an hour or two with that they got the fire under control, so off we went back to bed. The next day we saw the results of that fire. In one way it was a job well done, that fire, as the building had stood empty for about ten years and was getting worse looking, having not one pain of glass that was not broken and with people thieving anything that was saleable from inside.

Later that year, the building was sold to a developer and now we have a beautiful estate, having rebuilt what was damaged in the fire in the main building and turning that into nineteen flats. They have also built another block of six flats and about twenty beautiful houses.

The other major incident that took place was when part of the station bridge was washed away. As it happened we were the first people to be affected by this, as we were on our way home from Paula's. We came to the bridge where a policeman stopped us going over it saying it was not safe, due to part of it being washed away. The policeman showed me where the river was washing the bridge support away, so I went down under it and saw for myself.

It was clear to see that the water had started to wash away one of the bridge supports. Anyway, I turned the car around and went home via Holly Hill and the Green. The road was completely closed for a time and this caused a great strain on all people going to Catterick Garrison and also to the big store farm and garden suppliers. It affected a lot of people and later when they got organised and started to repair the bridge, they had single line traffic controlled by traffic lights.

It took a long time to repair and it did immeasurable damage to the farm and garden store sales and also to the swimming baths.

The following year, I changed my back garden again and made raised beds round one side. Once again I won a prize in the garden competition. I should have mentioned earlier, that after a lot of thought, I told Ken that I was packing in with the pigeons. I decided that it wasn't fair to Dorothy that she should give up her weekends because of me and the pigeon racing. It also meant that we had Saturday and Sunday free if we wanted to go anywhere. I resigned from the partnership and the clubs and became a free weekend man again. I was honoured by the Richmond club as they made me an honoury member. I still kept in touch, though, as the club continued to come to our garage to work out the results every weekend. We used to take the lads across at the garage a cup of tea, for which they were duly thankful. Ever since, Dorothy and I have been guests at the prize presentation and always received a Poinsettia plant or a beautiful bouquet of flowers. I had a complete year's rest from the pigeons but the next year I was asked if I would be chief cook and bottle washer, in other words run the Colburn Lodge Club. I said I would and still am today enjoying doing the admin side and keeping everything in order.

I'm very nearly up to date with my memories now but there are still one or two things worth mentioning. One was our Anne's 18th birthday. Hazel asked me if I would organise something for her party and after a bit of thought I came up with, or maybe Hazel thought of, doing 'This is your life Anne Bransby'. What a brilliant idea that was, no matter who thought of it.

So I started getting all her relatives, friends, workmates and teachers, in fact anybody who knew her, to write a greeting to her that I could read out if they weren't coming to the party. You couldn't invite everyone, as there are more than enough if all the family turn up. Now I'm known for always running a game or quiz at these sorts of gatherings, so when I got everyone in the sitting room I told Anne to sit in one particular spot. She still didn't know what to expect and when I got hush and said those famous words "Tonight Anne Bransby this is your life", she didn't know what to do.

Such a cheer went up that I had to wait till everybody had settled again. I had put a microphone on the mantelpiece just beside Anne, so as to record all the proceedings. I called in turn first her mother and her sisters and relations and so on to say what they remembered of Anne and to wish her a happy day. Finally it was her dad's turn and he spoke not just for himself but also for all of us, saying that we loved her and wished her all the best. That night there were tears of joy and emotional tears but all were for the best of intentions.

Drawing nearer and nearer to the present day, I remember Sonia saying to me that she was going camping with Sam and could I find a nice campsite to go to. She had bought a tent and Sam was looking forward to having a bit of time with his mam. First of all one of her sisters, be it Hazel or Moira, jumped on the wagon and said "okay I'll come camping with you". Then the other sister said "well you're not going without me", so what turned out to be a bit of quality time for Sonia with Sam turned out to be a family outing. What made me laugh, though, was they went to all this trouble for just one night. If that made me laugh, this made me howl, they were going camping but not one meal was cooked. They all went down to the local pub for their meals. That's not like the good old days, living under canvas and cooking beans for every meal, and washing in the river nearby.

Chapter Sixteen

I have now reached the grand old age of seventy-five in this year of our Lord 2004 and have been writing these memories for the past six months or more. After skimming through them, I realise I haven't mentioned the death of Dorothy's dad; also I only just mentioned about my dad's death in passing. Now I can't let this go uncorrected, can I.

These two great, generous, respected and very much loved men were all of that to me. Not only was my father all that I have just said but he was a character known throughout the town but mainly at the Buck Inn.

Being presented with 2nd Prize in the Garden Competition by the Mayor, Stuart Parsons, September 2003.

Dorothy's dad was also well-known and held in high esteem in the town by everyone. I am not going to end my story with just the deaths of these loved ones but will tell you a funny story about each of them, which I like to remember them by.

First, Arthur Wood, that's Dorothy's dad: We hadn't been married long when my in-laws decided to have their sitting room papered, and not been able to do it himself, he got two of his workmates to do it. To cut a long story short, they made a hash of it, and I put it right, more about that later. The funny side of this was, I became his chief decorator from then on. We were asked to decorate a house on Darlington Road for a friend. Dad said that we could do it and this was how I learnt to decorate.

Everything was going fine until he said that the ceiling had to be papered. I had never papered or even thought about papering a ceiling before and if anyone had seen us doing this ceiling they would have died laughing. There was I on a chair, sticking one end of the paper on the ceiling, while dad held the other end up off the floor with a brush. We had a good laugh about it when we eventually got it done.

My dad went into Scorton Hospital with breathing difficulties and when Ruby, a friend of mine, went to visit him, this is what she told us. She had gone into the ward and found his bed but he was not in it. After hearing a commotion at the other end of the ward, she went there, and there was my father having a game of bowls with the other patients using oranges as the bowls. That's the sort of character he was, always being happy, and that's the way I like to remember him.

Enough about that; as I previously said, I have decided to call it a day for the time being. What conclusion I have come to, though, is I now realise that I could write as much again about the life I have led without repeating anything. I have remembered so much more since writing these last chapters that I have decided to continue to write about them in another book.

Things like my diaries, which I kept daily, of what I did and where I went and so on. Such as my holidays as a single man and then as a married man, the craft fairs, more about the bands and the things that we got up to.

So I close with these sobering thoughts. Last Wednesday, August 11th, I went to our arts and crafts monthly meeting (I have to go as I'm the chairman) to hear and see a demonstration on beeswax candle making. Whilst there, I made a candle to bring home.

As long as the candle burns (for a long time yet I hope) I will continue to write and SHOUT ABOUT LIFE.